Polish-American Politics in Chicago 1888-1940

Edward R. Kantowicz

The University of Chicago Press
Chicago and London

EDWARD R. KANTOWICZ is assistant professor
of history at Carleton University in
Ottawa, Canada.

To Arthur Mann and Oscar Handlin,
the grandfather and great-grandfather
of the work

The University of Chicago Press, Chicago
60637
The University of Chicago Press, Ltd.,
London
© 1975 by The University of Chicago
All rights reserved. Published 1975
Printed in the United States of America

Library of Congress Cataloging in Publication Data

Kantowicz, Edward R
  Polish-American politics in Chicago, 1888–1940.

  Includes bibliographical references.
  1. Poles in Chicago. 2. Chicago—Politics and
government—To 1950. I. Title.
F548.9.P7K36   917.73'11'069185   74–16682
ISBN 0–226–42380–8

Contents

Contents

Maps and Tables

Maps

Tables

Preface

In the 1880s and 1890s, America experienced a marked shift in its immigration patterns. Instead of the Anglo-Saxons, Teutons, and Celts of northwestern Europe, Slavs and Latins from southern and eastern Europe began to predominate in the immigrant influx. In the twenty years preceding the First World War, Poles, Italians, Jews, Greeks, Lithuanians, and many other nationalities transformed the population of major American cities. Puzzled natives felt that the strange languages, customs, and religions of these "new immigrants" compared unfavorably with the familiar habits of those who came earlier. Unable to understand the newcomers, Americans often used them as scapegoats for the ills of urban industrial life. Consequently, when the U.S. Congress ended mass immigration in the 1920s, it instituted an immigration quota system which discriminated against the "new immigrant" nationalities.

Fear and suspicion of southern and eastern Europeans have subsided, but understanding has not increased correspondingly. Americans still know surprisingly little about these turn-of-the-century "new immigrants" and their descendants.

Historians are familiar with the broad immigration patterns, and politicians ritualistically intone ethnic appeals at election time; but detailed knowledge of specific ethnic groups has long been lacking. A few recent works, such as Moses Rischin's *The Promised City: New York's Jews* and Humbert Nelli's *The Italians in Chicago,* have examined the adjustment of particular immigrant groups to American urban life. Yet some ethnic groups are still virtually unknown. Polish-Americans, in particular, are dimly perceived through the stereotypes of the "Polish joke." A sociologist once remarked to me that social scientists know more about many primitive tribes in Africa and Asia than they do about Poles in Chicago.

Political historians have paid some attention to the newer immigrant peoples and their effect on the political system. Studies of "boss" politics, in particular, have usually examined the ethnic bases of boss power; and a few biographies of "new immigrant" politicians, most notably Alex Gottfried's *Boss Cermak of Chicago* and Arthur Mann's *LaGuardia,* have appeared. But the study of bossism still emphasizes the dominance of the older Irish leaders rather than the political activities of newer groups.

In recent years a number of studies have followed suggestions made by Lee Benson, in *The Concept of Jacksonian Democracy,* that ethnicity and religion, not economic class, have been the most important determinants of American political behavior. This "ethnocultural" approach to political history has been an important antidote to the rather culture-blind view of most political historians of the progressive tradition. It has produced an impressive series of studies describing the political behavior of many ethnic groups.[1] The outstanding weakness in all these studies, however, is that they look at ethnic groups "from the outside," through the filter of statistical correlations.

A need still exists for studies of ethnic politics from inside the group itself. Political history reflects the group's background, institutions, social structure, and values. Narrative flesh on the statistical skeleton of voting results can reveal what the group felt was important and why. Good political history is also social history.

This study presents a political history of Chicago's Polish-Americans from 1888 to 1940. I have attempted to describe the political leaders of the Polish community, to examine the voting patterns of Polish-Americans, to explain the issues which Polish voters deemed significant, and to determine the economic and psychological functions which American politics served for Polish-Americans. Finally, I have tried to evaluate the successes and failures of the Polish-American community in Chicago politics and to indicate what significance their political record holds for an understanding of ethnic politics in general.

Chicago has the largest Polish-American population in the United States; indeed, an old cliché has long claimed it to be the world's second largest Polish city, next to Warsaw. By the end of the period I have examined, Polish-Americans had become Chicago's largest white ethnic group.

The study begins in 1888, for this is the first year in which a small Polish voting group could be identified. In that year a redistricting placed most of Chicago's oldest Polish-American community in one ward. Also in 1888, this ward elected the city's first Polish-American alderman. I ended the study in 1940, since, after the Second World War, Polish-Americans dispersed more rapidly and widely throughout the city and suburbs. Less concentrated and less identifiably Polish, Polish-American society entered upon a new era after the war which would be best examined in a separate study.

A political history of Polish-Americans in one city will not tell us everything worth knowing about this large group of "new immigrants" and their descendants. But, I hope, it will illuminate both the phenomenon of group politics and the process of immigrant adjustment to American life.

Many people have helped me with this study. My note on sources acknowledges a few of the persons who graciously granted me interviews. One person whom I wish to single out for special thanks is Francis P. Canary. As a member of the Chicago Board of Election Commissioners, Mr. Canary cut through much red tape and gave me full access to the voting records and precinct registration lists which formed the statistical core of this study.

My dedication indicates the heavy intellectual debt I owe to Professors Arthur Mann and Oscar Handlin. Arthur Mann supervised my work in its initial stages as a doctoral dissertation and has since read all my revised drafts. His superb editorial judgment and his constant inspiration as a friend and mentor are largely responsible for whatever is of value in this work. The remaining shortcomings are strictly my own. I have never met Oscar Handlin, but his seminal book *The Uprooted* first introduced me to the excitement of immigration history; and the example of his sympathetic, scholarly approach to the "new immigrants" has spurred me on in my own work.

Finally, my wife, Jane Taylor Kantowicz, has given me her constant personal support in my work and has often contributed shrewd insights into American ethnic life drawn from her own experience as a native Chicagoan.

From Poland to Chicago

In the nineteenth century Poles in Poland and those in emigration clung to ideals of strength in unity despite the harsh facts of division and disunion.

In partitioned Poland the Poles rose in revolt against the occupying powers in 1794, 1830, 1846, and 1863, in vain hope of erasing the political division of their country. Throughout the century Poles realized that the failure of these revolts was partially due to a yawning social chasm dividing the politically conscious gentry from the inert mass of peasants. Peasant emancipation and persistent nationalist propaganda, though they did not close the gap, eventually threw a bridge of nationalist longing across the social abyss. When the First World War presented an opportunity for Poland's rebirth, Poles were still divided over tactics; but unlike the period of the insurrections, all social classes of the nation were united in the commitment to new strength in unity.

By the time of Poland's rebirth, however, almost four million Poles had left the country, the great majority settling in America. The three million Polish immigrants in the United States struggled for their own unification in a community they called *Polonja Amerykańska*. Polonia cherished its own ideal of strength in unity and constructed institutions to work towards the ideal. These immigrant institutions were strongest in the urban areas of the Great Lakes Basin where the Poles concentrated; and most made their headquarters in Chicago, the largest Polish-American center. Chicago became an informal capital for *Polonja Amerykańska*.

In Chicago, as elsewhere in Polonia, a few of the Polish immigrants were actively engaged in the politics of Polish liberation. Most took some part in the internal politics of the new Polonia institutions. And those immigrants and their children who were on the leading edge of the Americanization process found American politics vital to their new life in Chicago.

1 Polska and Polonia

In 1797 Poland's three neighbors, Prussia, Russia, and Austria, carved up the Polish remnant left from two earlier partitions; and the name of Poland disappeared from the map of Europe. During the Napoleonic wars a small part of Poland acquired semi-independence under Napoleon's tutelage as the Duchy of Warsaw (1807–15). When, upon Napoleon's downfall, the Congress of Vienna allotted this fragment to the Tsar of Russia, it retained a measure of autonomy and was granted a constitution as the Congress Kingdom of Poland. But when the Poles rose in unsuccessful revolt against the Tsar in 1830, even this small measure of autonomy disappeared. Though the Kingdom remained technically distinct from the Russian Empire and retained the Code Napoléon as the basis of its laws, for most practical purposes it became a subject province of Russia.

Thus from 1830 to the First World War, Poland's destiny was completely out of Polish hands, bound up with the development of three occupying nations. Russia ruled the majority of Polish territory, including the Congress Kingdom and the territories to the east which had been part of the Commonwealth of Poland in its days of independence. These latter were of mixed Polish-Lithuanian-Ukrainian-Byelorussian nationality. Austria held the large province of Galicia, along the rim of the Carpathian Mountains, a region of nearly equal Polish and Ukrainian populations with a large minority of Jews. Prussia's portion included the Baltic areas of West Prussia and Pomerania as well as Silesia and the Grand Duchy of Poznań, all of mixed Polish and German nationality.[1]

In the wake of the 1830 revolt, rebel leaders scattered into exile, the majority gathering in France to plot new conspiracies and rebellions. Weak risings in 1846, however, in the Prussian and Austrian territories proved their conspiratorial hopes unrealistic. The action of the Galician peasants,

3

Map 1. Partitioned Poland, circa 1870

who sided with the Austrian authorities and slaughtered their Polish land-
lords, sent a profound shock through Polish "patriot" circles. The rebel
leaders were mainly from the gentry class; and despite the promise of the
revolutionists' Poitiers manifesto to emancipate the serfs, they failed to overcome the peasants' long-standing class hatred and to secure their cooperation in the national cause. The naive gentry hopes of rebellion and reunification died in the "Galician days" of 1846; thereafter, most conservative
gentry advocated collaboration with the partitioning powers as the only
realistic course.

One final Polish insurrection broke out in January 1863 in the Russian
sector; but, after a year of bloody fighting, it too was crushed by Russian
troops. The Poles in the next half century abandoned the futile course of insurrection; and the three parts of Poland developed as unhappy, constituent
parts of their respective states. Galicia benefited politically from liberalizing
tendencies in Franz Joseph's Austria and enjoyed the greatest political participation, both in its provincial diet and in the imperial parliament, of any of
the three Polish fragments. However, its economic life stagnated, as the
province was cut off from its natural economic connections with the Vistula
River system. The Russian segment suffered the most repressive political situation, but it underwent considerable industrialization and agricultural mod-
ernization. The Prussian government also restricted political activity; but
Poles benefited economically from participation in the modern, rapidly developing Prussian (after 1871, German) state.[2]

The greatest obstacle to Polish unity, in some ways more serious than
political division, was the deep social chasm between the gentry and peasant
classes. The peasants made up over 70 percent of Poland's population; but
at the beginning of the nineteenth century they were still serfs, bound to the
soil they tilled but with no property rights to it. They had no political standing in the state. They owed their landlord burdensome labor services
(pańszczyzna) and were subject to him in matters of civil and criminal
justice.

Politically, Poland in the days of its independence and in the early years
of the partitions was a nobility nation. The Polish szlachta, or gentry, were
the most numerous noble class in Europe, forming 8 percent of Poland's
population on the eve of the second partition. In theory all gentry enjoyed
equal political rights under the Polish Comonwealth, though in practice the
great landowners among them dominated the state. The landed gentry also
held a virtual monopoly on Poland's principal economic activity, the grain
trade.

Gentry and peasant were tied together in the manorial farm-compulsory labor *(folwark-pańszczyzna)* system of agriculture. The lord gave some land to the village peasants, in usufruct not in property title, to till for their own subsistence, then required in turn that the peasants work the lord's own manor farm with compulsory labor. Though economically bound together, peasant and gentry could not be more divided socially. In the eighteenth century, some *szlachta* even believed they were descendants of the ancient Sarmatians, a different race than the peasants.

Poland contained two other classes, the clergy and the townsmen. But since the most influential clergy were drawn from the gentry and closely allied with them, and the townsmen were not numerous nor influential until late in the nineteenth century, the "old Poland" may be described, for simplicity's sake, as a politically and economically dominant gentry ruling over a dependent peasant class.

It was the gentry leaders of the "old Poland" who led the quixotic revolution of 1830 and were slaughtered by the peasants in the "Galician days" of 1846. The wide distance between lord and peasant made the early Polish hopes of reunification chimerical. However, as the nineteenth century progressed, the social system of Poland changed.

The peasants of the three fragments were emancipated gradually and at differing tempos. Unlike some other European countries where the entire feudal regime was wiped out at one stroke, many Polish peasants were declared legally free at an early date but had to wait as much as fifty years for full emancipation.

Napoleon and his Grand Army struck the first blow at serfdom in Polish lands. The constitution of the Duchy of Warsaw, which Napoleon dictated on July 22, 1807, decreed in article four that "slavery will be abolished." This made the serf technically a free man with the right to leave the lord's manor if he so chose. The Prussian state followed suit with a similar decree on November 11, 1807. Polish peasants in Austrian Galicia and in the Russian borderlands were untouched by these decrees, but over half the Polish peasantry was technically freed in 1807.

Such freedom meant very little, however, if the peasant was not granted title to the land he farmed and thus was given economic independence *(uwłaszczenie)*. In the Duchy of Warsaw, which was metamorphosed into Russia's Congress Kingdom after the Napoleonic wars, *uwłaszczenie* did not follow until 1864. In the Prussian lands the government did follow up the abolition of serfdom with a further reform confirming the peasant's title to his land. But this Prussian *uwłaszczenie* was partial, covering only the largest peasant holdings which could exist as self-supporting farms; and it was gradual, not being completed until about 1860.

In Austrian Galicia peasant emancipation followed the general European pattern of all-at-once reform. When revolution broke out across Europe in 1848, the Galician peasants were on the point of rising. The Austrian governor forestalled this by decreeing *uwłaszczenie*—an end to all compulsory labor and confirmation of peasant title to land.[3]

Though the processes were different, the final result of peasant emancipation, toward the end of the nineteenth century, was remarkably similar in the three divisions of partitioned Poland: a divided peasantry. Some peasants became moderately prosperous landed farmers while the majority became landless and impoverished.

The landowning peasants remained where they were, tried to buy more land from the gentry or from small peasant landholders, participated in agricultural improvement schemes and whatever political opportunities their occupying state allowed them, and eventually were converted to the Polish dream of national reunification by the persistent, though often secret and illegal, nationalist propaganda of the patriots. The landless peasants and small landowners were reduced to marginal subsistence; forced to work the lord's land as wage earners in conditions scarcely better than those of *pańszczyzna;* driven to migratory labor or industrial work in the cities; or else pushed out of Polish territory altogether as emigrants.

The waves of emigration began in the 1870s in Prussian territory, where the pressures of landlessness had been felt first. Most left for America, but many also went to industrial western Germany. By the time of the First World War, 1.2 million Poles had left the Prussian provinces east of the Oder-Neisse line. Emigration fever struck next in the Congress Kingdom, directed first toward Brazil, where the government offered free passage and promised land. But economic opportunities were lacking in Brazil, so most Poles went instead to the United States. In the years just before the war nearly one hundred thousand Poles per year were leaving Russian Poland; by 1914, about 1.3 million had emigrated. In the late 1890s, Galicians too began to leave, at the rate of fifty thousand per year. When the war broke out, a million Galicians had left, two-thirds of them Poles who went mainly to the U.S.; most of the rest were Ukrainians and chose Canada.

The overwhelming majority of these emigrants from all three areas were landless peasants or small peasant landholders who could no longer make a living from the soil. The landowning peasants left behind faced differing prospects in the three partitioned areas—those in Germany were the best-off economically, and those in Galicia enjoyed the most political freedom. But the winnowing processes of emancipation and emigration made the economic fugitives from tripartite Poland all of one class, the rural proletariat. Few of them had enjoyed any economic or political privileges under the partitioning states.[4]

Emigrants from the three parts of Poland were more united than some other European emigrants. A common language and common religion made them more alike than German and Russian Jews were. Their economic differences were slight compared to those separating northern and southern Italians. And the memory of a long history of independence gave Poles a firmer basis for nationalism than the South Slavs, who had been parceled out among different empires from time immemorial.

The divisions among the Poles were not totally erased by emigration. German, Russian, and Austrian Poles felt some mutual suspicion and noted each other's strange dialects and accents in the New World. But American natives viewed them all as simply Poles; and the immigrants themselves, aided by their fundamental similarities, soon adopted this identification. Polish subjects of Germany, Austria, and Russia all became Poles in the *Polonja Amerykańska.*

Polonia was a New World ideal of strength in unity, partially realized in the United States. In origin *Polonja* was simply the Latin word for Poland, but the immigrants did not use it in that sense. Poland was *Polska,* or sometimes *ojczyzna,* the fatherland, but never *Polonja.* To the immigrants Polonia was America. Or rather, they called those parts of America in which they settled *Polonja Amerykańska.*

Polonia meant different things to different people. Political emigrés of the gentry class, interested primarily in the fatherland, not the New World, considered Polonia a "fourth province of Poland." In this view the immigrant colonies formed a sort of Poland in exile, a place to keep faith in the Polish nation while waiting for the restoration of the Polish state.

To the sociologists, Thomas and Znaniecki, writing just after the First World War in their monumental study, *The Polish Peasant in Europe and America,* Polonia was not just a piece of Poland afloat in the New World but a fundamentally new society. Polish immigrants, uprooted from their peasant villages in Europe, suffered a kind of culture shock when they found themselves in America. The only way they could survive in this strange environment was by trying to re-create the Polish village, with its familiar customs and habits, on this side of the Atlantic. But the peasant village could not be re-created whole; so the result was "the formation of a new Polish-American society," neither Polish nor American. Polonia was then, in these sociologists' view, the foundation of a new nationality.[5]

To the ordinary immigrant, however, both of these concepts—Polonia as fourth province and Polonia as new society—were far too sophisticated. The peasant immigrant knew he was not alone in America. Indeed, one of the prime causes of his immigration had been the glowing letters he had received from kinsmen in the United States. Many of these kinsmen lived with him in the same community, and he knew that others lived elsewhere in the new land. *Polonja Amerykańska* was simply a vague collective term for all those who, like himself, had left Poland for America. Others words for this phe-nomenon, such as *wychodztwo,* literally "the emigration," were also in com-mon use.

Polonia in America grew rapidly in the late nineteenth and early twen-tieth centuries. In 1870, when mass immigration from partitioned Poland was just beginning, there were about fifty thousand Poles in America. By 1890 the number had grown to approximately eight hundred thousand. From 1897 until the First World War, the immigrant tide swelled, reaching its high point in 1912–13, when 174,365 Poles entered the United States. By the end of the war, over three million people inhabited Polonia.

These enumerations of Poles in America are only estimates. The U.S. Census identifies immigrant groups only in the first two generations, listing them by origin as "foreign-born" and "native-born of foreign parents." The third and subsequent generations disappear in census records into the listing "native-born of native parents." In this study, unless otherwise mentioned, any enumeration of Poles in America refers to the first two generations only.

There is an additional problem with the census enumeration of Polish immigrants before the First World War. The 1900 and 1910 censuses re-corded a person's nationality by "country of origin." Since there was no Po-land in a political sense in these years, all Poles appeared as either Germans, Austrians, or Russians. Other sources, such as school censuses, which listed immigrants by "native language" rather than "country of origin," have to be used to obtain estimates of Polish-American population in these years.[6]

Whatever their precise number, Polish immigrants scattered across three dozen states and thousands of local communities. Though the vast majority were concentrated in the industrial cities of the Great Lakes Basin, from New

York to Illinois, at least a third of the total lived in small, rural communities. The American Polonia was not a tightly-knit geographical entity. Polonia as a united, self-conscious community was largely an ideal cherished by the immigrant leaders. The reality was a series of isolated immigrant colonies scattered across the American continent.

Yet the Polonia ideal was not totally without foundation. The various immigrant colonies were similar in many ways. The Polish steelworker in Buffalo faced the same problems of poor housing, hard labor, low wages, and long hours as the coal miner in Scranton or the stockyards laborer in Chicago. Polish farm communities were different from Polish urban concentrations, of course, but were quite similar to each other. Radom, Illinois, had a social structure much like that of Wilno, Ontario, or Polonia, Wisconsin. And everywhere in Polonia, urban or rural, the immigrants faced the same language barrier, the same hostility and incomprehension from native Americans, the same need to reconstruct life patterns in a new environment.

The leaders of Polonia made remarkable efforts to establish communication between and forge a kind of unity among its isolated elements. As early as 1873 a group of Polish priests attempted to unite all the Polish colonies in America into one organization. This attempt failed, but the fledgling organization was revived in the 1880s as the Polish Roman Catholic Union. In 1880 the Polish National Alliance, a similar organization with more specifically nationalistic goals, was founded to work for the liberation of Poland.

These two leading Polish-American fraternal organizations differed in their underlying purposes. The PNA wanted to preserve the Polish immigrants as a coherent part of the Polish nation and as a strong force to work for its liberation. It cherished the "fourth province" conception of Polonia. The PRCU, on the other hand, focused attention on the New World. It wanted to preserve the Catholic faith and Polish heritage among the immigrants.[7]

But despite these differing aims, both organizations were trying to make Polonia a reality. They united many local associations into two super-territorial organizations based on the federal principle. The representatives of the locals met in yearly congresses, and the individual members read the organizations' journals for news of other immigrant communities and of Poland itself.

Other organizations also attempted to forge links between the various immigrant colonies. The priests of the Congregation of the Resurrection (C.R.), the most significant spiritual force in Polonia, crisscrossed the continent, attending to spiritual needs and keeping up communication between otherwise isolated settlements. The first three Resurrectionists arrived in the United States in 1866 and founded a mission among the Poles of Texas. Besides making the rounds on the Texas plains, they also answered calls to service from as far away as Chicago and kept in touch with other Resurrectionists in the U.S. and Canada as well as with their superiors in Rome and Cracow. They founded churches and schools and encouraged the establishment of publishing companies and newspapers to inform and unite Polonia.[8]

Their efforts, like those of the fraternal organizations, did not completely realize the ideal of a united Polonia. Yet they accomplished much. An immigrant who spoke no English and never left his local community could read in his own language news from Polish communities all over the U.S. He could read about events in Poland, hear firsthand reports from the national congresses of the PNA or the PRCU at his local association meeting, and inquire after faraway friends and relatives from his parish priest.

Polonia was an ideal of strength in unity for the Poles in America. But it was an ideal only partially realized. Thus Polonia is best understood by studies of its local communities.

2 Polonia's Capital

Among the numerous local communities inhabited by Polish immigrants, Chicago came to be preeminent.

Other Polish colonies were older. Small groups of gentry emigrés and adventurers from Poland had scattered across the U.S. throughout the eighteenth and nineteenth centuries. The first large-scale settlement of Polish peasants, who emigrated for economic rather than political reasons, was in Texas. In 1854 a group of Silesian peasants founded Panna Maria (Virgin Mary) on the plains near San Antonio. But as economic forces pushed more and more Poles across the ocean, most of them found they had neither the technical skill, the capital, nor the inclination to attempt prairie farming in America. Most Polish immigrants congregated in the seaports or in industrial cities along the internal lines of communication.[1]

Chicago, the growing metropolis of the Midwest, was favored as an immigrant collection center by its superb lines of communication with the seaboard and its opportunities for employment in trade and industry. In the late 1860s enough Polish immigrants had gathered there to form a mutual aid society and a Catholic parish. By the mid-1880s the Polish population of Chicago had grown to 45,000 in a city of over a million people.[2]

Other large cities of the Northeast and the Middle West also attracted the immigrants from Poland. New York, the point of arrival for almost all immigrants of every nationality, retained a large number of Poles, who eventually numbered about two hundred thousand in that city. Yet New York was so huge that it tended to swallow up the Polish immigrants. Poles were overshadowed by larger German, Irish, and Jewish populations, so that New York was never considered a major Polish-American center.[3]

On the Great Lakes Buffalo stood astride both the rail and water routes from New York into the interior; and many Poles, upon reaching this industrial city, went no further. Indeed, Buffalo eventually became a predominantly Polish city; but since the population of Buffalo was considerably smaller than that of other Great Lakes centers, the total number of Poles in Buffalo was limited, no matter how great a percentage of the population they became. Cleveland also attracted Poles as laborers for its industry, but many other immigrant groups settled there as well. A colony of Poles was founded in Milwaukee, but the heavily German character of that city tended to eclipse the Polish settlement. Outside Milwaukee numerous rural communities attracted Poles to try farming. By 1890 Wisconsin had the largest number of Polish settlements of any state in the nation. Even so, the entire Polish population of Wisconsin was exceeded by the number of Poles in Chicago.[4]

That left Detroit and Chicago as the two major Polish immigrant centers. At the time of the First World War, the Polish population of Detroit constituted nearly a fourth of that city's total population. Yet prewar Detroit, before the auto industry transformed it, was only a moderate-sized city. And when the production of automobiles began to swell the city's size in the teens and twenties of this century, the Polish population was greatly diluted by black and white migrants from the American South.[5]*

Thus Chicago, the fastest growing center west of New York, gradually gathered in more Poles than any other city in the nation. Though the Poles in Chicago never formed as large a percentage of the city's people as did the Poles in Buffalo or even in prewar Detroit, in absolute numbers they rapidly outstripped their kinsmen elsewhere. And unlike the situation in New York, the Polish colonies in Chicago were sufficiently large to attract notice and to make an impact on the city as a whole.

The Resurrectionist Fathers were the first to read correctly the implications of these population trends. In order to maximize the effectiveness of their limited manpower, they abandoned many of their missions in Texas and elsewhere in the United States and concentrated their efforts on Chicago. Other Polish-American leaders followed this example. The Polish Roman Catholic Union was organized in Chicago. In 1875 its first journalistic organ, the *Gazeta Polska Katolika* (Polish Catholic Gazette), originally published in Detroit, was moved to Chicago, where both the union and its various publications have remained ever since. Likewise, the organ of the Polish National Alliance, *Zgoda* (Harmony), first issued from Milwaukee; but in the late 1880s it too moved to Chicago. In 1898, when the Resurrectionists felt their position in the U.S. merited the establishment of a separate American province, Father Vincent Barzynski, C.R., a Chicago priest, became the first provincial superior.[6]

By 1910 Chicago had nearly a quarter-million Polish-American residents. The national organizations of Polonia—not only the PNA and PRCU
but the Polish Women's Alliance, the Polish Falcons, and the Polish Socialists
as well—had established their headquarters and were publishing their official
organs in Chicago. The city supported four Polish-language daily papers,
with circulation extending far beyond the city limits.

By the time the First World War brought to an end the greatest waves
of Polish immigration, Chicago had established itself as the informal capital
of Polonia in America.

Polonia's capital looked back to Anthony Smarzewski-Schermann as the
first permanent Polish settler in Chicago. He came from German Poland in
1851 and settled with his family on the northwest side of the city. That he
was the first arrival in Chicago is doubtful, for municipal records show evidence of a few Polish names from the very beginning of the city's history in
the 1830s. But Smarzewski-Schermann's family formed the nucleus of
Chicago's first cohesive Polish neighborhood; by the time he died in 1900
at the age of eighty-two, he was revered as the founder of Chicago's Polonia.[7]

At the time of the American Civil War, Chicago's Poles numbered about
five hundred. Towards the end of the war, in 1864, Smarzewski-Schermann,
three of his fellow pioneers in Chicago, and Peter Kiolbassa, a young cavalry
captain on leave in the city, organized the St. Stanislaus Kostka Benevolent
Society, the first Polish organization in the city. In 1867 the St. Stanislaus
Society laid plans for the founding of Chicago's first Polish parish. Previously, Polish Catholics had been obliged to worship at nearby English- or
German-speaking parishes, where the language barrier had been both inconvenient and humiliating.

At first St. Stanislaus Kostka Parish had no permanent home and no
regular priest in residence. Then in 1870 the founding society purchased
four building lots for a church at Noble and Bradley streets in the then lightly-
settled Polish area about a mile and a half northwest of the city's business center. That same year the Reverend Adolph Bakanowski, C.R., one of
the three original Resurrectionist missionaries in Texas, came to Chicago as
the parish's full-time pastor. A year later a combination church and school
building was completed.[8]

During the next twenty years, Polish immigration to Chicago—coming
largely from the German-occupied section of Poland—increased greatly. The
little colony around St. Stanislaus expanded, new Polish colonies crystallized
around various industries in Chicago, and St. Stanislaus Kostka fathered new

Polish parishes. Like Polonia as a whole, Polonia's capital comprised numerous isolated settlements, tenuously united by the efforts of priest, press, and fraternal order.

Determining the location and approximate founding date of a Polish community is relatively simple. Since nearly all Polish immigrants were Catholics who, as soon as possible after their arrival, tried to organize a parish, the founding dates of Polish churches form a rough outline of the origins of Polish settlements. Poles themselves called their communities by parish names. In Polish, the addition of the suffix *owo* to a parish name formed a community name. Thus Smarzewski-Schermann's colony around St. Stanislaus Kostka became the *Stanisławowo,* the "St. Stanislaus District" in cumbersome English translation.

By 1888, the *Stanisławowo* had expanded to form a large, wedge-shaped Polish settlement between the North Branch of the Chicago River and Milwaukee Avenue, with northern and southern boundaries roughly at Fullerton and Chicago avenues, respectively. Noble Street, on which St. Stanislaus Kostka Chuch stood, was the "main street" of the district; and the triangular corner of Milwaukee, Division, and Ashland avenues was the business hub. Two other Polish churches had already joined St. Stanislaus in the area: Holy Trinity (1872), directly south on Noble, and St. Hedwig (1888), about a mile to the northwest. Just across the river to the north, a group of Kaszubs, a Slavic group from Pomerania, closely related to the Poles, had founded St. Josaphat's Parish in 1884.[9]

Much of this territory was included in the city's Sixteenth Ward in a redistricting in 1888. The area as a whole formed the largest component in Polonia's capital, and had many nicknames. English-speaking Chicagoans styled it variously the St. Stanislaus district, Little Poland, and Polish Downtown. The last term is, perhaps, most appropriate, for it rightly denotes this area as the heartland of Chicago's Polonia.

By 1910 Polish Downtown was a thoroughly Polish area. The Sixteenth Ward contained 42,845 Poles, forming two-thirds of the ward's population, while two neighboring wards contributed roughly the same number of Poles to give Polish Downtown a population of nearly 100,000.[10]

In 1888 the Sixteenth Ward was already congested and unhealthful, with a death rate higher than that of the city as a whole. Years later social worker Edith Abbott, in a housing canvass of the city, described the area thus:

Evidences of congestion are still to be seen on every side. There are very few vacant lots, and vacant apartments or houses are very rare. Along one

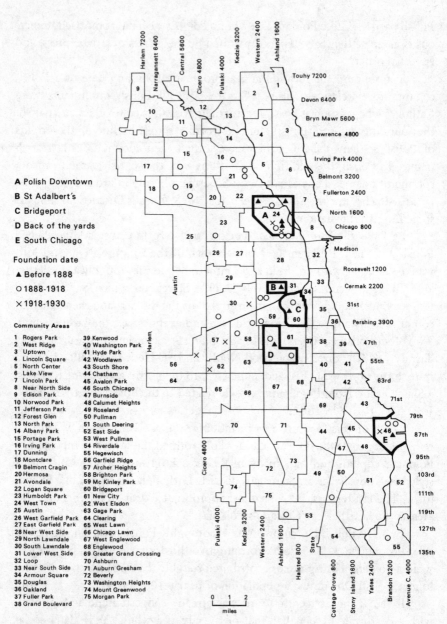

A Polish Downtown
B St Adalbert's
C Bridgeport
D Back of the yards
E South Chicago

Foundation date

▲ Before 1888
○ 1888-1918
✕ 1918-1930

Community Areas

1 Rogers Park	39 Kenwood
2 West Ridge	40 Washington Park
3 Uptown	41 Hyde Park
4 Lincoln Square	42 Woodlawn
5 North Center	43 South Shore
6 Lake View	44 Chatham
7 Lincoln Park	45 Avalon Park
8 Near North Side	46 South Chicago
9 Edison Park	47 Burnside
10 Norwood Park	48 Calumet Heights
11 Jefferson Park	49 Roseland
12 Forest Glen	50 Pullman
13 North Park	51 South Deering
14 Albany Park	52 East Side
15 Portage Park	53 West Pullman
16 Irving Park	54 Riverdale
17 Dunning	55 Hegewisch
18 Montclare	56 Garfield Ridge
19 Belmont Cragin	57 Archer Heights
20 Hermosa	58 Brighton Park
21 Avondale	59 Mc Kinley Park
22 Logan Square	60 Bridgeport
23 Humboldt Park	61 New City
24 West Town	62 West Elsdon
25 Austin	63 Gage Park
26 West Garfield Park	64 Clearing
27 East Garfield Park	65 West Lawn
28 Near West Side	66 Chicago Lawn
29 North Lawndale	67 West Englewood
30 South Lawndale	68 Englewood
31 Lower West Side	69 Greater Grand Crossing
32 Loop	70 Ashburn
33 Near South Side	71 Auburn Gresham
34 Armour Square	72 Beverly
35 Douglas	73 Washington Heights
36 Oakland	74 Mount Greenwood
37 Fuller Park	75 Morgan Park
38 Grand Boulevard	

Map 2. Location of Polish-language
Roman Catholic churches and five
original Polish neighborhoods in Chicago

TABLE 1   CHICAGO'S POLISH-LANGUAGE ROMAN CATHOLIC CHURCHES

Name	Date	Neighborhood
St. Stanislaus Kostka	1867	Polish Downtown
Holy Trinity	1872	Polish Downtown
St. Adalbert	1873	Lower West Side
Immaculate Conception	1882	South Chicago
St. Mary of Perpetual Help	1883	Bridgeport
St. Josaphat	1884	Polish Downtown
St. Joseph	1887	Back of the Yards
St. Hedwig	1888	Polish Downtown
St. Casimir	1890	Lower West Side
St. Michael the Archangel	1892	South Chicago
St. John Cantius	1893	Polish Downtown
St. Stanislaus B. and M.	1893	Cragin
St. Hyacinth	1894	Avondale
SS. Peter and Paul	1895	McKinley Park
St. Mary of the Angels	1897	Polish Downtown
St. Salomea	1898	Kensington
Assumption B.V.M.	1902	West Pullman
St. Anne	1903	Lower West Side
St. Florian	1905	Hegewisch
Holy Innocents	1905	Polish Downtown
St. John of God	1906	Back of the Yards
Good Shepherd	1907	South Lawndale
Five Holy Martyrs	1908	Brighton Park
St. Francis of Assisi	1909	Humboldt Park
St. Barbara	1910	Bridgeport
Sacred Heart of Jesus	1910	Back of the Yards
St. Mary Magdalene	1910	South Chicago
Immaculate Heart of Mary	1912	Irving Park
Transfiguration	1912	Lincoln Square
St. Wenceslaus	1912	Avondale
St. Helen	1913	Polish Downtown
St. Ladislaus	1914	Irving Park
St. James	1915	Cragin
St. Constance	1916	Jefferson Park
St. Szczepan	1919	Polish Downtown
St. Bronislawa	1920	South Chicago
St. Fidelis	1920	Polish Downtown
St. Pancratius	1924	Brighton Park
St. Bruno	1925	Archer Heights
St. Turibius	1927	West Elsdon
St. Thecla	1928	Norwood Park
St. Roman	1928	South Lawndale
St. Camillus	1928	Garfield Ridge

TABLE 2   POPULATION OF CHICAGO'S POLISH NEIGHBORHOODS, 1910

Community Name and Ward Number	Total Population*	Estimated Polish Population and % of Total**	Other Prominent Nationalities,%
Bridgeport (4)	49,650	10,707 (22)	German, 16 Lithuanian, 7 Irish, 7 Italian, 7
Brighton Park-McKinley Park (5)	57,131	8,480 (15)	German, 23 Irish, 15 Lithuanian, 8
South Chicago-Hegewisch (8)	65,810	18,004 (27)	German, 11 Swedish, 8
Back of the Yards (29)	81,985	17,708 (22)	German, 20 Czech, 10 Irish, 9 Lithuanian, 8
St. Adalbert's (11)	57,664	14,837 (26)	Russian (Jewish), 18 Czech, 15 German, 13
Polish Downtown (16, 17, 28)	203,505	96,243 (47)	German, 13 Italian, 7 Russian (Jewish), 4
Avondale and Far N.W. Side (27)	112,793	14,496 (13)	American, 32 German, 25
City-wide	2,185,283	213,776 (10)	German, 21 Scandinavian, 9 Czech, 5 Jewish, 5 Italian, 3

*Source: U.S. Bureau of the Census, Thirteenth Census of the United States.

**Source: Chicago Board of Education School Census, 1910.

street after another there are rows of tall and narrow brick tenements, usually three stories high, some four stories, built on twenty-five foot lots. Looking down narrow passageways, numerous frameshacks are to be seen on the rear of the lots. . . . Many of the rear shacks can only be described as miserable fire traps that should be torn down. They are dirty, ill kept, and reported by one investigator to be 'overrun with bugs and rats.'

Even today rear tenements, buildings resting several feet below the grade of the street, and dark narrow passageways between the buildings characterize this district, to which urban renewal has come only lately. If an observer looks down any alley just before the garbage is collected, he can easily visualize the turn-of-the-century conditions of Polish Downtown.[11]

Yet to thousands of Poles this area was home in the New World; and, for Polonia's capital, it was truly "downtown." The fraternal organizations located their national offices along Division or Milwaukee avenues; the most influential newspapers of Polonia were published nearby; Poles from elsewhere in the city sometimes came here to shop; and St. Stanislaus Kostka was by far the largest and best-known Polish church in Chicago.

Chicago's second oldest Polish community formed around a number of small factories on the near west side of the city. In the 1860s a few Poles began to settle among the Czechs and Slovaks of St. Wenceslaus Parish at Desplaines Avenue and DeKoven Street, just one block from the barn where Mrs. O'Leary's mythical cow would soon ignite the great Chicago fire of 1871. The very year of the fire, these Poles, desiring a church of their own, formed the Society of St. Adalbert Bishop and Martyr, which succeeded in obtaining a pastor for the new St. Adalbert's Parish at Seventeenth and Paulina in 1873.[12]

The *Wojciechowo,* as the Poles called this neighborhood (*Wojciech* is the Polish word for Adalbert), was neither as old nor as congested as Polish Downtown in 1888. Chicago's Ninth Ward, in which St. Adalbert's was then located, had only half the population density of the Sixteenth; and the health and mortality statistics were not yet alarming. By the mid-nineties, however, the area had begun to decline; and the social conditions which shocked Jane Addams at Hull House, one mile to the east, had moved into this neighborhood as well.[13]

The West Side of Chicago, around St. Adalbert's and farther west, never became as heavily Polish as the *Stanisławowo.* In some respects the ethnic situation of the West Side resembled that of Manhattan Island in New York, where other groups swallowed up the Poles. Along the city's east-west axis of Madison Street, middle-class Irish and old-stock Americans preempted the West Side's most desirable neighborhoods. To the south of Madison Street, in North Lawndale, a prosperous Jewish community developed out of the old "ghetto" area just west of Chicago's Loop; and the Italians of Hull House also moved into Lawndale.[14]

The West Side's Poles were confined to a narrow strip between Ogden

Avenue and the Sanitary and Ship Canal. Within this strip three new parishes
marked the Poles' expansion in a straight line from St. Adalbert's to the city
limits. But even within this narrow strip, the Poles were outnumbered by the
large Czech communities of Pilsen and Cêske Kalifornia. The area later came
to be dominated politically by a Czech leader, Anton Cermak, rather than by
a Pole.[15]

Across the South Branch of the Chicago River from the polygot West
Side lay Bridgeport, the site of Chicago's third Polish community. Bridgeport,
more than most city neighborhoods, is a natural geographic unit, surrounded
by branches of the river on two sides and enclosed by railroad tracks on the
other two. Irish laborers, imported to dig the Illinois and Michigan Canal,
which began at the northern border of Bridgeport, first settled the area in the
1830s. In the 1880s and 90s, numerous breweries, foundries, and brickyards
along the waterways and railroads, as well as the nearby Union Stock Yards,
attracted unskilled Poles and Lithuanians into the area to form a vast labor
pool.

The first few Polish families founded Our Lady of Perpetual Help
Parish in 1886. Many of the Irish moved out, leaving behind such names as
Lyman, Farrell, and Quinn on the street signs. A good number, however,
stayed to be near Bridgeport's rich mine of industrial employment. By the
time of the First World War, the neighborhood was composed of roughly
equal numbers of Poles, Germans, and Irish, as well as smaller clusters of
Lithuanians and Italians. The population, well protected by Bridgeport's
natural boundaries, still retains approximately the same ethnic character it
had assumed by 1914.[16]

Bridgeport was rich in industry and jobs but small in area. The gigantic
Union Stock Yards, which had arisen directly south of Bridgeport in 1865,
attracted far more workers than the neighborhood's constricted boundaries
could contain. Thus the expanse of prairie south and west of the yards began
to be settled by the slaughterhouse workers. This ill-defined neighborhood,
called Back of the Yards, or else, euphemistically, "New City," was located
in the Town of Lake, which was outside Chicago's city limits when the first
Poles began obtaining jobs at the yards in the mid 1880s. These Poles
founded the parish of St. Joseph in the area in 1887, with the grand boundaries of Bubbly Creek (a branch of the Chicago River) on the north, Lake
Michigan on the east, the township limits on the west, and then running all
the way to St. Louis, Missouri, on the south. Two years later Chicago annexed
the Town of Lake as well as other surrounding areas, bringing the Poles of

Packingtown within the limits of Polonia's capital. In the next twenty years, two additional Polish churches arose back of the yards to diminish St. Joseph's grand expanse.[17]

Population density around the stockyards was far lower than in Polish Downtown or other older parts of the city. There were few tenements in the yards district, most of the dwellings being simply frame cottages hastily erected on the prairie. Yet the congestion within these cottages was frightful, for often two or more immigrant families shared a house, and families frequently took in lodgers.[18]

Worse still were the outside surroundings of the houses. Mary McDowell, the Jane Addams of the stockyards, has described her first glimpse of the yards' surroundings when she first took the job of head resident of the University of Chicago settlement house.

At the close of the summer of '94, I came to live in Packingtown near the corner of Ashland Avenue and 47th street, two blocks from Whiskey Point and three from the great packing houses. . . .Packingtown as I then knew it, had many features of the frontier town. . . . It was separated from the other side of town by forty-two railroad tracks, and one square mile of stock yards. On the north was the backwater of the Chicago River, . . . Bubbly Creek. The streets were unpaved, the houses had no sewer connections, and the ditches were covered with a germ-breeding scum.

The slaughter pens; the hair-drying fields, where cattle hair was laid out to decay in the sun; and Bubbly Creek, an open sewer for industrial waste, gave the Packingtown air a permanently offensive odor. The garbage dumps in clay pits to the west added to the stench and vermin of the area.[19]

In the midst of this scene, thousands of foreign-born workers of many nationalties made their homes. By 1910 Poles made up about 15 percent of the work force at the yards and 22 percent of the area's population. They shared the yards district with Irish, Germans, Scandinavians, Bohemians, Lithuanians, and even some Negroes.[20]

The industrial community of South Chicago, ten miles south of Chicago's Loop along the lakefront, was the fifth Polish colony founded in Chicago before 1888. Actually, like Back of the Yards, it was outside the city limits, in the Town of Hyde Park, until the annexation of 1889 swallowed it up. South Chicago was similar to the yards district in many other ways. It, too, owed its founding to the movement of a large industry, in this case the Illinois Steel Company, to more spacious surroundings from a former site near the center of the city. It, too, was a one-industry community made up of numerous ethnic groups of unskilled laborers. As in the stockyards area, the dominant industry affected the physical environment for the worse; but instead of the foul odor of the slaughterhouse, the South Chicago air was filled with a black pall of smoke which shut out the nearby lake and the neighboring meadows.[21]

Seventy Polish families in South Chicago organized a mutual aid society in 1882. The bishop of the diocese then gave permission for the construction of a wooden church, dedicated to the Immaculate Conception, at Eighty-eighth and Commercial Avenue, a few blocks from the mills. The steel mills kept booming through most of the years preceding the First World War, and South Chicago grew rapidly. Two more Polish churches were founded by 1910, when Poles in the steel community numbered almost twenty thousand, ranking about equal with the Polish colony near the stockyards.[22]

Contemporary observers often compared these original Polish neighborhoods and other ethnic colonies, dominated by the twin spires of church steeple and factory smokestack, to self-contained medieval villages. Later writers generally accepted these descriptions and termed the ethnic colonies in American cities "ghettoes." The closed ethnic ghetto as the residence of first-generation immigrants is perhaps the most common generalization found in immigration history. Recently, however, historians have questioned whether immigrant groups, in fact, clustered together as tightly as they were presumed to have done. It is becoming clear from recent studies that clustering in ghettoes was not a universal experience of all immigrants but something of a special case, limited mainly to southern and eastern European "new immigrants" in the largest American cities. It would be reasonable to expect, then, that Poles in Chicago would have been one of these special cases; and this is, in fact, what the evidence indicates.[23]

The city wards in which the five original Polish neighborhoods were located were not wholly Polish. In 1910 only one ward in the city, the Sixteenth in Polish Downtown, was more than 50 percent Polish. But in the other Polish wards there was still much concentration and clustering. Poles were the largest single group in these wards. Of all the Poles in the city, 73.7 percent lived in the five original colonies in 1910.

The index of dissimilarity, or segregation index, by wards was 63 for the Poles. This statistical measure of residential segregation employs a scale from 0 to 100. An index of 0 indicates perfect integration and an index of 100 indicates complete segregation. Any index above 25 shows significant segregation. The Polish index of 63 is unusually high for an immigrant

group. It means that 63 percent of all Chicago Poles would have had to move
to another ward in order for an even distribution of Poles to be obtained
throughout the city.[24]

Actually, Poles were even more clustered than these ward figures indicate. The area of a ward usually included several neighborhoods, and the
smaller-area data which are available show that Poles clustered together on
specific city blocks within these wards. The Immigration Commission picked
out several sample Polish blocks in Chicago. On the Cleaver Street block in
Polish Downtown, 95.1 percent of the households were Polish; and on
Buffalo Avenue between Eighty-second and Eighty-third streets in South
Chicago, 90.3 percent of the households were Polish. Even in the more mixed
yards district, Wood Street from Forty-seventh to Forty-eighth streets was
61.6 percent Polish.[25]

By inspecting registration lists I found that in the 1890s the registered
voters in six electoral precincts of the Sixteenth Ward were over 80 percent
Polish; and in three more precincts they were over 60 percent Polish (these
precincts were generally one or two square blocks in area). Thus nine of the
ward's twenty-eight precincts were overwhelmingly Polish, and these nine
precincts formed a solid Polish area three-quarters of a mile long and one-
half mile wide. Several precincts in South Chicago were also over 50 percent
Polish at this time. By 1910 there were overwhelmingly Polish precincts in
all five of the original Polish neighborhoods. This use of political registration
lists undoubtedly understates the extent of Polish clustering, for the majority
of Poles in America before the First World War were not citizens and would
not appear on voters' lists. There is not enough data available to compute an
index of dissimilarity based on small areas, but it seems clear that such an
index would be considerably higher than the 63 percent figure based on
wards.[26]

Thus Chicago Poles clearly did cluster together, and the traditional concept of ethnic ghettoes does apply at least to this group. Furthermore, even
when Poles did share a relatively small neighborhood with other groups,
demographic mixing would not necessarily lead to social mixing. Language
barriers alone would prevent this; but, in addition, the organization of Catholics into separate, national parishes, the institution of ethnic fraternal organizations, and the founding of small businesses by members of each nationality
to serve their countrymen would tend to keep groups apart. A ghetto was a
social organization as much as a geographic or demographic entity.

Though Chicago's Poles did experience an initial ghetto experience, the

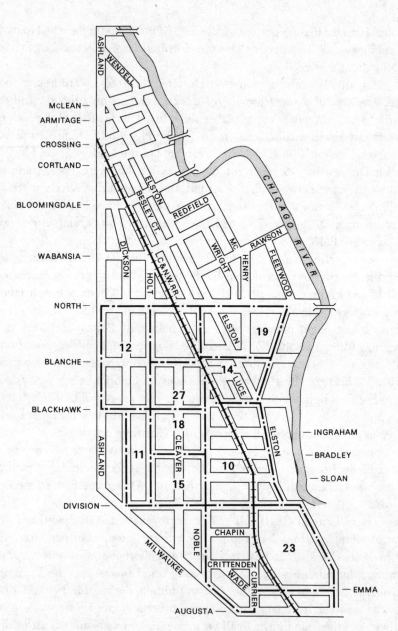

Map 3. Precinct boundaries in Polish
Downtown, 1896. In precincts 10, 11, 14,
15, 18, and 27 more than 80 percent of
the registered voters were Polish; in

precincts 12, 19, and 23 over 60 percent
were Polish.
Source: registration lists at the Chicago
Board of Election Commissioners.

five original colonies did not hold them for long. Before the First World War, new Polish communities grew up farther out from the city center. The Polish immigrant somehow saved a portion of each week's meager pay to buy a house or rent a more spacious flat out beyond the congestion. The greatest expansion of the Polish mass into more desirable, middle-class neighborhoods took place to the northwest, along Milwaukee Avenue, and to the southwest, along Archer Avenue. Many Poles had become acquainted with the open spaces along these streets as they rode to the two Polish cemeteries beyond the city limits.[27]

Expansion northwest began early in the 1890s. Rather than moving in a continuous wave along Milwaukee Avenue, the Poles leaped over an established community of Germans and Scandinavians around Logan Square and purchased home lots about a mile and a half out from Polish Downtown in the area known as Avondale. In 1894 about forty families from St. Stanislaus owned lots in Avondale and were impatient for a church of their own. Father Barzynski, pastor of St. Stanislaus, was reluctant to spend his scarce money and manpower on such a small establishment. But the Avondale settlers forced his hand by engaging a schismatic priest and threatening to establish an independent church. Father Barzynski swiftly abandoned his reluctance and used Resurrectionist money to buy up the schismatic's plot of ground and found there the parish of St. Hyacinth.[28]

In the next decade Avondale filled in slowly with Poles. The Milwaukee Avenue horsecar line was electrified, providing speedier connections with Polish Downtown and Chicago's Loop. Small factories sprang up along the two railroad lines running through Avondale, and the empty land and spacious building lots looked attractive to residents of the overcrowded *Stanisławowo*. In 1912 the bishop opened a second Polish church in the area. Before the end of the First World War the Poles had moved even farther out and founded parishes in the far northwest neighborhoods of Irving Park and Jefferson Park.[29]

On the southwest, expansion along Archer Avenue proceeded more slowly, as the majority of Poles remained near Bridgeport's industries or spread out back of the yards. But by the time of the First World War, Polish parishes had also been opened near Archer Avenue in the communities of McKinley Park and Brighton Park. The Santa Fe railroad tracks west of Kedzie Avenue formed a temporary barrier, and the land beyond was still empty prairie.[30]

These diagonal movements northwest and southwest contained the main body of Polish community expansion. Elsewhere in the city, however, smaller communities of Poles also sprang up around some local industry, and even more parishes were born. Five miles straight west of Polish Downtown, the little industrial village of Cragin grew along the Chicago, Milwaukee, and St. Paul Railroad tracks, where a small cluster of Poles organized St. Stanislaus Bishop and Martyr Parish in 1893. Poles from South Chicago trekked to the southern limits of the city and founded parishes in Hegewisch, West Pullman, and Kensington. By the time of the First World War, Polonia's capital had outposts in nearly every corner of the city, thirty-four parishes in all in 1916, and had pushed over the three hundred thousand mark in a city of two million people.[31]

Like the greater Polonia in the United States, this far-flung Polonia in Chicago was struggling to realize itself as a united community, although it never really succeeded in this aim. Long distances, impassible barriers, and poor transportation facilities kept individual communities apart. For instance, on a map, St. Adalbert's appears very close to the community of Bridgeport; indeed, the two are only about a mile and a half apart. There was, however, no direct physical link between the two districts. Halsted Street, slightly east of both communities, possessed the only bridge over the barrier formed by the Ship Canal and its corridor of railroads.

Having neither time, means, nor occasion to venture elsewhere, the residents of each community confined their activities largely to home, church, and factory, all within the immediate neighborhood. Even when the Poles joined the outward expansion of the city, their new neighborhoods were largely self-sufficient, with jobs, schools, churches, and stores in reasonable walking distance.[32]

The Polonia leaders never stopped trying to unite these communities. In the early days Resurrectionist priests commuted by horse and wagon from St. Stanislaus to Cragin and South Chicago before permanent pastors could be found to offer Mass in these areas. The PNA and PRCU leaders printed their papers in Polish Downtown and distributed them to all parts of Polonia's capital, including news items from nearly every Polish parish.

Still, their efforts were not completely successful. Poles in outlying areas sometimes felt that the leaders in Polish Downtown either ignored them or else put on airs in considering the *Stanisławowo* the intellectual and spiritual heart of Polonia's capital. In South Chicago, particularly, such resentment rankled. In 1906, upon the initiative of the pastor of Immaculate Conception

Parish, the South Chicago Poles established their own weekly newspaper, *Polonia*. The pioneers in this venture felt that the leaders of Polish Downtown only recalled South Chicago's existence when they needed money. The new paper was intended to assert the neighborhood's growing importance in Chicago's Polonia.[33]

Thus Polonia's capital, spreading out on the Chicago prairies between 1888 and 1914, was a fragmented giant, made up of relatively isolated, self-conscious, sometimes jealous "villages," struggling with an ideal of strength in unity.

3 Influences and Institutions

The separate "villages" of Polonia's capital, despite their relative isolation from each other, shared many occupational, economic, and social characteristics. The Immigration Commission, which reported its findings in 1911, provides some information on such characteristics. Though this Commission manifested a strong anti-immigrant bias and attempted to use its findings as a justification for immigration restriction, the raw data it accumulated afford a useful glimpse at the population of Polish newcomers.[1]

The great mass of Polish immigrants were peasants; fully 81.5 percent of the commission's sample had been farmers or farm laborers in the old country. The majority were unskilled laborers in the new. Fifty-four percent of the Polish-born male heads of households listed their occupation in Chicago simply as laborer. Many of the other occupations listed by name, however, were essentially unskilled jobs; so the true total of the unskilled reached roughly two-thirds of this sample. About 22 percent reported a job in a skilled trade, whereas the remainder were divided about equally between small businessmen and the unemployed (five percent in each case).[2]

The unskilled laborers were largely on their own in the ceaseless hunt for employment, taking their places with other immigrants in the long lines waiting for work at the factory gates. Labor unions had made little effort to organize the unskilled, and the Immigration Commission found that only 9.5 percent of Chicago's Polish workers were unionized. Yet when an enlightened union approached the unskilled and made the effort to address the Poles in their own language, as the Amalgamated Meat Cutters did prior to the stockyards strike of 1904, Poles joined the union and fought for better wages and working conditions. Mary McDowell, during the 1904 strike, heard a Polish worker exhorting his fellows in four different languages to hold out for 2½¢ an hour raise, avowing that, without this raise, "You know that you can't give your children an American living." A steady job and an "American living" were constant goals of the unskilled Poles, but, until the labor organizing drives of the 1930s, they made the quest largely without the aid of unions.[3]

Nor did socialism exert much influence on Polish labor. The Catholic church, of course, was vehement in its denunciation of socialist agitators; and the fact that many socialist leaders were of German or Jewish birth made the movement repugnant to Poles. The Polish Socialist Alliance was mainly a group of emigré intellectuals, and it was generally more nationalistic than socialistic anyway. Polish laborers, however, realized that social and economic conditions needed amelioration. By 1905 or 1906 enough interest in practical socialism had developed for the American Socialist party to organize a Polish-language section and begin issuing a Polish daily, The *Dziennik Ludowy* (People's Daily), in Chicago. The newspaper reached a circulation of about twenty thousand nationally at its highpoint in 1920, and as many as 10 or 15 percent of the Polish voters in Chicago occasionally cast a ballot for a particular Socialist candidate. But in the long run, the Socialist party failed to build a mass base in Polonia. The extremely anticlerical tone of *Dziennik Ludowy* hindered the party's chances among the Catholic Poles.[4]

Unskilled labor was the lot of the "typical" Polish immigrant; but many American Poles worked as carpenters, butchers, or in other trades requiring a skill. Others owned small businesses, and some even built up moderate fortunes. A Polish business directory for 1905 reveals that most of the small businessmen owned saloons, meat markets, groceries, tailor shops, or bakeries, generally serving the immediate needs of their laboring-class neighbors. In the 1880s Ladislaus Dyniewicz capitalized on the immigrant's need for reading matter in his own language with a flourishing print shop, and Ladislaus Smulski built up a small publishing empire of Polish-language books and newspapers. Smulski's son, John, who inherited the family business upon his father's death, used the capital from the publishing enterprise to organize an influential bank in Polish Downtown, in 1907. He and a few compatriots speculated far and wide in real estate and even in western mining strikes. By the time the First World War broke out, John Smulski had become a millionaire.[5]

Other early settlers in Polonia's capital had earned professional degrees in law or medicine before leaving Poland, and thus they provided sorely needed services for Chicago's Poles. Likewise, many ambitious sons of immigrants studied law, medicine, or business in the night school of a local

university and began practice among their kinsmen. John Schermann, son of
Chicago's first Polish settler, was fairly typical of the Polish business class,
selling fire insurance, speculating in real estate, and dabbling in politics.[6]

These small businessmen were part of the "respectable" half of the
leadership class in Polonia's capital, and most of them held office in one or
more of the fraternal organizations. But another group of influential businessmen, less respectable in the eyes of English-speaking Chicagoans, coexisted
with them, the saloonkeepers. It took about five hundred dollars to start a
small saloon at the turn of the century, and many an immigrant hoarded his
laborer's salary in order to save that amount. In fact, saloonkeepers formed
over 3 percent of the Polish population and were the second most numerous
occupational group after common laborers.

The saloonkeeper was an important figure in his community. Like the
other small businessmen, he was his own boss and a model to the mass of
toilers around him. Furthermore, he was the heir of a great tradition; in the
old country an innkeeper or public-house owner was a man of distinction. Finally, since his saloon was often the only bright spot in the lives of most immigrant laborers, and he could act as genial host to all, quick with a bit of advice
and maybe even some real assistance with a glass of beer, the saloonkeeper
was a man of considerable influence.[7]

But no one in Polonia's early days, neither respectable businessman nor
saloonkeeper, could rival the influence of the Catholic priest. In partitioned
Poland the peasant had suffered much deprivation and disorganization. His
language and his religion remained, however, to help him define who he was;
and in the rapidly changing world of nineteenth-century Europe, "the task of
the priest [among peasants] was to maintain in the mind of the peasant the
idea of order in the universe." The priest in Poland, then, served as a pillar
in the center of the peasant community.[8]

Upon emigration to America the Polish peasant needed such a pillar all
the more. Disoriented and bewildered in a strange land, the peasant needed
leaders and institutions which could assure him he was still the same man. The
Polish priest in a parish church did this. If it were merely a question of religious services, the Polish immigrant could easily have attended a German or
Irish parish. Indeed, the Mass was offered in a language equally incompre-
hensible to all nationalities, in Latin. But the parish church in Polonia was
more than a place for religious services; it was a community center, and thus
it had to be run by a priest who spoke the Polish language. In his preaching

and his community activities, the Polish priest embodied religion, language, and national culture in his own person.[9]

The Polish Roman Catholic Union attempted to strengthen the local priest's influence by federating parish associations into a Polonia-wide Catholic fraternal organization. From its founding in 1873, the PRCU published a weekly journal for the instruction and edification of its membership. Though the name and editorship changed periodically in the early days, the PRCU organ has borne the title *Naród Polski* (Polish Nation) from 1897 to the present.[10]

The career of Father Vincent Barzynski, C.R., who directed St. Stanislaus Kostka parish from 1874 to 1899, illustrates the prodigious activities and influence of a vigorous immigrant pastor. Vincent Barzynski had lived an adventurous early life in Europe. Born in 1838 in the Congress Kingdom of Poland under the Russian domination, he was ordained a secular priest and took an active part in the 1863 insurrection against Russian authority. Fleeing to Cracow in the Austrian sector after the rebellion failed, Barzynski was arrested and jailed in Austria for ten months, then deported to France, where he joined a large community of Polish emigrés.

In Paris he came into contact with a group of Resurrectionist priests, whose work and life style attracted him. The Congregation of the Resurrection had been founded in 1836 in Paris by three Polish emigré priests for the purpose of uniting Catholicism with the cause of Polish national rebirth. Its headquarters in Poland was established in Cracow under the relatively lenient rule of the Austrians. Barzynski joined the congregation in 1865 and was sent as one of the three pioneer Resurrectionist missionaries to Texas in the following year. Two of his brothers, Joseph Barzynski, C.R., also a priest, and John, a layman and journalist, followed him to America. In September of 1874 Vincent was called to Chicago as pastor of St. Stanislaus. Chicago remained his home until his death in 1899.[11]

The growing parish of St. Stanislaus Kostka would have taxed the energy of any one man. Father Barzynski built the massive, cathedral-like church which stands on Noble Street, raising almost $100,000 to complete its twin towers in 1892. He also built a new rectory, a convent, and a parish school containing the largest auditorium in Polonia's capital. The parish hall of St. Stanislaus housed varied activities, from the Society of Polish Singers to political meetings. In the Chicago World's Fair year of 1893, St. Stanislaus was billed as the largest Catholic parish in the world, with over two thousand baptisms, almost four hundred weddings, and one thousand funerals in that year. Father Barzynski was overseer of the parish's numerous associations and clubs. He even founded a parish savings and loan association. This not only ensured safe keeping for the meager savings of the Polish immigrants, who mistrusted banks, but also provided Barzynski with a pool of capital for his ambitious building projects.[12]

Yet Father Barzynski did not rest content with merely building the largest parish in the world; his activities stretched throughout Polonia's capital. He had a hand in organizing some twenty-five other parishes in Chicago, staffing them with Polish-born Resurrectionists like himself. He stirred up opposition among parishioners who resented what they interpreted as his desire to dominate them. Father Vincent, however, had the ear of the Chicago bishops, who consulted him on most decisions that would affect the diocese's Polish Catholics and backed him with their own authority when disputes arose. Besides parish-building, the tireless pastor of St. Stanislaus also founded a Polish orphanage, hospital, and secondary school; persuaded one order of Polish sisters to come to Chicago and established another order of American-born nuns; participated in the organization of the Polish Roman Catholic Union; and, in 1887, set up the Polish Publishing Company to fill the need for Catholic literature printed in the Polish language.[13]

This entry into the publishing field proved to be one of Father Barzynski's most important means of maintaining the church's influence in Polonia. The company published a full line of missals and devotional books; but it also put out a short-lived polemical weekly, *Kropidło* (The Holy Water Sprinkler), in 1887 and 1888, to attack the Masonic, socialist, and anticlerical enemies of the church. Then in 1890 the board of directors of the Polish Publishing Company—Father Barzynski, three other priests, and three laymen—founded the first Polish-language daily newspaper in Chicago, the *Dziennik Chicagoski* (the "Chicago Daily News" literally, but always referred to as the "Polish Daily News" to distinguish it from the English-language *Chicago Daily News*). Under the active direction of Father Francis Gordon, C.R.—another Polish-born Resurrectionist and Father Barzynski's successor as the dominant spiritual leader in Polonia's capital—the *Dziennik Chicagoski* had a wide circulation and exerted a powerful influence on the community.[14]

This daily newspaper followed faithfully the credo of Father Barzynski and the other Resurrectionist priests working in America: "That each Pole should retain his Catholic Faith, learn the language and history of Poland, but be given the chance to become a good Yankee." Despite the secular cast of many Resurrectionist activities—building edifices of brick and mortar, handling money at a savings and loan, and publishing newspapers—the order's primary aim was spiritual. Father Barzynski and his colleagues knew that even the devout Polish immigrant lived not by faith alone and that by providing for mundane needs they could maintain their spiritual influence more effectively.

The second part of the Resurrectionist creed, learning the language and history of Poland, was intertwined with the first. Language, history, and religion formed a cultural trinity for nineteenth-century Poles; maintenance of this trinity of values among their peasant flocks was a primary task of the Resurrectionists. During his Chicago years Vincent Barzynski was no longer involved in the politics of liberation. He realized the futility of the insurrections in Europe; absorbed in his new work, he considered the spiritual-cultural unity of all American Poles as a more immediate and attainable goal than the liberation of Poland.[15]

The final guiding principle of the Resurrectionists was "that each Pole be given an opportunity to be a good Yankee." In its very first issue, *Dziennik Chicagoski* restated the point this way:

[Among] the principles guiding us shall be ... to regard highly the Constitution of the United States, as citizens of the country. We must participate actively in the public life of our country. ... Specifically, we Poles must not consider ourselves as visitors but as an integral part of this country.[16]

The widespread influence of the church and clergy in Polonia's capital was often challenged by nonconforming individuals, by the independent church movement, and by the Polish National Alliance. A popular stereotype of Polonia as a monolithic society directed by the Catholic clergy leaves out of account both the opposition which the wide-ranging activities of the Polish priests stirred up and the persistent factionalism of Poles. The great scope of Father Barzynski's efforts was not wholly the product of zeal and devotion on his part. Often he was moved to action by a challenge from independent-minded parishioners or schismatic priests, as when the residents of Avondale forced his hand in the founding of St. Hyacinth Parish. The Polish-American church experienced some of the same troubles from trusteeism that the native American church had undergone in the early nineteenth century. The trustees of St. Stanislaus Kostka, having founded the parish by their own effort, wanted to keep title to the church lands rather than turn them over to an Irish bishop. The first Resurrectionist pastor of the parish had to persuade them to sign over the title of ownership to the bishop, as the American hierarchy had decreed at the councils of Baltimore.[17]

The independent church movement posed a constant threat to the Catholic clergy in the early days. Independence was, at first, a reaction to the dominant position which the Resurrectionist Order had gained. In at least one case an ambitious priest founded an independent parish, not because of doctrinal differences nor in an attempt to cause a permanent schism, but only to cause such a controversy that the church authorities would mediate the dispute and confirm his position as pastor.[18]

The independent movement, however, fed on a number of real grievances. Many Polish Catholics saw no reason why they should be ruled by German and Irish bishops; others, far ahead of their time in Catholic thinking, desired the language of the Mass to be changed from medieval Latin to the Polish vernacular. Independent-minded Poles, furthermore, exhibited a Protestant-like resentment at the charging of money stipends for the Mass and the sacraments, and a democratic urge for the parishioners, not the bishops, to administer the land and money of the parish.

Stung by these grievances, a Polish priest, Reverend Francis Hodur, gathered together a number of independent churches and in 1896 founded the Polish National Catholic Church, with headquarters in Scranton, Pennsylvania, and himself as first bishop. Bishop Hodur conceded that the Roman church and the Resurrectionist order had done much heroic work among Polish immigrants but avowed that they overstepped their authority and perverted the message of Christ. He organized his church, schismatic in the eyes of Rome, around a number of leading principles:

> The owners and administrators of the church's wealth in America should be the Polish people, and the bishops and priests are custodians of the churches and schools as delegates of the people.
> Sacraments administered for money are invalid, sacrilegious, and simoniacal.
> Religion is a living relation between God and man and not a machine for making money and keeping the people in ignorance.
> The great sacrament of the Christian and National Church . . . is the preaching of and the listening to the Word of God.
> The religious rites should be performed in the Polish language, because they are external expressions of the Polish spirit, the Polish nation's relations to God.[19]

The existence of this alternate church in Polonia and the fact that seven Polish National parishes, including the Cathedral of All Saints, were even-

tually organized in Polonia's capital, gives the lie to any monolithic interpretation of the Roman clergy's influence. Yet a close reading of Bishop Hodur's
statement of principles, particularly his bitter reference to the Roman church
as a "machine for making money and keeping the people in ignorance," reveals a grudging admission of the Catholic church's strong, persisting influence. The Polish National Church never attracted more than a few thousand adherents in Polonia's capital, but it was a sign of diversity and dissent
among the Poles.

The independent church movement was often supported in specific con-
troversies by the Polish National Alliance, which had its own ideological
reasons for opposing church influence. The PNA, though its mass membership was due more to low-cost burial insurance and opportunities for socia-
bility than to ideology, was led by politically conscious emigrés. These leaders
carried with them from Poland a resentment of the usually conservative role
the church had played in Polish politics. Their organization was anticlerical

TABLE 3   LEADING POLISH-AMERICAN ORGANIZATIONS AND INSTITUTIONS

Name of Organization or Institution	Nature of Organization	Date and Place of Founding
Congregation of the Resurrection (C.R.)	Religious order of priests	1836, Paris 1866, America
Polish Roman Catholic Union (PRCU)	Catholic fraternal order	1873, Chicago
Polish National Alliance (PNA)	Patriotic fraternal order	1880, Philadelphia
Polish Falcons of America	Patriotic gymnastic organization	1830s, Poland 1880s, America
Alliance of Polish Socialists	Political organization	1880s, America
Polish National Catholic Church	Religious denomination	1896, Scranton, Pa.
Polish Alma Mater	Youth-oriented fraternal order	1897, Chicago
Polish Women's Alliance	Women's society	1898, Chicago

in tone and had no religious test for membership, admitting Polish Jews, schismatics, and nonbelievers as well as Catholics. The PNA opposed the PRCU and the Resurrectionist priests vociferously in its weekly organ, *Zgoda,* and later in its daily paper, *Dziennik Zwiazkowy* (Alliance Daily News).

TABLE 4   IMPORTANT POLISH-AMERICAN NEWSPAPERS IN CHICAGO

Name	Dates	Frequency	Affiliation
Gazeta Polska Katolika (Polish Catholic Gazette)	1874-84	weekly	Polish Roman Catholic Union
Wiara i Ojczyzna (Faith and Fatherland)	1887-99	weekly	Polish Roman Catholic Union and Polish Publishing Co. (C.R.)
Kropidlo (The Holy Water Sprinkler)	1887-88	weekly	Polish Publishing Co. (C.R.)
Zgoda (Harmony)	1880-	weekly	Polish National Alliance
Dziennik Chicagoski (Polish Daily News)	1890-1971	daily	Polish Publishing Co. (C.R.)
Naród Polski (Polish Nation)	1897-	weekly	Polish Roman Catholic Union
Dziennik Ludowy (Peoples' Daily)	1907-24	daily	Polish Section American Socialist Party
Dziennik Zwiazkowy (Alliance Daily News)	1908-	daily	Polish National Alliance
Polonia	1906-48	weekly	South Chicago Poles
Telegraf	1892-1939	irregular	Personal Organ
Dziennik Narodowy (National Daily News)	1848-1923	daily	Independent
Dziennik Zjednoczenia (Union Daily News)	1928-39	daily	Polish Roman Catholic Union

The Alliance and the National Church both cherished the "fourth province of Poland" ideal. Besides their many other grievances against Barzynski, the Resurrectionists, and the Roman church, both groups felt that the Catholic priests were insufficiently interested in Poland. The Catholic priests, in their opinion, submitted too meekly to the "foreign" hierarchy in

America and did not support Polish liberation efforts actively enough. Though the Congregation of the Resurrection was a nationalist organization in Europe, its priests in America were too busy building religious institutions for their local flocks to agitate against Poland's conquerors. The Alliance and the independent churchmen resented this. Bishop Hodur summed up the apologia for his church thus:

The Roman clique and its agents, the priests, have done some creative things in Poland and America, but without the Alliance, without the Falcons, without the free popular Polish press, and the Polish workers party, and without the Polish National Catholic Church, there would not be living, enlightened people with a warm feeling for Poland.[20]

Minus the polemics, this sentence and what it contains between its lines aptly describes the constellation of influences affecting life in Polonia and its capital. The "Roman clique and its agents" possessed the dominant voice; but other organizations and institutions created a diversity, dissension, and factionalism which were not always apparent to the eyes of outsiders.

4 Politics in Polonia

The ordinary immigrant in Polonia's capital, as throughout Polonia, was primarily concerned with the day-to-day struggle for survival. All community activities—founding mutual aid societies, building parish churches, federating local societies into fraternal organizations, printing Polish-language newspapers—were related to this prime concern. Mutual aid was a necessity of physical survival, and a Polish church was imperative for spiritual existence. Fraternalism provided a social life, and the Polish press preserved the rudiments of language and culture.

Once the fundamental social structures of the immigrant community had been established, political activities began to appear. Polish immigrants and their children engaged in three different kinds of politics, corresponding to the three worlds in which they lived. There was the politics of Poland, aimed at the liberation of the fatherland from the partitioning powers. There was the politics of Polonia, involving internal clashes over a new Polish-American society struggling to be born. Finally, American politics beckoned.

Though Polish immigrants cherished keen memories of their homeland and longed for an end to the century-long humiliation which Poland had suffered at the hands of its three neighbors, very few engaged in political effort on Poland's behalf. These few were generally political emigrés, aristocrats or burghers who had participated in one or another of the insurrections of the nineteenth century and then fled to America upon the failure of the rebellion. These emigrés considered themselves temporary residents of the United States and seldom lived among the mass of Polish immigrants. Rarely becoming American citizens, they considered themselves Poles in every way.

In the 1890s these temporary immigrants organized the Alliance of Polish Socialists. This group was connected with the Polish Socialist Party (PPS) in Poland, which later, under Joseph Pilsudski, played a large role in the resurrection of the Polish state during the First World War. But in America this alliance numbered only a few thousand members and had little influence in Polonia as a whole.[1]

The original founders of the Polish National Alliance, an organization which was large and influential, were also avid workers for Poland's liberation. But the rank and file of the organization were primarily interested in the fraternal and practical aspects of the Alliance's local associations. The average peasant immigrant was unequipped to take part in the high politics of liberation, as the Alliance leaders hoped he would.[2]

Thus, before the First World War radically altered the power balance in Europe and all Polish-American leaders began to collect funds for the relief and liberation of Poland during the war, most inhabitants of Polonia did little for the homeland but wait and pray.

The institutions struggling to build a viable Polish-American society, mainly the church and the large fraternal organizations, practiced their own brand of politics.

The Congregation of the Resurrection, like any religious organization, from the powerful Jesuit order to the smallest convent, had its own internal politics. Resurrectionist priests occasionally found a trip to Rome necessary to explain their unconventional activities to superiors. Father Vincent Barzynski, C.R., often found himself in ecclesiastical hot water due to his freewheeling spending of the congregation's money and his neglect of careful bookkeeping and detailed reports to Rome.[3]

The Resurrectionists also engaged in delicate political negotiations with the largely Irish and German hierarchy of the American church. In 1871 the congregation signed a contract with Bishop Foley of the Chicago diocese which gave it, for ninety-nine years, exclusive rights to staff with its own members, or else to appoint other priests, to all of Chicago's Polish churches.[4]

Such clerical arrangements might seem remote from the ordinary immigrant churchgoer; but, in fact, the whole Polish community sometimes became embroiled in ecclesiastical politics. For instance, in 1872 a new church was erected as a branch of St. Stanislaus Kostka Parish. However, a serious rivalry broke out between the parishioners of the new church, who wanted to be free from Resurrectionist domination, and the pastor of St. Stanislaus. The dispute dragged on for twenty years. The new church, Holy Trinity, was periodically closed by the bishop, and for several years lapsed into schism. Finally, in 1893 Rome's apostolic delegate to the United States settled the matter by abrogating the Resurrectionists' exclusive contract and bringing in a Polish priest from another religious order as pastor of Holy Trinity. A similar quarrel in the 1890s over Resurrectionist control of another new parish even led to mob action against several priests and litigation in the American courts. Polonia took church politics seriously.[5]

The two largest fraternal organizations, the PRCU and the PNA, also had their own internal politics. These organizations were, after all, federated bodies organized along representative lines. The members of local associations elected representatives to a national congress, and the congress elected the organization's officers and appointed its functioning committees. Such intraorganizational politics was frequently quite lively. Besides, for the peasant immigrants, who had had no part in the politics of the old country, these elections of representatives in the fraternal organizations were useful lessons in the democratic process.

The PRCU and the PNA, despite the similarity of their structures and functions, were, in the early days of Polonia, bitter rivals. The two organizations fought each other in their journals and vied for membership and influence among the immigrant masses. An often quoted paragraph from one of the earliest histories of Polish America described the situation thus:

For sometime neither Catholics nor Poles existed in America, but only Unionists (PRCU) or Alliancists (PNA); who was not a member of the Alliance, him the PNA did not regard as a Pole; while whoever was not a member of the PRCU, the PRCU did not regard as a Catholic.[6]

This slightly overstates the case. The mass of immigrants took their organizational politics almost as seriously as their church politics, but both concerns were secondary to the struggle for survival. The Union and the Alliance were, after all, insurance and mutual help organizations as well as ideological groupings. An immigrant joined one or the other, and frequently both, for primarily practical reasons.

Thus the politics of Polonia—the politics of church and fraternal organization—were of more immediate concern to the average immigrant than the politics of Poland, but only insofar as they were relevant to his spiritual and material survival in the New World.

American politics were, at first, a complete mystery to the Polish immigrants. For European peasants government had been a matter beyond their ken and control, an affair of nobles, armies, and distant bureaucrats. Few would have had the opportunity to vote in one of the three partitioning states.[7] Upon their arrival in America, they retained this aloof attitude toward government; however, they gradually realized that American politics could serve several vital functions in Polonia.

American government in the nineteenth century was far different from a European bureaucracy. In particular the government of American cities, where most of the immigrants gathered, was the despair of sophisticated European observers, such as James Lord Bryce, who called it "the most conspicuous failing of American democracy." But the very features which European observers condemned made American politics relevant for Polonia.

City governments were boss-directed patronage organizations. These organizations presented themselves to the immigrants in immediate, personal terms. The bosses were gregarious human beings whose power was based on personal relations with people around them.

To the inhabitant of Polonia's capital, or any other city in Polonia, the political boss seemed vaguely reminiscent of the feudal lord in the old country. Like the lord, the boss was a man of importance who lived well and held the keys to government and business. The boss was someone you went to for a job or a favor. Like the best of the old lords, he frequently helped the people out in times of need, bringing a bucket of coal or a basket of food to a cold and starving immigrant family. But unlike the old lord, the American boss asked relatively little in return for his benevolence. The European peasant had owed his lord burdensome labor duties (*pańszczyzna*) or at least a money rent. But the boss asked only for a vote on election day, a small enough price for the immigrant to pay.

Another important difference between the Old World lord and the American boss was that seemingly anyone could become a boss in America. European lordship was a matter of birth and blood, but the political boss was a man very much like the new immigrants themselves. Most likely his parents had also been immigrants, and he himself had worked as a common laborer in his youth. Thus, an ambitious citizen of the American Polonia might aspire to be a boss in his own right some day.

For the individual in Polonia, therefore, American politics fulfilled practical functions. The politicians performed rudimentary social welfare services; and for the lucky or talented few, politics could be a ladder for social mobility and personal gain.

But besides these immediate benefits, American politics also helped the whole immigrant community, all of Polonia, to feel more secure in the new land. When a presidential candidate addressed them in person, sometimes haltingly uttering a few words in their own language; when the local bosses helped them with jobs and favors; when they saw their own sons entering American politics and holding offices at city hall, the inhabitants of Polonia felt an upsurge of pride in their growing importance in the new land. One of the shrewdest of Chicago's politicians, Mayor Carter Harrison II, understood the importance of political recognition to an immigrant group. Reminiscing about his career as five-time mayor of Chicago, Harrison wrote:

For the past half century Bohemians, Poles, Italians, Jews, Lithuanians, Hungarians, Croatians, Slavonians, Slovaks have been coming to our country in hosts. Ours is a strange country to them, ours a strange language. The habits, the customs of their adopted surroundings are new and startling. At best they do not know if they are welcome or not. With a timid heart they enter into citizenship. They realize the greatness of this citizenship, indeed it weighs upon them, it almost overwhelms them. Not certain that they are really wanted among us, they are fearful that in some way, by some mishap they may lose this citizenship. . . .
    Then comes an appointment of one of their very own to some place, perhaps of a most trivial character. Instantly everything is changed. Certainty, security has come to them; now and hereafter they are part, parcel, and fibre of the government under whose flag they work and live.[8]

    Thus American politics fulfilled economic, occupational, and psychological functions in Polonia. Furthermore, participation in American politics, even at the lowest level of exchanging a vote for a material favor, marked a definite step in the Americanization of the Polish community. Everywhere in the United States, an immigrant, in order to vote, had at least to declare his intention of becoming a citizen; in the state of Illinois, actual citizenship was required. Under U.S. naturalization laws this took five years of American residence. The immigrant who became a citizen and registered to vote had taken the first step away from being a Pole to becoming a Polish-American. Those who went further and climbed the political ladder themselves had turned away from the Old World decisively and were well along towards being simply Americans of Polish descent.

    American politics concerned only a part of Polonia. But this part was on the leading edge of the Americanization process. For those immigrants and their children who most keenly felt their status as outsiders in America, participation in politics became an important means for coming inside.

▌▌ Chicago Politics in the Progressive Era

During the twenty-five years preceding World War I, Chicago politics was a jungle of rival bosses and factions. No organization like the Tammany machine in New York dominated the scene. The Republicans generally held sway in state and national elections, but the Democrats had more success in purely local campaigns.

William Lorimer, a former streetcar conductor, rose to preeminence among the Republican bosses. A majority of the wealthy and respectable businessmen voted Republican, without inquiring too closely about the men who wielded actual power in the party; and the English-language press rendered near-unanimous support to the Republican ticket.

The Democrats relied mainly on their power base among the Irish and on the personal charisma of the two Carter Harrisons, father and son, each of whom served as Chicago mayor for five terms. In the late 1890s John P. Hopkins, the city's first Irish Catholic mayor, and his protégé, Roger Sullivan, began laying the foundations for the Democratic machine which finally emerged three decades later. Factional squabbles

between the Harrisons and the Irish frequently split the party.

The bosses and factions in each party faced repeated challenges from civic reformers during these years. Issues of honesty versus corruption, fair dealing in city franchises versus aldermanic boodling, and direct democracy versus boss rule made this an era of progressive ferment.

Polish-Americans in Chicago emerged in the late nineteenth century as a small but growing Democratic bloc, with a remarkably consistent voting record. Their political leaders were of two types: bosses and heelers in the Democratic party, or respectable business and professional men in both parties. The political issues of the progressive era had little impact on the Polish bloc. Its allegiance was determined by bread-and-butter favors from individual bosses, appeals to the group by the popular Harrisons, and, particularly, by the Democrats' greater sympathy for the Catholic, working-class Polish community.

Polish voters followed a strategy of party solidarity in pursuit of unity, recognition, and progress for Polonia's capital.

5 The Emergence of the Polish-Democratic Bloc

In 1888 Chicago's Sixteenth Ward on the northwest side elected August J. Kowalski the city's first Polish-American alderman. An electoral redistricting early in the year had placed Polish Downtown within the boundaries of this new ward, and almost a third of the ward's population of fifty-five thousand was Polish. Yet, ironically, Kowalski was not the choice of the Polish voters. Since many Poles were not yet citizens, less than one-fourth of the ward's registered voters were Polish (1,736 out of a total registration of 6,264); and in only three of the ward's thirteen precincts did Polish voters form an absolute majority. In these three precincts the voters selected not Kowalski but another Polish candidate, Peter Kiolbassa. Thus the first Polish-American alderman in the city was not the Polish choice at all, but rather the selection of the Sixteenth Ward's German and Scandinavian Republicans.[1]

Kowalski and Kiolbassa were both Republicans in 1888, when Coroner Henry L. Hertz, who had long ruled the near northwest side for the GOP, chose Kowalski as his aldermanic candidate. It is not clear exactly what Kowalski's background was. The *Chicago Tribune* first reported him to be a grocer; later, the same paper, when denouncing him as Hertz's pawn, called him a saloonkeeper. In any case, he was a small businessman who had married Frances Schermann, the daughter of the neighborhood's first settler.[2]

Kiolbassa enjoyed greater status in Polonia. Born in Silesia, he had come to Texas before the Civil War with the first large group of Polish emigrants to the U.S. He served for a year in the Confederate cavalry; but, after being taken prisoner by Northern troops, he enlisted in the Union cause. The young cavalry captain, having spent some of his furloughs in Chicago, settled

Parts of this chapter and of Chapter 8 originally appeared in "The Emergence of the Polish Democratic Vote in Chicago" in *Polish American Studies* (vol. 29, pp. 67–80), and are used here with permission.

in the city when the war was over and took a leading part in the founding of
St. Stanislaus Kostka Parish.

Kiolbassa held several minor political offices for the GOP in Chicago
and even served a term in the state legislature. Near his home he also ran a
notary public's office, which provided a modest living and a base of operations. The simple notary's office was actually a combination of social service
agency, legal aid bureau, and secular confessional. Kiolbassa was familiar
with American ways and could help newly arrived Polish immigrants "learn
the ropes" in America. His notary's office kept him in touch with his constituency, and his timely advice and sympathy to his fellow residents made him
something of an institution in Polish Downtown.[3]

Boss Hertz probably chose Kowalski to run for alderman because he
deemed him more controllable than Captain Kiolbassa. Kiolbassa, refusing
to accept the decision, broke party ranks and ran as an independent. A German contractor running on the Democratic ticket and several minor party
candidates further complicated the race; but among the ward's Polish voters,
the choice lay between Kowalski and Kiolbassa.

This contest was enlivened and embittered by the old rivalry between
the church organizations and the Polish National Alliance. Kiolbassa, soon
to be elected president of the Polish Roman Catholic Union, was clearly the
choice of Father Vincent Barzynski, a close personal friend. Kowalski, on the
other hand, was cashier of the Polish National Alliance and was recommended by that organization's organ, *Zgoda,* as the Alliance candidate.[4]

When the ballots were counted, Kowalski carried the ward by over 150
votes; but in the three overwhelmingly Polish precincts, Kiolbassa ran far
ahead. Had Kiolbassa run as a Democrat, he probably would have won; for
the combination of his 858 votes and the Democrat's 305 exceeded Kowalski's total of 1,019.[5]

The Alliance leaders totally misread the significance of this election.
Zgoda estimated that Polish voters in the Sixteenth Ward outnumbered those
of other nationalities by five to one, and thus Kowalski's election was a re-
sounding mandate from Polonia. This contention was absurd, since the Poles
were themsleves outnumbered four to one on the voters' lists. *Zgoda* also went
on to gloat over its triumph:

We are glad that the candidate of Fr. Barzynski met defeat and the office-
holder of this Alliance gained the majority of votes. If it had been necessary
to go to the polling place through the confessional, Kowalski would have
been defeated. . . . But this Barzynski crowd, with whom Kiolbassa was

TABLE 5   POLISH VOTERS IN THE SIXTEENTH WARD, 1888

Precinct	No. of Polish voters	Total No. of voters
1	1	464
2	0	512
3	2	459
4	4	384
5	2	286
6	10	484
7	2	543
8	27	447
9	189	415
10	292	378
11	573	714
12	633	836
Total	1,736	6,264

Source: Chicago Daily News Almanac, 1889, p. 160.

running in the election campaign, lost the race, because the majority of the
parishioners acted rightly. . . .[6]

In fact, the majority of parishioners voted with the "Barzynski crowd";
but there simply were not enough Polish voters yet in the ward to beat Henry
Hertz's Republican machine in a multicandidate race. In the next few years
Barzynski and Kiolbassa would enjoy greater success at the head of a Polish
voting bloc; but they would use the Democratic party as a vehicle.

Kowalski, Kiolbassa, the Schermanns, and other pioneers of Polonia's capital
were originally Republican in politics, due perhaps to memories of the Civil

TABLE 6   ELECTION RETURNS: SIXTEENTH WARD ALDERMANIC ELECTION, 1888

Precinct	Kowalski (R)	Kiolbassa (Ind.)	Besse (D)	Others
1	117	50	6	78
2	102	35	36	39
3	101	43	23	53
4	83	40	23	34
5	61	25	15	16
6	97	63	33	30
7	117	42	19	36
8	70	64	37	46
9	50	93	14	24
10	58	75	20	13
11	73	105	20	12
12	81	163	59	12
Total	1,019	858	305	393

Note: Polish precincts underlined.

War and, more practically, because of the local dominance of Hertz's party. But the mass of Polish-Americans beginning to vote in Chicago tended to be heavily Democratic. In the 1888 aldermanic race, national pride directed the Polish voters' attention to the two feuding Republicans, Kowalski and Kiolbassa; but in city-wide elections, where Poles were generally not candidates, Polonia's capital voted consistently Democratic.

In the five mayoral contests from 1889 to 1895 (four regular biennial elections and one special election to fill the vacancy left by Carter Harrison's death), the Polish vote averaged over 75 percent Democratic. Only in 1895, when the Democrats bore the political blame for the economic depression then at its worst, did their Democratic percentage fall below that level (58

percent). The Polish voters also recorded high Democratic majorities in the
several state and national elections during this period.[7]

Timing was one factor determining this Democratic allegiance. Had
mass immigration from Poland begun before 1860 and large numbers of
Poles participated in the Civil War, Polonia might have been fused into the
Republican coalition. But when most Poles arrived in America, the Republican party was a long entrenched political establishment, Protestant in character, business-oriented in ideology, and unresponsive to the needs of new
groups.

TABLE 7   ELECTION RETURNS (IN PERCENTAGES): MAYOR, 1889-1895

| Year | No. of Polish Precincts | Polish Vote (City-wide Vote) | | |
		Republican	Democratic	Independent
1889	5	Roche 23.07 (43.81)	Cregier 76.86 (55.42)	
1891	7	Washburne 7.83 (28.82)	Cregier 77.92 (28.60)	Harrison 10.42 (26.35)
April, 1893	11	Allerton 11.20 (44.05)	Harrison 87.87 (54.03)	
December, 1893	11	Swift 20.80 (49.16)	Hopkins 78.38 (49.69)	
1895	11	Swift 37.11 (55.08)	Wenter 57.96 (39.48)	
Average		20.00 (44.18)	75.80 (45.44)	

The Democrats, for their part, were the perennial "out" party after the
Civil War; and, as underdogs, "they tried harder." With the Irish Catholics
and a few old Jeffersonians as their only source of votes in Northern cities,
they had everything to gain by cultivating the new immigrants.

Carter Harrison the elder showed the Democrats the way to appeal to
immigrant groups. He firmly advocated "personal liberty," which, in the

political code of the day, meant the right to drink beer, wine, or spirits without restriction by blue laws. Harrison was a Protestant but no puritan, having
been raised in the relaxed Protestant tradition of a Southern plantation. Extensive travels in Europe and long residence in Chicago taught him that the
"Continental Sabbath" was a cherished institution of Central and Eastern
Europeans. Thus, during his terms as mayor, Harrison opposed all Sunday
closing ordinances, curfews on saloon hours, and higher license fees for
saloonkeepers. If a hostile city council passed such laws, the mayor made
certain that police enforcement was not rigorous.[8]

To the Poles Democratic opposition to prohibition was one sign that the
Democrats understood and tolerated their Catholic religion. Opposition to
anti-Catholic secret societies was another. In 1889 the local Democrats exposed Republican mayor John Roche as a member of the secret Order of
Deputies, an anti-Catholic group. In 1894 a Democratic state platform unequivocally declared its opposition to all such societies:

> Hostility to secret political societies is a tenet of the democratic faith which is
> fundamental, and standing by this doctrine now as in the days when the party
> presented an unbroken front to the cohorts of know-nothingism . . . , the
> democracy of Illinois denounces as cowardly, unpatriotic, and dangerous
> . . . the American Protective Association, which seeks to proscribe men on
> account of their religion or birthplace.

Illinois Republican platforms were silent on secret societies, but political
rumors branded the APA a Republican front.[9]

The *Dziennik Chicagoski,* in an 1894 editorial, summed up the religious
argument for Democratic allegiance, combining it with an economic argument of Democratic sympathy for workers:

> For whom should the Poles vote?
> For the Democrats.
> Why should we vote for the Democratic party?
> Because in reality it is the people's party and it stands for freedom.
> Who opposes all restrictions?
> The Democratic party.
> Who are the true friends of the working people?
> The Democrats.
> Who are restraining millionaires and exploiters?
> The Democrats.
> Who condemns Pullman so severely?
> The Democrats.
> Who condemns the wicked APA?
> The Democrats.

Who are ruining and endangering the country?
The Republicans.
Are there any Polish candidates on the Republican ticket?
No, there are none.
Why?
Because, when a Pole tried to run for county commissioner the Republicans placed a Negro on their ballot.
Therefore, let the Negroes vote for them.
And who else?
The Pullmans.[10]

The masses were ahead of their leaders in the formation of a Democratic bloc. The Polish National Alliance, in its weekly organ, *Zgoda,* and later in its daily paper, *Dziennik Zwiazkowy,* did not show much interest in American politics; and when it did, it professed a high-minded, nonpartisan line. Yet a close reading of these papers reveals that, beneath the nonpartisan rhetoric, they nearly always supported the Republican ticket. PNA leaders probably preferred the Republican party because it was more respectable and as the dominant national party, it was in a position to do more for Poland. Later, when the church leaders became Democratic advocates, the Republican leanings of the PNA were reinforced by the old rivalry.[11]

The church leaders had no clear political leanings before 1890. Father Barzynski originally groomed Peter Kiolbassa to make a political breakthrough for Polonia, and Kiolbassa was a Republican. But a combination of circumstances turned the church leaders Democratic. Kiolbassa's rebuff by Boss Hertz in 1888 was the first step, but Kiolbassa did not leave the party immediately after his independent aldermanic race. During the spring elections of 1889, he presided over a meeting of the Polish Republican Club at St. Stanislaus, where Republican mayor John Roche and Republican alderman Kowalski addressed the parishioners. Then, in 1891 we find him on the rostrum of a Sixteenth Ward campaign meeting for Carter Harrison, the Democrats' champion vote-getter. And in its very first issue in December 1890, the new Resurrectionist daily, *Dziennik Chicagoski,* expressed a preference for the Democratic party.[12]

What determined this new Democratic preference of the church leaders was the growing anti-Catholicism of the Republicans and, in particular, a bitter controversy over the Catholic-school question.

The Illinois state legislature in 1889 passed a compulsory school law requiring every child between the ages of seven and fourteen to attend some recognized school for at least sixteen weeks each year. The law further provided that no institution which did not teach reading, writing, arithmetic, United States history, and geography in the English language would be recognized as a school under the act. This, in effect, declared hundreds of German, Polish, and Bohemian parochial schools, where the medium of instruction was not ordinarily English, illegal. The law passed the legislature with bipartisan support, but it was commonly known as the Edwards Law, after Professor Richard Edwards, the Republican state superintendent of public instruction. The Democrats responded to the public outcry by repudiating the law.

The state's German population, whose well-established Catholic and Lutheran schools were affected by the Edwards Law, were in the forefront of opposition. The Democrats rode the school controversy to victory in the 1890 state elections; and John Peter Altgeld, the Democrats' German-born candidate for governor in 1892, also made a successful campaign issue of it. Governor Altgeld succeeded in having the legislature repeal the Edwards Law in 1893. This, coupled with his emotional identification with the workingman and his bitter protest against suppression of the Pullman strike in 1894, made Altgeld a hero in the Polish community.[13]

The school issue was crucial to the Polish church leaders, for many of them had spent their early lives in Poland opposing similar campaigns waged by Russia and Germany against the use of Polish in schools. It seems probable that this was the deciding factor which pushed Barzynski, Kiolbassa, and others into the Democratic camp. Just before election day in 1892, thousands of copies of the Edwards Law were distributed to the parishioners of St. Stanislaus; and Father Barzynski personally urged a mass meeting in the parish hall to oppose the school law by voting for Altgeld.[14]

The rank and file of Polish voters had already shown a Democratic preference; by the early 1890s, the influential church leaders had followed and baptized the party. *Dziennik Chicagoski* wrote, "The Democratic party, the true people's party, the party with a high regard for religion, ought to be our party. There is no room for us in the Republican party." Only the PNA and the small Socialist contingent opposed this trend.[15]

To Polish voters the Republicans were the party of big business, puritanical prohibitionists, fanatical anti-Catholics, and narrow-minded educators trying to stamp out the Polish language. The Democrats were the party of workingmen's democracy and broad-minded toleration. The political allegiance of Polonia's capital was firmly set.

The first important beneficiary of the Polish bloc voting was Peter Kiolbassa, once he had finally switched parties. In 1891 political circumsances overtook Kiolbassa and transferred him from his notary's office to one of the most important positions at City Hall.

DeWitt Cregier, the incumbent Democratic mayor, was seeking reelection in 1891; but Carter Harrison, who had retired four years before after serving four terms as mayor, was trying to stage a comeback. Kiolbassa conducted mass meetings for Harrison in the Sixteenth Ward and served as a Harrison delegate to the party convention. But Cregier rammed a renomination through the convention, and Harrison prepared to run as an independent.[16]

At this juncture lightning struck for Kiolbassa and the Polish community. The man slated for city treasurer on the Cregier ticket, George A. Weiss, bolted to Harrison, leaving that spot vacant. The mayor wanted another German to' replace him; but all the leading German politicians were either backing Harrison or the Republican candidate, Hempstead Washburne. Then, apparently someone at Democratic headquarters had a brainstorm. Why not appeal to the Polish voters, whose numbers on the registration lists were increasing every year, by slating a Polish-American for treasurer? A committee approached Kiolbassa, but he was reluctant to run, probably because he was already committed as a Harrison man and because his losing aldermanic race had soured him on office-seeking. But the intervention of Father Barzynski, who saw this as a golden opportunity for the Polish community, convinced him to accept.[17]

During the campaign Kiolbassa avoided criticism of the popular Harrison and simply stated that Cregier had offered Polonia an influential position whereas Harrison had not. He stressed that he was a reluctant candidate, running not out of personal ambition but rather to give Polish-Americans some political influence. When the ballots were counted, he garnered 85 percent of the Polish votes and carried Cregier along with nearly 78 percent of Polonia's voters. In the city-wide totals Cregier and Harrison were both defeated in the mayoral race by the Republican Washburne. However, Kiolbassa ran ahead of the rest of the Democrats and registered an upset victory for city treasurer. His two opponents, both Germans, evenly divided the city's large German vote; the massed vote of the few thousand Polish voters gave Kiolbassa his margin.[18]

Peter Kiolbassa's election was the first important triumph in American politics for Polonia's capital, but the new city treasurer's problems were just

beginning. He was, of course, without influence in the Republican administration of Hempstead Washburne; and the Democrats, who had only turned
to him as a last-minute choice, were also cool toward him. The six downtown
banks required by a recent city ordinance to sign a $15 million bond for the
city treasurer, in return for the privilege of holding city funds, decided to
forego that privilege and refused to act as sureties for Kiolbassa. The new
treasurer was thus forced to present a bond signed by forty-four private individuals, including the defeated Carter Harrison, who saw political advantage in championing the cause of the underdog.[19]

TABLE 8   ELECTION RETURNS: MAYOR AND CITY TREASURER, 1891

	MAYOR			
	Washburne (R)	Cregier (D)	Harrison (Ind.)	Others
City totals	46,957 (28.82%)	46,588 (28.60%)	42,931 (26.35%)	26,403
Average of seven Polish precincts	7.83%	77.92%	10.42%	

	CITY TREASURER			
	Nettlehorst (R)	Kiolbassa (D)	Tiedemann (Ind.)	Others
City totals	41,760 (25.64%)	50,056 (30.73%)	45,639 (28.02)	25,409
Average of seven Polish precincts	5.12%	85.30%	5.77%	

The office of city treasurer had been the subject of scandal and controversy for a number of years in Chicago. The law prohibited the treasurer from
deriving any personal gain from the use of public money, but it had been
common practice for years for the treasurer to deposit the city's funds in
private banks and then pocket the interest which accrued. The previous mayor,
Cregier, had taken note of the rising public sentiment against this practice and
had asked the city council to pass remedial legislation. The council passed an
ordinance designating the banks of deposit but neglected to require the interest earned to be turned over to the city.

Kiolbassa found it impossible to comply with the new ordinance, since the designated banks refused to cooperate; however, he felt, as a matter of principle, that the public outcry against private gain in the treasurer's office was just. Therefore, he deposited the city's funds in several other banks and kept a careful account of all the interest earned. In his first annual report, he informed the city council that the city had earned $44,500.70 on its money, $16,600 of which he had applied to the expenses of running his office and $15,000 of which he kept as compensation, since the council had also neglected to vote him a salary. The remainder, $12,900.70, belonged to the city. At the end of his two-year term, he reported that $106,000 had accrued in interest and that $38,991.52 of that had been saved for the city coffers.[20]

Kiolbassa as treasurer, therefore, established by precedent what the city government had failed to establish by law. In Polonia's capital this action earned him the nickname of "Honest Pete" and a reference in all of Polonia's commemorative books as the "first city treasurer who gave the interest money back to the city."

At the end of his two-year term in the treasurer's office, Kiolbassa had had enough of abuse and controversy; so he returned to his notary's office in Polish Downtown. That same year, 1893, Carter Harrison finally made his comeback, winning election to a fifth term as mayor just in time to play host to the Chicago World's Fair. Using his timely support of Kiolbassa's surety bond as his main talking point in Polonia, Harrison garnered 87 percent of the Polish vote.

Peter Kiolbassa eventually returned to politics, but he never became a power in the Democratic party and he never again matched his victory of 1891. In 1896 he finally won the Sixteenth Ward aldermanic seat which had eluded him years before. Following his one term in the city council, he served in a minor elective post as township supervisor for his West Town area from 1899 to 1901. Carter Harrison II, who followed in his father's footsteps as a long-time mayor of Chicago, then kept Kiolbassa employed in one or another patronage job until the death of "Honest Pete" in July 1905.[21]

To the Polish voters of his day, Peter Kiolbassa was an honest, sympathetic man of integrity, an exemplary individual to represent Polonia in American politics. As an early settler in America, a founder of the *Stanisławowo*, the first of his nationality to hold city-wide office, and an honorary president of the Polish Roman Catholic Union, he was esteemed by the younger Polish-Americans in Chicago as the Grand Old Man of Polonia.

To the other citizens of Chicago, Kiolbassa was a minor political figure.

His one big triumph, election as city treasurer in 1891, was largely a political accident. Had it not been for the unusual circumstances of that election, he would only have served a term or two as alderman and then lived out his days in minor patronage posts, as indeed he did for the rest of his life after retiring from the treasurer's office.

In the long run, the major significance of Peter Kiolbassa's career lies in his shift from Republican to Democrat in the early 1890s. Kiolbassa saw which way the Polish voting bloc was headed and he joined it in time to gain the first city-wide political office for Polonia's capital. His election as city treasurer in 1891 marks the emergence of the Polish Democratic bloc in Chicago.

6 The Banker and the Boss

In the mid-1890s reform came to Chicago like a series of gunshots.

The first blow was literally a gunshot. On the last day of the Columbian Exposition in 1893, a disappointed office seeker shot and killed Mayor Carter Harrison I. The assassination shocked Chicago into action against the spoils system, just as the earlier murder of President James Garfield under similar circumstances had shocked the nation. In 1895 Chicago became the first city west of the Atlantic seaboard to adopt a comprehensive civil service law. But the fight against political jobholders was just beginning. Successive mayors picked legal holes in the law and often circumvented it. Civil service reform became a continuing political issue in Chicago.[1]

The next blast was a verbal one, fired by an English journalist, William T. Stead. Stead arrived in Chicago the day of Carter Harrison's murder and found that not only murder but vice, gambling, police graft, and political payoffs were comon occurrences in the World's Fair city. The journalist published his revelations early in 1894 in a sensational book, *If Christ Came to Chicago,* whose four hundred pages of brimstone left no doubt that Christ would be displeased with the city. This exposé stirred the "better element" in the city, Republican businessmen and professionals, to organize a reform group called the Civic Federation. The Federation set in motion a wide variety of relief efforts for Chicagoans affected by the industrial depression and focused attention on the city's untidy streets and rickety street railways which detracted from "civic beauty." It also organized committees in Chicago's election districts to keep an eye on the aldermen and other public officials.[2]

The city council badly needed watching. For years the "Gray Wolves" of the council, bosses like Johnny Powers and Maurice O'Connor in the river wards, and Michael "Hinky Dink" Kenna and "Bathhouse" John Coughlin,

overlords of the First Ward, had been receiving generous payoffs from businessmen seeking city franchises. Like most American cities at the time,
Chicago had grown rapidly, and it needed a complete rebuilding of physical
facilities and municipal services. Private contractors spread large amounts
of boodle around the council and the state legislature to obtain lucrative street
railway and utility franchises. On February 25, 1895, Mayor John Hopkins
and his protégé, Roger Sullivan, engineered two of the most audacious franchise grabs. The city council passed an ordinance granting virtually unlimited
franchise rights to the Cosmopolitan Electric Company and the Ogden Gas
Company, dummy corporations whose most prominent shareholders were
Messrs. Hopkins and Sullivan. The graft technique was simplicity itself.
Selected Gray Wolves from the council had been cut in as shareholders; after
the ordinances passed, the valuable franchises were used to blackmail legitimate utility companies with the threat of actually operating Cosmopolitan
Electric and Ogden Gas as competitors. The ploy proved successful. A few
years later, after selling their franchises to utility corporations, Hopkins,
Sullivan, and their cohorts were rich men.[3]

The Ogden gas grab moved the Civic Federation leaders to form a new
organization, the Municipal Voters' League, to fight for an honest city council. The MVL organized at the grass-roots level of wards and precincts to
support honest aldermanic candidates, regardless of party. Social settlement
workers, businessmen, and just plain concerned citizens built a civic machine
which reached into most of the city's wards and often tipped a local election
toward an honest candidate. The league had such success in purging the council of many of its Gray Wolves that by 1903, when the muckraker Lincoln
Steffens visited Chicago, he proclaimed the city "half free and fighting on."[4]

The final call to reform was uttered by a young Republican lawyer, John
Maynard Harlan. In 1897 he ran an independent campaign for mayor on a
one-line platform, "The streets belong to the people." The most lucrative
franchise which the city had to offer was the right to lay streetcar tracks in
the city streets. Most of these "traction rights" (so called after the traction
process of powering cable cars) had been bought up by the tycoon Charles
T. Yerkes. The very year that Harlan entered the fight, Yerkes secured from
the state legislature an enabling act, the Allen Law, empowering the city
council to extend the traction franchises for fifty years. Harlan waged a
brilliant speaking campaign against Yerkes and the Allen Law, arguing that
the people should reclaim the city streets through municipal ownership of
street railways.[5]

Harlan lost the election to Carter Harrison II, the martyred ex-mayor's son; but he gave Chicago politics a perennial issue for the next decade, the traction question. And though the battle for municipal ownership finally failed, Yerkes also suffered defeat. Mayor Harrison rallied the greatly improved city council against implementation of the fifty-year franchises; and after several years of wrangling, the various streetcar companies were forced to pay an adequate compensation to the city before their franchises were renewed.[6]

This series of shocks, scandals, and revelations defined the main reform issues in Chicago at the turn of the century: civil service, honesty in government, and carefully regulated utility and transport franchises with adequate compensation for the city. The era of progressive reform had come to Chicago politics. After the turn of the century, many other typically progressive reforms, such as the direct democracy devices of primary, referendum, and popular election of school board members, were advocated as well.[7]

During this reform-conscious era, Chicago politicians were typed by the public as either "good guys" or "bad guys," as reformers or bosses. In the Republican ranks William Lorimer led the boss faction until 1912, when the U.S. Senate declared his election to that body fraudulent and expelled him. The reformers rallied around John M. Harlan and his lieutenant, Harold L. Ickes, and were often supported by wealthy businessmen, powerful civic groups like the Municipal Voters' League, and Republican newspapers such as the *Tribune, Daily News,* and *Record-Herald.*

Among the Democrats Roger Sullivan built a machine around the remnants of the Gray Wolves. The reform element in the Democratic party was weaker than in the Republican; but in 1905 they found a champion in Judge Edward F. Dunne, who pledged himself to fight for immediate municipal ownership of street railways.

Between the extremes of boss and reformer, both parties contained a vast middle ground. Politicians of this "mixed faction" often used machine-like methods, but they were personally honest and they sometimes worked for reform goals. Republican Charles Deneen from the middle-class neighborhood of Englewood on the southwest side was such a politician. The reformers mistrusted his tactics; but in his rise from state's attorney to governor of Illinois to the U.S. Senate he could always count on a good deal of respectable support. The Deneen faction acted as a powerful counterweight to the Lorimerites throughout this period.

Squarely astride the middle ground in the Democratic party stood Carter

Harrison II. The younger Harrison was the despair of the purists for his foot-
dragging on civil service, his long alliance with Hinky Dink and Bathhouse
John in the First Ward, and his almost demagogic appeals to the immigrant
vote. But, like his father before him, he never took a penny of city money and,
in a relaxed way, he tried to administer public business efficiently. Furthermore, his firm stand against Yerkes and the fifty-year franchises gave him a
powerful reform appeal which his father had never had.[8]

Among the first generation of Polish-American politicians, from the heyday
of the pioneer Kiolbassa until the First World War, there was also a rough
division into two groups, reformers and bosses. Actually, the term "reformers" is not accurate; none of the Polish-Americans were in the forefront
of progressive reform. A better term would be "respectables." They came
from Polonia's business and professional class and were leaders in church and
ethnic organizations. Unlike the bosses who arose in Polonia, the respectables
met with the approval of the English-language press and the American community in general. There was no Polish-American equivalent to the mixed
politicians and this later proved to be a political handicap.
    Each group developed one side of the double legacy left by Peter Kiol-
bassa. The respectables continued the tradition of honesty, integrity, and good
government which Kiolbassa's strict accounting of city funds symbolized. The
bosses carried on the important allegiance to the Democratic party which
the pioneer had come to value. These two lines of political development un-
folded concurrently. Polish voters usually supported both groups, simply because they were Poles; but conflict occasionally arose between the two camps.
    The oustanding leader of the Polish respectables was John Francis
Smulski. Born in Poznań, German Poland, in 1867, Smulski came from a
middle-class family. His father, Ladislaus Smulski, left him a flourishing publishing business in Chicago; but John was more interested in the law than
the printing press. He earned a law degree at Northwestern University in
1890 and began practice in Polish Downtown. Local politics held no great at-
traction for Smulski, but an ambitious lawyer could ill afford to ignore politics. Eventually he played an active role in the affairs of the Republican party.[9]
    John Smulski chose to remain with his social class in the Republican
party rather than follow the mass of his countrymen as Peter Kiolbassa had
done. In fact, he was defeated by the Democrat Kiolbassa in the Sixteenth
Ward aldermanic election in 1896, Smulski's first try for public office. Two
years later, however, he succeeded in gaining a one-year city council term to

fill a vacancy in the Sixteenth Ward; and he was returned to a council seat for full terms in 1899 and 1901.

In these early electoral battles, Smulski enjoyed considerable support from Chicago reformers. In 1896 the Municipal Voters' League endorsed both Smulski and Kiolbassa for alderman, instructing voters to "take your choice." In Smulski's first successful race, however, and in his subsequent re-election campaigns, the MVL unequivocally supported him over his Democratic opponents.[10]

Just to the south of Polish Downtown, in the Seventeenth Ward, Graham Taylor, the head resident of Chicago Commons settlement house, organized an active local chapter of the Civic Federation. In 1901 a redistricting placed Smulski and the southern portion of Polish Downtown in this ward. Smulski wanted to leave politics and give more attention to his business and his law practice, but Graham Taylor and the settlement reformers asked him to run in his new ward to continue the high standard of aldermanic representation they had been building. Smulski accepted and waged a vigorous campaign among the Germans, Scandinavians, and Poles of the ward, appearing with Graham Taylor and John Maynard Harlan at a final mass meeting in the Chicago Commons hall. He was elected by a comfortable margin in this normally Democratic ward, due to the strong support of the settlement reform club.[11]

Smulski was an honest and efficient alderman but not a vigorous reformer. He lined up with Mayor Harrison and the council majority on all the crucial council votes in 1898 which defeated Yerkes' fifty-year franchise measure, but in 1900 he also followed the majority in allowing Roger Sullivan's sale of the Ogden Gas Company without any compensation to the city. The only reform measures he originated were resolutions calling for more equitable water rates, a stricter enforcement of the civil service law, and a ban on dances in saloon halls. Smulski apparently held strong opinions on the latter subject; in a letter to the Northwestern University settlement house in his ward, he explained:

These dances work a great deal of harm to the young people of Chicago. . . .
While it is perfectly legitimate for societies and clubs to hold dances in halls of good reputation, the city authorities should not permit these so-called "Saturday night dances" in saloons or in rooms attached to saloons. . . .
The saloon dance hall offers increased facilities for the young people of the city to be debauched and degraded.

These reform resolutions all died a quiet death in city council committees.[12]

The Polish voters did not flock to Smulski's cause. On the contrary, he won his first electoral victories despite the Polish vote. In 1896 and 1899, Peter Kiolbassa and August Kowalski, having finally found the right party, beat Smulski soundly in the Polish precincts of the Sixteenth Ward. In 1898 a non-Polish Democrat ran two-to-one against Smulski in the Polish areas. Only in 1901 in the Seventeenth Ward, where even Polish voters were influenced by the strong settlement-house campaign, did Smulski carry the majority of Polish voters along with him.[13]

By the time Smulski cut his political teeth in the city council, he had established solid credentials as a respectable in American politics and became associated with the Deneen faction in the Republican party. The moderates in the party had grown tired of sending losing candidates, dictated by Boss Lorimer, against the popular Carter Harrison and in 1903 were looking about for a businesslike, good-government prospect for mayor. The crusading John M. Harlan was too radical for most Republicans; so the party settled on Graeme Stewart, who, according to the *Tribune*, would provide "more business ability and less politics," a "higher standard of efficiency," and "rigid economy." Since Smulski also fitted these specifications, he was slated for city attorney.[14]

Mayor Harrison's popularity slipped in 1903, but he managed to save his mayoral chair by a narrow margin of eight thousand votes. He won almost two-thirds of the Polish vote. However, with a Polish candidate on the ballot for the Republicans, Polish voters split their tickets in massive numbers. The chance to win an important office for Polonia overcame the strong Democratic allegiance. Smulski's 68.06 percent of the Polish vote helped him win a narrow, upset victory. Clearly the Polish vote held the balance of power in this close election. The Democrat Harrison carried 47 percent of the city-wide vote with a 64 percent margin in Polish precincts. In the race for city attorney, these figures were reversed; the Republican Smulski garnered 47 percent of the city-wide vote with over 68 percent of the Polish voters behind him.[15]

As a Republican city attorney serving with a Democratic mayor, John Smulski had little chance of exercising much influence on the administration's policies. Instead, he turned to his duties as Chicago's chief lawyer and tried to impose some order upon his untidy department. As one Chicago newspaper commented, "He devoted himself to the business of the office with as much eagerness, enthusiasm, and persistence as he could put into his own business."

In 1906, during his second term as city attorney, he made news with his annual report, which exposed a ring of ambulance chasers, both lawyers and physicians, who were milking the city with fraudulent or exaggerated personal injury claims. The city had paid over $300,000 the previous year to cover claims for broken arms and legs and other minor injuries. Smulski placed the blame for this large bill not only on the shyster lawyers "who teach the otherwise honest and respectable citizen the methods of the grafter" but also on inefficient city inspectors who allowed holes in streets and sidewalks to go unrepaired. Though the prose of this report was generally legalistic and restrained, its contents must have been the envy of many a muckraking journalist. At one point in the document, Smulski let his feelings about municipal corruption break through:

One cannot avoid a feeling of intense disgust at the inattention and the seemingly wilful neglect in the performance of public duty in this city. I wonder frequently if there is anyone in Chicago who really looks after its public affairs.[16]

The impact of this report led to speculation that Smulski might be mayoral timber. But such speculation was premature; in 1906 Smulski was slated for the office of state treasurer by his friend Charles Deneen, who had moved on to the governor's mansion in Springfield. Smulski won this office handily, but, as in his earlier campaigns, he did it in spite of the Polish vote. The Democrats put up another Polish businessman, N. L. Piotrowski, to oppose him; faced with a choice between two Polish respectables, the Polish vote split about evenly, with a slight edge for Piotrowski. The downstate Republican vote, however, swamped the Democratic candidate.[17]

At the state treasury in Springfield, Smulski confronted the same issue of fiscal reform which Peter Kiolbassa had faced in Chicago. The practice whereby city, county, and state treasurers in Illinois enriched themselves with the interest earned on public funds had been a by-product of the state's antiquated constitution. When the constitution was drawn up, it was assumed that all public money would remain in governmental treasuries. But modern banking practices and the vast increase in public revenues had made it obvious that these funds should be let out to private banks to earn interest. Yet state law had not caught up with the practice; thus individual treasurers, not the public treasuries, had profited.

In the progressive era this abuse became intolerable. Peter Kiolbassa had established a precedent of fair dealing for city treasurers in 1893, and in 1903 the Cook County treasurer returned the interest money in his keeping to the county. In his 1906 campaign for state treasurer, Smulski pledged that he would do likewise with state money. He kept his pledge, turning over to the state $70,000 in interest for fiscal 1907. The following year his friend Governor Deneen had the legislature confirm this practice by law.[18]

Thus John F. Smulski was the second Illinois official of Polish nationality to accomplish a significant fiscal reform. This enabled him to approach the Polish voters as a second Kiolbassa and the rest of the electorate as a sound, businesslike progressive. But Smulski was not the man to capitalize on these political assets. He resigned his post as state treasurer late in 1907 to give more attention to business; and after a short stint as president of Chicago's West Park Board, he resigned that office as well. He made one more entry into the political arena, in 1911, running for the Republican nomination in Chicago's first direct mayoral primary. Although he enjoyed overwhelming Polish support, there simply weren't enough Polish Republicans; and he failed to win the nomination.

For the rest of his life Smulski remained a Deneen Republican, and he occasionally endorsed candidates and made speeches on their behalf. But of his many roles—businessman, lawyer, and political leader—the role of politician interested him the least. In 1905 he founded the Northwestern Trust and Savings Bank, Chicago's first distinctively Polish bank, in the heart of Polish Downtown at Division Street and Ashland Avenue; and this enterprise absorbed more and more of his attention. When the First World War broke out, he was a Polish-American leader in the "high politics" of Polish relief and liberation, serving under Ignace Paderewski on the Polish Central Relief Committee and the Polish-American National Department (*Wydział Narodowy*). These activties won for Smulski the French Legion of Honor and the new Republic of Poland's highest honor, the Order of Polonia Restituta, as well as some valuable contacts in Washington. But he never sought to convert these honors into political capital.

To the Polish-American "respectable," American politics was not an all-consuming passion; so John Smulski remained a minor figure of the progressive era.[19]

Unlike reformers or respectables, machine politicians made politics their whole life.

The outstanding political boss of Polonia's capital was Stanley Henry Kunz. Born in Wilkes-Barre, Pennsylvania, in 1864, Kunz had been brought to Chicago when he was two years old. Throughout his lifetime, his only profession was politics. Indeed, his only other interest was horse racing. He

TABLE 9   JOHN SMULSKI'S ELECTORAL RECORD, 1896-1911

1896   Sixteenth Ward Aldermanic Race

        Smulski (R)   Kiolbassa (D)
        3,222 (48.74%)   3,389
        Smulski's average Polish vote--28.64%

1898   Sixteenth Ward Aldermanic Race

        Smulski (R)   Winter (D)
        3,363 (50.69%)   3,273
        Smulski's average Polish vote--34.91%

1899   Sixteenth Ward Aldermanic Race

        Smulski (R)   Kowalski (D)
        4,468 (46.72%)   3,509
        Smulski's average Polish vote--40.25%

1901   Seventeenth Ward Aldermanic Race

        Smulski (R)   McGrath (D)
        5,689 (54.24%)   4,400
        Smulski's average Polish vote--68.12%

1903   City Attorney Race

        Smulski (R)   Owens (D)
        141,192 (47.27%)   132,955
        Smulski's average Polish vote--68.06%

1905   City Attorney Race

        Smulski (R)   Noak (D)
        154,929 (48.81%)   136,138
        Smulski's average Polish vote--63.72%

1906   State Treasurer Race

        Smulski (R)   Piotrowski (D)
        142,565 (55.08%)   80,451 (city-wide vote only)
        Smulski's average Polish vote--46.60%

1911   Republican Mayoral Primary

        Smulski   Merriam   Thompson
        23,138 (20.07%) 53,089   26,406
        Smulski's average Polish vote--88.79%

claimed that a friend for whom he had obtained a job in the city department of animal husbandry first interested him in horses, and Kunz eventually had his own stable in Tennessee and a string of racehorses.[20]

Kunz won his first political office in 1888 when the voters of Polish Downtown sent him to the state legislature as a Democratic representative. In 1891 the same three-way vote split that catapulted Peter Kiolbassa into the city treasurer's office made Kunz Sixteenth Ward alderman. With a few brief interruptions, Kunz held a council seat for the next thirty years; and he was usually Democratic ward comitteeman as well.

Stanley Kunz was a table-thumper, a yeller, a screamer, and a fighter, who always acted as if he owned the Sixteenth Ward. In his later years he carried a cane, often using it to rap on a table for emphasis. Political insiders were certain that many a rival precinct official also felt the hard wood of this cane. Kunz's reputation outside Polonia was distinctly unsavory. The Chicago newspapers dubbed him "Stanley the Slugger" and the "terrible Pole." During one aldermanic campaign the Municipal Voters' League summed up his "disgraceful record" with dry understatement: "A man of force, which is usually directed to bad ends."[21]

Within Polonia's capital vilification from the American respectables was of little consequence. Most Polish-Americans did not read the American press, and the Polish papers generally backed Kunz because he used his influence to gain jobs and favors for Poles. Such jobs and favors were the key to any ward boss's power among immigrant groups.

Jane Addams once remarked that former peasants respect nothing so much as the good man, and to them the ward boss was very good indeed. Other settlement workers also understood that the seemingly blind adherence of immigrant masses to a boss had a rational basis. As one of them remarked, "Ward politics is a kind of crude socialism, basing itself upon the feeling that the power of the ballot ought to bring with it tangible economic betterment to the people." And Charles Merriam, a political scientist who learned some valuable lessons as an active participant in reform politics, summed up the power of the boss:

There is no mystery surrounding the power of an organization to control and deliver votes. . . . To the newcomer, unfamiliar with the environment and economically dependent, the outstanding issue may well be a job given him, or some favor or adjustment important in his world. . . . Considering the exploitation of the immigrant in the United States, it is not remarkable that he . . . clings to the Little Father of the Community, who is always there and ready to help as best he can.[22]

Stanley Kunz was such a father to the community of Polish Downtown and a well-known figure to Poles elsewhere in Chicago. For many years a common expression in Chicago's Polonia, whenever anyone had a problem, was "Go to Kunz, he can settle it."[23]

Polonia's church leaders, already committed to the Democratic party, usually backed Boss Kunz. Father Vincent Barzynski never opposed Kunz in any way, and Father Francis Gordon, who became pastor of St. Stanislaus in 1906 and gradually grew as influential in Polonia as Barzynski had been, cooperated with the boss for the greater good of the community.

During the interim between 1899, when Vincent Barzynski died, and 1906, when Francis Gordon became pastor, a less politically minded priest, Father John Kasprycki, presided over the *Stanisławowo*. Father Kasprycki interested himself more in youth work and in expansion of the parish's physical plant than in political advancement for his community; under his mild rule, Father Andrew Spetz, a parish assistant with reformist ideas, enjoyed free rein to mount a challenge to Boss Kunz.[24]

In 1903 Kunz was not up for reelection, but the other aldermanic seat in the Sixteenth Ward was at stake. Father Spetz and the "church party" in the ward proposed Vincent J. Józwiakowski, a young journalist on the staff of the Resurrectionists' *Dziennik Chicagoski,* as the Democratic candidate in the ward's party convention. Józwiakowski not only had the confidence of the Polish priests but of the Municipal Voters' League as well, which called him a "first class man, who would reflect credit upon his ward." However, Kunz controlled a majority in the convention, which chose August Klafta, one of Kunz's ward heelers, as the Democratic nominee. Jówiakowski and his reform backers decided to run an independent campaign; and the Republicans in the ward, realizing that they were too weak to mount a challenge on their own, endorsed the independent.[25]

The campaign was a heated one, with disputes and fist fights breaking out at nearly every polling place on election day. But, when the votes were counted, Józwiakowski had won by a comfortable margin; over 71 percent of the Polish voters had defied Kunz by supporting the independent. In the neighboring Seventeenth Ward, the Chicago Commons Community Club also registered another victory, electing Lewis D. Sitts, a German-American, to succeed John Smulski. Father Spetz of St. Stanislaus, elated by his own reform triumph, gave a congratulatory speech at the Seventeenth Ward victory dinner at Chicago Commons; but in this ward the Polish vote had split evenly between the two parties and had not been a factor in Sitts's election.[26]

Buoyed up by their success in 1903, the reform element in Polish Downtown put up another independent in 1904 to challenge Kunz himself. The Polish voters, however, were less eager to scratch the boss than they were his creature; and Kunz was reelected with a safe 58 percent of the Polish vote. When Józwiakowski came up again at the polls the following year, Kunz groomed another of his lieutenants, John M. Nowicki, to oppose him. Nowicki ran only a little better than Klafta had two years before, gaining a scant 40 percent of the Polish vote; but this time the Republicans refused to unite behind Józwiakowski, putting forward a Polish candidate of their own. In this triangular race, with the anti-Kunz vote divided, precinct machinery carried the day and Nowicki squeezed into office. A short time later, when Father Gordon became pastor of St. Stanislaus and made his peace with Kunz, the reform drive of the church party petered out.[27]

Ironically, Stanley Kunz was finally defeated for alderman in 1906, not by reformers, but by a man who skillfully used Kunz's one reform vote in the city council against him. Early in 1906 a citizens' reform meeting had been held at the Auditorium Theater in Chicago to discuss the city's high crime rate. It decided that a thousand additional policemen were needed immediately; and in order to finance the hiring of new personnel, the reformers hit upon an ingenious proposal—raise the saloon license fee from five hundred to a thousand dollars annually! Not only would money be raised for new policemen but, by driving some saloonkeepers out of business, the new license fee might in itself help solve the crime problem.[28]

When an ordinance to this effect was introduced in council, Kunz voted against it on all the preliminary motions and engaged in attempts to delay its passage or substitute a lower fee than the proposed thousand dollars. But when the final vote on the measure came up, Kunz and his Sixteenth Ward puppet, Nowicki, both voted for the higher license fee, an act which led to disaster for Kunz at the polls.[29]

There is no conclusive evidence to explain why Stanley Kunz experienced this sudden change of heart, but three explanations are possible. First of all, the brewery agents were lobbying heavily against the ordinance, and there almost certainly was a payoff involved for aldermen who would vote against it. Perhaps Kunz was not cut into the boodle or thought his share insufficient and thus voted for the measure. Or perhaps Kunz was alarmed by the three-year reform fight against him in his own ward and believed that a vote for reform on this measure would help recoup his position with the church party. Or, as a third possibility, Kunz may have known that his vote would be political suicide but had already decided to retire and go out on a positive note. He had recently been quoted as saying that he was sick of politics and would like to retire to his horse farm and "become a gentleman." This last possibility is unlikely, for politics was Kunz's life; but it is impossible to tell which of the first two alternatives was decisive.[30]

In any case, in the April elections that year, John Schermann, former Republican alderman from the ward, conducted his campaign against Kunz in the form of a walking tour of the ward's 329 saloons. Most reform issues were not matters of immediate import to the Poles, but any attempt to prohibit, or raise the price of, beer and liquor was important to them. Schermann succeeded in convincing the saloon proprietors and patrons of Kunz's responsibility for the higher license fee, and, although Kunz managed to retain a slim 55 percent of the Polish vote, he lost the election by a few thousand votes.[31]

Kunz, however, did not retire and become a gentleman. He still retained his post in the state senate, to which he had been elected a few years earlier. He defeated Carter Harrison's brother, Preston, in the Democratic primary for U.S. congressman and then narrowly lost the congressional election, largely due to widespread defections by bitter Harrisonites. This incident soured relations between Kunz and the Harrisons for the rest of their careers. Kunz jumped back into his old aldermanic seat in 1907 and was not seriously challenged again until 1915.

Stanley Kunz eventually became the first Polish-American congressman from Chicago in 1920. Holding on to his power base as ward committeeman in Chicago, he served six consecutive terms in Washington until his defeat in 1932. Ironically, for a man of his reputation, he won his last victory in 1930 in a recount, making good on charges of vote fraud against his Republican opponent.[32]

The difference between John Smulski and Stanley Kunz was aptly summed up by some unknown wit in the Aldermanic Club. At the Club's St. Valentine's Day dinner in 1900, the printed program included a list of all the aldermen with a humorous little verse about each. The verses for Smulski and Kunz, who at the time were both aldermen, ran as follows:

> Smulski: Beware the snares of Washington,
>   O Statesman dear, beware;
>   But ere this caution you need heed,
>   Get there, me boy, get there.
> Kunz: A man of spirit very often,
>   A man of spirits all the time.[33]

Even at this early date, Smulski was recognized as a statesman, not a

TABLE 10   ELECTORAL RECORD OF STANLEY KUNZ'S TROUBLED TIME, 1903-1906

1903   Sixteenth Ward Aldermanic Race

        Klafta (D)   Józwiakowski (Ind.)
        2,901 (37.66%)   4,522 (58.70%)
        Average Polish vote--71.62% (Ind.)

1904   Sixteenth Ward Aldermanic Race

        Kunz (D)   Czarnecki (Ind.)
        3,927 (57.89%)   2,548 (37.56%)
        Average Polish vote--57.85% (D)

1904   Congressional Race*

        Harrison (D)   McGavin (R)
        13,025 (33.48%)   20,107 (51.69%)
        Average Polish vote--37.83% (D)

1905   Sixteenth Ward Aldermanic Race

        Nowicki (D)   Przybylski (R)   Józwiakowski (Ind.)
        3,251 (38.88%)   2,033 (24.31%)   2,343 (28.02%)
        Average Polish vote--40.31% (D)

1906   Sixteenth Ward Aldermanic Race

        Kunz (D)   Schermann (R)
        2,683 (41.88%)   3,029 (47.29%)
        Average Polish vote--55.11% (D)

1906   Congressional Race **

        Kunz (D)   McGavin (R)
        11,336 (39.70%)   11,421 (40.00%)
        Average Polish vote--73.71% (D)

---

*Kunz lost the congressional nomination to Preston Harrison, then
 knifed Harrison in the general election.

**Harrison lost the congressional nomination to Kunz, then knifed
 Kunz in the general election.

politician. And, in fact, he eventually did play the statesman's role in Washington, meeting frequently with President Woodrow Wilson and other government leaders to discuss the Polish question during the First World War. Kunz, on the other hand, was typed as a man who liked his glass of spirits; and they might have added his love of the ponies as well. But the aldermen also detected the fierce spirit of Kunz—his drive and ambition—which he employed in quest of power and recognition for himself and the Polish community.

Throughout the ups and downs of his career, Stanley Kunz nearly always retained at least a majority of the Polish voters in his own ward; but many times when Smulski was running for office the Poles voted against him. This was not primarily because Smulski was a respectable or a reformer and Kunz a boss. Reform was largely irrelevant to the Poles, except for the liquor question. They voted against Smulski simply because he belonged to the wrong party. They voted for Kunz because he was powerful, benevolent, and near at hand.

Excepting Smulski, most Polish respectables were confined to appointive positions, such as the Library Board, the Board of Education, or the Board of Health. The few elective positions which fell to Polish-Americans before the First World War were snared by machine politicians. Usually Kunz and a protégé held the two aldermanic posts in the Sixteenth Ward, and the Democrats of South Chicago's Eighth Ward often picked a Polish-American for one of that ward's council seats.

When Smulski and the other respectables earned a reputation for honesty and service, and when they lobbied in the corridors of the White House for the freedom of Poland, Chicago's Poles respected and admired them, enjoying the prestige brought to Polonia. When Kunz and his cohorts hammered their way into the councils of the Democratic chieftains, the Poles rejoiced in that too, glad of the power and material benefits gained for the community. The efforts of boss and respectable, though in political conflict with each other, were complementary from Polonia's standpoint. Only later, when Chicago's Polish-Americans were seeking wider recognition in politics, did the lack of a mixed breed of political leader who could combine the strengths of both boss and respectable hinder Polonia's progress in politics.

7 The WASP as Ethnic Leader

Among American politicians in Chicago, the Democratic bosses were generally sensitive to the Polish community, at least at election times; the Republican reformers were uniformly haughty. Harold Ickes typified the latter attitude when he called John Smulski "a Polish stuffed shirt who was frequently used as window dressing."[1] But the middle-ground, mixed politicians of both parties best understood the possibilities of the growing Polish vote strength. Charles Deneen was Smulski's mentor for the Republicans, and the Democrat Carter Harrison II enjoyed the greatest Polish support of any WASP politician in the city. In fact, Harrison was the outstanding ethnic vote-getter of his generation in Chicago politics.

Carter Harrison II, born in 1860, was educated in private schools in Germany and at St. Ignatius College in Chicago. These two biographical facts gave him political advantages in a city where Germans were the second largest ethnic group and Catholics outnumbered Jews and Protestants. The younger Harrison, furthermore, married a Catholic and had his two children baptized and brought up in that faith. Young Carter owed his start in politics solely to his father's name and to his father's political cronies who organized his first mayoral election in 1897; but he soon introduced his own modifications of the Harrison style and governed the city for five terms, very much in his own right.[2]

The younger Harrison was a different man, in temperament and personality, from his father. He was more thoughtful and less gregarious, and he lacked his father's mastery of a crowd from the speaker's platform. Yet he carried on many of his father's most successful practices, modifying them to fit changing times or his own personality. He kept open court for the public in his City Hall office nearly every day, as his father had; and he presided without an absence over every city council meeting during his five terms. Not able to cover the city on horseback as his father had, he supported the turn-of-the-century fad for cycling and distributed a large photo of himself in cycling gear during his 1897 campaign. Beneath the photo, the caption read: "Not the Champion Cyclist, but the Cyclist's Champion."[3]

As for issues, defense of personal liberty on the liquor question was his mainstay. Only when discussing this issue before an immigrant audience did he feel completely at ease on the stump. Harrison also, through most of his career, shared his father's "live and let live" attitude toward vice and gambling, choosing to segregate the evil in one compact vice district rather than trying to stamp it out. The only issue which was peculiarly his own, and not inherited, was the traction issue. Harrison had moved with unaccustomed vigor against Yerkes and the Allen Law; and, ever after, he never missed a chance to remind the voters of how he thwarted the "Traction King."[4]

Like his father, Carter Harrison II cultivated the immigrant groups. Both used the personal liberty issue and City Hall patronage for this purpose, but a subtle difference of style reflected their differing personalities. The elder Harrison loved to give rip-roaring speeches to Polish audiences, but the son took a more intellectual approach. Late in the 1890s, he held a little after-dinner chat with the priests of St. Stanislaus and a few selected parishioners in the parish rectory. Any ordinary political hack would have tried to flatter the Poles with references to Pulaski and Kosciuszko, those great Polish lovers of liberty who came to America during her revolution to fight for freedom. Harrison did not neglect to mention these figures, but he continued by giving the Polish priests a flattering, but largely accurate, lecture on Polish cultural history:

A nation's . . . true greatness lies in what its people have contributed to the religion, the intellectual, the scientific, the artistic development of civilization. In these particulars the unhappy kingdom of Poland holds high rank. . . . Poland was a Catholic country and for centuries perfect freedom of religious worship was permitted to the people. In this respect it was a prototype of religious freedom of belief in our own country. . . . Freedom of religious belief led to liberty of the press and thus we find that early in the 15th century there were probably more printing presses in Poland than in any other country of Europe. . . . Copernicus, the founder of the modern system of astronomy, taught the world how the earth and the other planets revolve about the central sun. . . . The great university city of Cracow . . . today possesses the original block from which a world map was printed in the early days of 1500, . . . one of the oldest maps in the world which gives the name America to the Western Hemisphere. . . . Such was the cultivation, the learning of Poland four and five centuries ago. To show its people have not

fallen from the high standards of the past requires but little effort.If we
turn to music we find a Chopin charming the world with his wild harmonies
. . . a Paderewski looming like a giant among the piano virtuosos of the day.
In literature Poland gave the world, in Synkiewicz, one of the greatest
masters of fiction who ever wrote. . . . The English speaking nations claim
that Shakespeare, the great playwright, was the master literary figure of all
time, and yet we have to turn to a Polish actress, the great inspired Madame
Modjeska to interpret properly some of Shakespeare's greatest roles.[5]

No filiopietist historian could have assembled a better list of Polish
cultural achievements. The educated priests of St. Stanislaus, who lived every
day with the vulgarities of Kunz and the other bosses and who were disturbed
by the contempt of the reformers, must have been mightily impressed.

Harrison also grasped some of the psychological tensions of the immigrants. He realized that his policy of granting patronage jobs to newcomers
was not only politically shrewd but also a sound means of giving confidence
to the immigrants and encouraging them in their growing Americanism. In
an interview he gave late in his mayoral career, he explained:

Personally I stand by a belief which comes from the bottom of my heart
in the wisdom of recognizing officially members of the nationalities now in
the process of welding into the composite that will be the ultimate American.
I have seen enough of the resulting encouragement, of the pride
fellow racials feel therein, of the stimulus given thereby to an entire
nationality, to feel the firm conviction that nothing makes more surely for
good citizenship, for true Americanism among these peoples, than the
assurance that they are held worthy of a place in our public life. . . .
It is among the nationalities which have been furnishing the bulk of the
immigration of recent years that the recognition bears its richest fruits. . . .
Ours is a strange country to them, ours a strange language. The habits, the
customs of their adopted surroundings are new and startling. At best
they do not know if they are welcome or not. With a timid heart they enter
into citizenship. They realize the greatness of this citizenship, indeed it
weighs upon them, it almost overwhelms them. Not certain that they are really
wanted among us, they are fearful that in some way, by some mishap they
may lose this citizenship. . . .
Then comes an appointment of one of their very own to some place,
perhaps of a most trivial character.
Instantly everything is changed. Certainty, security has come to them;
now and hereafter they are part, parcel, and fibre of the government under
whose flag they work and live. I have seen the effects upon a nationality of
a thing intrinsically so petty as the naming of a young lawyer as an assistant
prosecuting attorney.[6]

Despite a certain pomposity and self-satisfaction evident in these remarks, Harrison's insight was sharp. He not only knew that ethnic recognition worked, something which any good pol knew instinctively; he knew why it worked.

The Polish-language press spread Harrison's fame throughout Chicago's Polonia. A typical headline in the *Dziennik Chicagoski* at election time read, "Carter H. Harrison, a True Friend of the Poles and a True Democrat." The newspaper then went on to explain what made Harrison so true:

Harrison always was a sterling and dependable friend of the Poles, just as his father, who left $1500 in his will for the Polish Nazareth Hospital, also was. His son, today's candidate for the office of mayor, carried out this wonderful bequest.

He appointed to his cabinet, in the time of his former administration as mayor of the city, our fellow-countryman, Peter Kiolbassa. No other mayor ever did anything of the sort.[7]

A legacy from his father and the shrewd use of patronage were sterling credentials for the young WASP as ethnic leader.

Harrison's personal charisma among Poles and other immigrants paid off handsomely. He served four consecutive terms as mayor, from 1897 to 1905; then after six years of retirement he made a comeback in 1911 to equal his father's five elections. In each of his mayoral victories, Harrison enjoyed solid support from the Polish vote. Of course, any Democrat at this time could win a majority of Polish voters, but a glance at the statistics shows that Harrison was more than just any Democrat. In the eight mayoral elections from 1893 to 1907, Harrison was a candidate half the time. In the four elections when he was not running, the Democrats averaged 66.67 percent, exactly two-thirds, of the Polish vote; but when Harrison led the ticket, he drew an average of 72.59 percent of the Poles.[8] In other words, he could raise the Democratic tendency of Polonia by six percentage points. If the Polish vote numbered about fifteen thousand (a conservative estimate by the end of this period), this 6 percent represented about one thousand votes. Added to the numbers of ordinarily Republican Germans, Italians, and Scandinavians that Harrison attracted, these extra votes often formed the margin of victory in a close election.

Harrison's final victory in 1911 provides a good case study of his ethnic appeal, and it also illustrates another important point: Harrison could play the progressive without damage to his ethnic appeal.

The year 1911 was the climax of many years of progressive agitation in Chi-

TABLE 11   ELECTION RETURNS (IN PERCENTAGES): MAYOR, 1893-1907

Year	No. of Polish Precincts	Polish Vote (City-Wide Vote)			
		Republican	Democratic	Independent	Socialist
Dec., 1893	11	Swift 20.80 (49.16)	Hopkins 78.38 (49.69)		
1895	11	Swift 37.11 (55.08)	Wenter 57.96 (39.48)		
1897	14	Sears 9.75 (20.09)	Harrison 82.91 (50.23)	Harlan 4.01 (23.53)	
1899	17	Carter 23.54 (35.15)	Harrison 68.75 (48.58)	Altgeld 6.13 (15.43)	
1901	18	Hanecy 23.54 (43.14)	Harrison 72.56 (52.66)		Collins 2.74 (1.80)
1903	18	Stewart 31.51 (44.75)	Harrison 64.37 (47.24)		Brecken 2.89 (3.59)
1905	17	Harlan 29.73 (42.19)	Dunne 64.99 (49.65)		Collins 4.78 (7.09)
1907	20	Busse 31.89 (49.02)	Dunne 65.44 (45.18)		Koop 2.29 (3.99)
Average		25.98 (42.32)	69.42 (47.84)		3.18 (4.12)

Average Polish vote for Democrats, 1893-1907, 69.42
Average Polish vote for Democrats without Harrison, 66.67
Average Polish vote for Democrats with Harrison, 72.59

cago. After Harrison's first retirement in 1905, both parties had slated reformers to deal with the traction issue. John M. Harlan finally attained his
party's regular nomination, and the Democrats put forward Edward F. Dunne,
an Irish Catholic judge of rigid integrity. Harlan still avowed that "the
streets belong to the people," but he had become aware of some of the legal
and financial complexities involved in municipal ownership; thus he urged a
gradual, cautious approach. Judge Dunne, on the other hand, campaigned
vigorously for immediate municipal ownership of the traction lines, a position
capsulized in three letters, IMO. The voters chose the man with the definite,
immediate program, electing Dunne by a large margin and sending Harlan to
final political oblivion. Among Polish voters IMO may have sounded catchy
and perhaps desirable, but it was not a major issue. The fact that Dunne was
a Democrat and a Catholic was sufficient.[9]

As mayor, Dunne ran into the complexities which Harlan had predicted;
after a complicated series of legislative maneuverings, court battles, and referenda, he failed to attain municipal ownership, settling finally for a grant of
greatly improved franchises to the existing streetcar companies. At the end of
his two-year term, his Republican opponents capitalized on voter frustration
with the mayor's unkept promises and elected Fred Busse, a benign-looking,
phlegmatic North Side boss, to the city's first four-year mayoral term. Busse's
regime was quiet and lackluster, marked only by some unsensational improvements in the civil service and a general slackening of reform fervor. But
by 1911, when his term expired, the Republican progressives were ready to
mount a new campaign; and Carter Harrison had decided to inject his personal brand of politics back into the local scene.[10]

In 1911 Chicago was scheduled to have its first direct mayoral primary,
so the time seemed right to upset the old factions by appealing to the people.
Yet since the political demise of Harlan, the Republican progressives had
been leaderless and disorganized. When the first gun in the 1911 scrap was
fired by Charles E. Merriam, a political science professor at the University of
Chicago, it came from an unexpected quarter. Merriam was just finishing his
first term as a Republican alderman in the city council. At the head of a council committee on municipal expenditures, he made a forceful fight for honesty
and efficiency in government. Harold Ickes, the veteran manager of the Harlan campaigns, in surveying the field of possible candidates, informed Merriam, "It looks to me as if you are the only man in sight." At Ickes' urging,
Merriam got a jump on the competition by announcing his candidacy in early
November of 1910.[11]

From the beginning of the campaign, Merriam tried to connect his own cause with the national Republican Progressive movement. In a January 4 speech he stated:

An aroused sentiment standing for courageous, progressive ideas has
in many places in this country achieved notable public victories. I believe
the people of this city are in sympathy with this movement.[12]

His platform was none too specific, but in it he called for public honesty and efficiency, home rule, city planning, and a just settlement of all outstanding public utility and traction questions. Above all, Merriam appealed to youth for a change in the old machine and faction system of graft politics. A *Chicago Tribune* editorial, entitled "Ring out the old, Ring in the new," captured the spirit of the Merriam campaign perfectly:

Mr. Harrison . . . made a more capable and efficient administration of
municipal affairs than some other Chicago mayors whom we might mention,
and he is really deserving credit for important services which he rendered the
public. But after all, Mr. Harrison is objectionable because he is an exponent
of a bad and vicious system and theory of municipal government—a system
which Chicago has outgrown. The old system has been that municipal offices
are the legitimate reward of politicians for political services in carrying
elections.[13]

In the February 28 primary, the progressive professor earned his nomination with a clear majority over four other Republican candidates.[14]

In the meantime, Carter Harrison had to buck strong opposition to his comeback in the Democratic primary. Ex-mayor Dunne, sensing, like Merriam, that the time was right for reform, came forth as a candidate; and Roger Sullivan's organization put forward Andrew J. Graham, a West Side banker. In this triangular fight, the real contest was between Harrison and Dunne, with Graham fading into the background. But among Polish voters, Graham caused Harrison some worries, thanks to the maneuverings of Stanley Kunz. Kunz still nurtured evil feelings toward the Harrisons, due to his two bitter congressional campaigns against the mayor's brother, and in recent years had edged closer to the Sullivan faction. This year, Stanley appeared openly with Sullivan on the platform, denouncing Harrison and all his works; and on election day he used all his power in support of the Sullivan man.

The results of the battle between the Polish power of Kunz and the magic name of Harrison were mixed. In his own Sixteenth Ward, Kunz managed to carry a scant 51 percent of the Polish vote for Graham, to 37 percent for Harrison and 10 percent for Dunne. Yet of twelve heavily Polish

precincts in the ward, Harrison carried four and gave Graham a close battle
in four more. The overall Graham plurality in the ward was only twenty-four
votes. Elsewhere in Polonia's capital, the power of Kunz was insufficient to
stop Harrison. In the nine wards where identifiable Polish voting blocs
existed, Harrison carried 46 percent of the Polish vote to 35 percent for
Graham and 18 percent for Dunne. In any case, Harrison won a very narrow
primary victory and the right to challenge Charles Merriam.[15]

Harrison realized that this was a progressive year, so he immediately set
out to capitalize on his reputation as a champion against the utility and traction interests.

We plan to wage this fight on the theory that public utility corporations
should be our servants instead of our masters. I believe the gas company
can sell its product at not more than 70 cents for 1000 cubic feet.

Seventy-cent gas gave Harrison a concrete issue that he could sell to his immigrant constituency and throw up against the vagueness of Merriam's calls
for honesty and efficiency. He also adopted the entire range of progressive
issues: "A business administration in the interest of all the people. . . . Strict
regulation of public utility corporations. . . . The construction of a system
of outer docks and harbors, with recreation areas, under public ownership
and control. . . . Home rule for Chicago."[16]

Thus in 1911, as so often in the progressive era, each candidate claimed
that he was the real progressive.

Yet Harrison shrewdly emphasized the difference in his brand of
progressivism. Whenever possible, he portrayed Merriam as a high-minded
but impractical and bookish reformer, and himself as an experienced man
of affairs. In an attempt to keep the allegiance of the immigrants, he branded
Merriam a potential prohibitionist.

The political action committee of the United Societies for Local Self-
Government—a coalition of ethnic politicians and community leaders organized to fight prohibition legislation—endorsed Harrison; and word spread
rapidly that Merriam was an uncertain factor whereas Harrison could be
safely trusted not to "clamp down the lid." Late in the campaign, Harrison
mailed thousands of letters to individual saloonkeepers in the "foreign districts," warning of the danger to personal liberty if Merriam should be
elected.[17]

When election day came, the voters chose Harrison's brand of progressivism by a narrow seventeen-thousand-vote margin.[18] Three factors proved

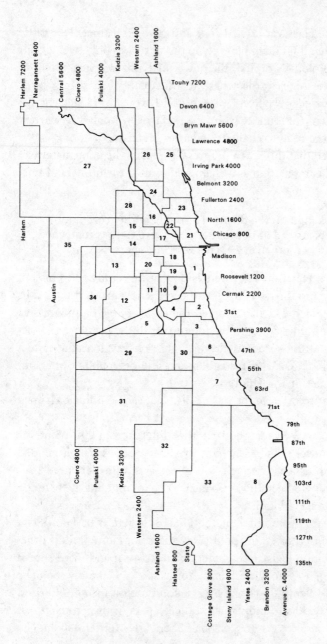

Map 4. Chicago ward boundaries,
1901–1921

TABLE 12   DEMOCRATIC PRIMARY ELECTION RETURNS (IN PERCENTAGES): MAYOR, 1911

Ward	No. of Polish Precincts	Harrison	Graham	Dunne
4th				
Polish vote	2	40.89	28.98	30.12
Ward average		27.60	25.22	47.17
5th				
Polish vote	1	32.00	20.00	48.00
Ward average		22.91	21.51	55.56
8th				
Polish vote	6	58.68	20.60	20.71
Ward average		44.64	17.78	37.56
11th				
Polish vote	3	52.94	36.94	10.20
Ward average		49.20	29.34	21.44
16th				
Polish vote	13	37.69	51.62	10.52
Ward average		41.95	42.71	15.33
17th				
Polish vote	1	33.96	43.39	22.64
Ward average		40.25	33.94	25.80
27th				
Polish vote	3	44.85	22.69	27.97
Ward average		41.90	19.27	38.81
28th	4	69.05	20.77	10.17
Ward average		52.12	26.91	20.95
29th				
Polish vote	4	37.70	31.33	30.95
Ward average		31.11	18.71	50.17
City-wide				
Polish vote	37	46.21	35.55	18.13
City average		37.39	26.17	36.43

crucial: the refusal of many regular Republicans to back the reformer Merriam, the tremendous flophouse vote for Harrison in the river wards, and the loyalty of the immigrant nationalities to Harrison. The newspapers discussed the first of these factors most thoroughly the day after the election. The Republican papers, in particular, were filled with reports of the "knifing" that occurred in supposedly Republican wards. Yet this defection from the Republican ranks was, to some extent, compensated by a similar defection of Dunne and Graham men from the Democratic ticket. The flophouse vote was

certainly an important element in the Democratic margin, with Hinky Dink
and Bathhouse delivering, as usual, the vote of their motley constituents. Yet
Harrison's plurality in the two river wards was 6,836, not enough in itself to
explain his victory.[19]

    The loyalty of the immigrant groups was the critical factor. Both can-
didates realized this in their retrospective writings on the election. Harrison
noted in his autobiography, "Beyond a shadow of a doubt I owed my victory
to the loyalty of the foreign nationalites backed up by the flophouse vote,"

TABLE 13   ELECTION RETURNS (IN PERCENTAGES): MAYOR, 1911

Ward	No. of Polish Precincts	Merriam (R.)	Harrison (D.)	Rodriguez (Soc.)
4th				
Polish vote	2	37.07	58.21	4.34
Ward average		29.39	64.98	4.70
8th				
Polish vote	1	34.64	62.20	2.75
Ward average		32.48	62.81	3.83
8th				
Polish vote	6	18.69	78.05	2.59
Ward average		42.94	51.16	4.91
11th				
Polish vote	3	27.19	75.87	6.68
Ward average		30.47	60.27	8.07
16th				
Polish vote	13	19.52	74.61	3.92
Ward average		23.59	68.42	7.06
17th				
Polish vote	1	35.36	57.14	6.69
Ward average		32.94	59.57	6.95
27th				
Polish vote	3	25.53	59.25	14.27
Ward average		44.02	40.73	14.11
28th				
Polish vote	4	22.52	68.24	8.14
Ward average		42.19	45.37	11.42
29th				
Polish vote	4	36.20	57.97	5.80
Ward average		32.20	60.49	6.46
City-wide				
Polish vote	37	24.40	68.91	5.60
City average		43.80	48.52	6.76

and Merriam conceded that "Harrison's traditional strength among the nationalistic groups aided him greatly." Polish voters were not the most important element in this immigrant coalition, for their vote could be counted
on as safely Democratic. It was the Germans and Scandinavians, who often
voted Republican and were likely to appreciate Merriam's progressive rhetoric, that Harrison needed and apparently won with his prohibition scare.
Still, Polish Democrats were an integral part of the coalition, and they backed
Harrison with nearly 69 percent of their votes. Even Stanley Kunz realized
that his followers would not be deterred from voting for Harrison, and on the
eve of the election, he abandoned his knifing attempt. After this last-minute
conversion, the alderman got up early on election day and had nearly his
whole ward voted by noon.[20]

Carter Harrison's victory in 1911 was a model of successful progressive
politics in a city composed mainly of immigrants and their children. First of
all, he was a member of the "right" party insofar as the Poles and some other
immigrants were concerned, whereas Merriam faced an uphill battle simply
because he wasn't a Democrat. Second, Harrison, like his father before him,
had played skillfully upon the nationalistic loyalties of the immigrants,
thereby raising the Democratic percentages among Poles and other normally
Democratic groups and attracting just enough of the more Republican-
oriented ethnic groups. Finally, Harrison made his progressivism concrete
and proved that it was safe. Seventy-cent gas meant much more to a poor immigrant than municipal efficiency; and Harrison, the champion of personal
liberty, was trusted, whereas Merriam, who hobnobbed with silk-stocking
temperance men, was not.

The fifth and final administration of Carter Harrison, from 1911 to 1915,
proved to be something of a springtime for Polish politicians. Not only had
the Democrats recaptured City Hall with strong ethnic support, but a year
previously they had also swept most of the important Cook County offices,
after a long period of Republican dominance. Then, in 1912, former mayor
Dunne reached the Springfield statehouse as governor and Woodrow Wilson
gained the White House. Democrats now controlled every level of Chicago
government—federal, state, county, and city—and there were patronage jobs
aplenty for deserving members of the immigrant groups who had helped
make this possible.

A number of Polish-Americans who had been previously unsuccessful in
politics found a resting place in one or another of these jobs. For instance,

N. L. Piotrowski, the unsuccessful challenger of Smulski for state treasurer, was appointed to a position in the city's law department. Throughout the four years of his last term, Harrison made certain that there were always two Polish-Americans on the Board of Education. His most notable Polish appointee to the board was Julius Smietanka, a South Chicago businessman and banker who was much like John Smulski in everything but his political affiliation. Many a young Polish-American who later distinguished himself in public life got his start during this Democratic springtime. Edmund K. Jarecki, later the county judge for thirty-two consecutive years, began in 1911 as Stanley Kunz's aldermanic running mate in the Sixteenth Ward. During this period Chicago's Polonia elected its first member of the bench, Joseph S. LaBuy (name changed from Labaj), who in 1912 ran successfully for municipal court judge.

When a Polish-American was appointed to a supervisory position, he brought other countrymen with him as subordinates. Thus, Piotrowski had two Polish attorneys as his deputies in the law department; and when Frank Danisch became clerk of the municipal court, he appointed thirty Polish assistant clerks within a period of three years.[21]

Many in Chicago had doubted Harrison's professions of progressivism during the 1911 campaign. Clarence Darrow, for instance, speaking at a Merriam rally, had declared that "Mr. Harrison standing upon a progressive platform is like a bust of Martin Luther on a Roman Catholic cathedral."[22] Yet in his fifth term Harrison took a number of courageous stands which eventually made his reelection for yet another term impossible.

Harrison revived the efficiency division in the Civil Service department and backed it to the hilt, greatly improving the performance of his municipal personnel. Urged on by the sensational report of a church group's vice commission, the mayor also moved against the segregated vice district of the First Ward. This action, though a response to public pressure, finished Harrison politically.

Harrison, as his father before him, had always believed in segregation, not repression, of vice; and his two strongest political allies were Hinky Dink and Bathhouse, the lords of the First Ward dens. However, in 1911 Mayor Harrison publicly confessed that "my ideas of the vice question have been wrong. . . . Segregation means protected vice. Chicago is through with the segregated vice idea. . . . Repression means treating it just as any other crime is treated." The police moved into the south end of Chicago's First Ward, padlocking the brothels and arresting the madams. The crackdown was not permanent, but it was damaging enough to alienate Hinky Dink, the Bath, and their allies, driving them into the arms of Roger Sullivan. When primary time came around again in 1915, Sullivan had a well-oiled machine and a strong candidate, Robert Sweitzer, waiting for the mayor. Harrison the reformer met the same fate that Kunz had met after his one essay in reform.[23]

Polish voters, for the most part, were loyal to Harrison to the end. They did not have a personal interest in the survival of the vice dens as they did in the preservation of the saloons, so they were largely indifferent to the hue and cry about repression of vice. Instead, they remembered all the jobs they had received in the last four years. The Polish National Alliance's *Dziennik Zwiazkowy* editorialized:

What concerns Poles is that Mayor Harrison showed himself to be a true friend. He demanded from the central committee of the party that Poles be represented on the ticket for the better offices, and thanks to his protection and intercession, we have today many Poles in high offices. . . .

In Sweitzer's office there are almost 250 positions to be filled and of these 250 we hold only two.[24]

In the Polish wards throughout the city, Sweitzer did carry a number of precincts, most notably those in the Sixteenth Ward, where Stanley Kunz finally got his revenge on the Harrisons. But city-wide, Harrison held on to a slim 51 percent of the Polish vote. This clearly would have been much larger had Kunz released his constituents to vote their real feelings. As Harrison himself remarked, "I had the sentiment, but Sweitzer had the sediment."[25] Ironically though, Kunz was so busy helping Sullivan's man that he neglected his own race for aldermanic reelection. While carrying 57 percent of his ward's Polish voters for Sweitzer, he pulled only 47 percent of the Polish vote for himself and lost to a Harrison man, Vincent Zwiefka.[26]

Polonia regretted the passing of Harrison. *Dziennik Zwiazkowy* lamented that though Harrison had given in to the ministers, the professors, and the so-called reformers, these same people were of no help to him when he needed them; for most of them voted in the Republican primary. At a testimonial dinner for the ex-mayor in May of 1915, Father Francis Wojtalewicz, pastor of Immaculate Conception Parish and a power among the Poles of South Chicago, gave the invocation; and the reception committee included every prominent Polish politician in the city, with the exception of Stanley Kunz.[27]

As Jane Addams had said, immigrants appreciated nothing so much as the good man; to Chicago's Poles, Harrison had been a very good man indeed.

TABLE 14   DEMOCRATIC PRIMARY ELECTION RETURNS, SIXTEENTH WARD:
            MAYOR AND ALDERMAN, 1915

Precinct*	Mayoral		Aldermanic	
	Sweitzer	Harrison	Kunz	Zwiefka
1	215	219	175	235
2	184	139	152	170
7	166	126	132	163
8	200	156	154	163
9	181	77	149	111
11	159	115	123	154
12	139	176	119	158
13	126	106	103	119
14	194	88	188	104
15	103	96	84	111
16	144	121	113	163
17	139	93	119	125
18	120	96	93	129
19	162	152	139	180
20	197	98	183	113
24	216	119	162	175
Ward total	4,226	3,290	3,495	4,063
	55.81%	43.44%	46.24%	53.75%
Average Polish vote	57.04%	42.22%	47.47%	52.56%

*Precincts listed are those with at least a 60 percent Polish majority.

8 Polonia and Progressivism

In Polonia's capital progressive reform issues—honest government, civil service, municipal ownership of street railways, direct democracy, and the like—had little resonance. Polish voters entered into the politics of progressivism largely by inadvertence.

Of the four local leaders carrying a progressive banner in mayoral elections between 1895 and 1915, Polish voters supported two and rejected two. John Maynard Harlan, an independent in 1897 and a Republican in 1905, and Charles E. Merriam, the Republican candidate in 1911, failed to stir up any interest in Polonia. But when Edward F. Dunne ran in 1905 on the most progressive platform the local Democrats had yet put forth, and when Carter Harrison II adopted the pervasive progressivism of 1911, their ethnic support was in no way diminished. Progressivism was not a deciding factor in these choices. Party allegiance, personal loyalties, and easily understood platforms carried the day for Dunne and Harrison; whereas Harlan and Merriam, due to their party, religion, and background, were anathema to Polonia.

Polonia's leaders were aware of the progressive ferment in the city. The Polish National Alliance's daily organ, *Dziennik Zwiazkowy,* discussed the leading progressive issues from time to time and consistently adopted a good-government, progressive stance. At the height of the progressive era, in early 1911, this paper examined the various "direct democracy" reforms in a page one article:

In many states the people are demanding the introduction of the so-called referendum, initiative, and recall. . . . These reforms, so greatly progressive, have called forth many opponents, particularly in the circles of the so-called "interests." Evidently these great "interests" have more confidence in the legislature today than in the people themselves who elect it. But after all, for whom are the laws, if not for the People? Why then cannot

these same people be able to have the majority of their votes decide what
they want and what they think best for their own good?

The progress of enlightenment has overthrown the despotism of the
lord and has given the lawmaking power, by the vote of the people, to a
relatively small group of persons. Still further progress of this enlightenment
is gradually taking shape by transferring the greatest part of this lawmaking
work from the legislature to the generality of the citizens.[1]

In a similarly philosophic tone, this paper remarked on another occasion:

The world is progressing, life goes forward, and with life everything
else must follow, especially individuals and parties in politics. . . . The first
step in the struggle of the people with the so-called special interests must
be the defeat of all the so-called machine candidates.[2]

These sentiments echoed the editorials of English-language papers such
as the *Chicago Tribune* and the *Chicago Daily News*. In fact, it is quite possible that the Polish Alliance editors took their opinions directly from one of
the English papers, a not uncommon practice for the ethnic press. In any case,
the tone is high progressive.

The *Dziennik Zwiazkowy* also advised its readers on how to vote in the
numerous referenda which appeared on city ballots during this period, generally recommending a favorable vote for progressive improvements in the
city. When Carter Harrison initiated a crackdown on police graft in late 1911,
the Alliance paper heartily welcomed the move, giving its endorsement of the
mayor's action an interesting ethnic twist:

At last action is being taken to purge the police department of those depraved
guardians of the public safety who . . . arrest and beat peaceful citizens while
they leave undisturbed the ordinary criminals with whom they live in
accord. . . . The practices now followed by the citizens of the Emerald Isle
who have been provided with clubs will be ended.

The newspaper even found a few words to say about the moderate socialists
of Milwaukee, recently elected to lead that city's administration. According to
the editors, they could "contribute to the elimination of various social and
economic ills."[3]

The newspapers published by the Resurrectionist Fathers in Polonia
were more critical of the solutions proposed by progressive reformers. The
Dziennik Chicagoski published a fair appraisal of the arguments for and
against civil service reform just after the Chicago civil service law was passed
in 1895, but it then went on to give its own opinion:

We feel that we ought to point out that as much as civil service is convenient for the people born in this country or those who speak English and have been trained in English schools, it also is equally inconvenient for the various immigrant groups.[4]

On questions of civil service, direct democracy, and nonpartisanship, the Resurrectionist papers seemed more aware than the Alliance papers that these progressive reforms were tailored to a homogeneous native-American citizenry which did not exist in Chicago. Except for the brief revolt led by Father Spetz against Stanley Kunz, the church party in Polonia's capital was generally content to work with Democratic bosses and let idealistic schemes of good government alone.

Throughout the first decades of the twentieth century, the voters of Chicago were called upon in numerous referenda to give an opinion on policies dear to the progressives. A quick glance at the referendum results in the Polish areas seems to indicate that Polonia followed the good-government advice of the Alliance papers and voted at least as progressively as the rest of the city. In a selection of thirty referendum propositions which appeared on the ballot from 1904 to 1916, the Polish vote overwhelmingly favored such typical progressive measures as immediate municipal ownership of street railways, popular election of the Chicago School Board, adoption of direct primaries, and adoption of voting machines. Polish voters generally decided against the floating of bond issues and the raising of taxes for such civic improvements as bathing beaches, new dock facilities, a municipal garbage treatment plant, and a new county court house; but on many of these same issues, the city as a whole also voted down additional expenditures.

In this sample of thirty referenda, Polish voters were generally a little less likely to vote in favor of the various propositions (54.93 percent average Yes vote as opposed to 62.04 percent average Yes vote city-wide); but in the majority of cases their Yes vote percentage was close (within ten points) to the city-wide percentage. Significantly, in 80 percent of the cases, the result of the referendum (either approval or disapproval) would have been the same if the whole city were composed of only Polish voters.[5]

And yet these referendum results are misleading if taken as a reliable cross section of opinion in Polonia's capital. Though Polish citizens who expressed their opinions on the ballot were generally just as progressive or just as conservative as the other voters in the city, a much smaller percentage of Polish voters bothered to mark referendum ballots. Comparing the top of the ticket in various elections during the period with the vote on referendum

TABLE 15   POLISH-AMERICAN AND CITY-WIDE VOTE ON THIRTY SELECTED REFERENDA, 1904-1916

| | Percentage Voting "Yes" | |
Proposition	Poles	City-wide
1904		
Adoption of the Mueller Law authorizing the city to operate street railways*	82.17	83.49
Immediate implementation of the Mueller Law*	81.89	70.79
Interim licensing of street railways, until municipal ownership can be achieved*	79.56	71.48
Popular election of the Board of Education	74.69	66.86
Constitutional amendment authorizing the legislature to grant home rule to cities	87.56	93.52
Adoption of voting machines	81.63	89.44
Adoption of direct primaries	88.28	92.09
Popular veto of state laws	87.64	89.69
1906		
Approval of municipal operation of street railways*	57.27	57.49
Issuance of street railway certificates, a financing measure under the Mueller Law*	55.63	50.77
Immediate municipal ownership of street railways*	58.03	50.87
1907		
Adoption of street railway franchises	40.15	55.48
Adoption of city charter	14.22	32.89
Changes in the municipal court	56.83	56.44
1911		
Issuing bonds to build bridges	66.16	76.47
Issuing bonds to pay city debts	55.74	67.65

Table 15--Continued

| | Percentage Voting "YES" | |
Proposition	Poles	City-wide
1912		
Issuing bonds for harbor improvements	37.75	58.63
Issuing bonds for bathing beaches	33.01	50.78
Issuing bonds for contagious disease hospital	39.02	56.51
Issuing bonds for police department	31.09	44.13
Issuing bonds for fire department	34.09	48.89
Bonds and taxes for county hospital and poorhouse	47.78	54.80
Bonds and taxes for county court house	33.95	41.33
Tax equalization amendment to constitution	51.02	68.62
Primary election reforms	50.91	70.45
Shortening the ballot	49.46	69.52
1916		
Bonds for municipal garbage reduction plant	34.12	40.37
Improvement of beaches	34.94	42.13
Consolidation of local governments	35.53	38.49
Amendment to banking law	67.74	72.15
Average of thirty referenda	54.93	62.04

*Issues requiring three-fifths majority for approval.

No. of cases where Polish and city-wide votes are separated by ten percentage points or less--17

No. of cases in which Polish and city-wide votes agree, as to approval or disapproval--24 propositions, farther down on the ballot, we can detect a wide divergence between Polish-Americans and other voters. In six elections from 1904 to 1916, only 58 percent of Polish-Americans who voted for the head of the ticket also marked their ballots on the propositions; whereas 76 percent of the electorate at large voted on the referenda. This means that almost half of Chicago's Polish voters were neither progressive nor conservative on the issues of reform in the progressive era, but simply indifferent.[6]

Progressivism, therefore, was not of major importance to the Polish community in Chicago. Polonia's leaders knew of its existence, generally understood it, and occasionally discussed it in their newspapers; but they did not give it any major portion of their time and attention. About half of the Polish voters expressed opinions on progressive policies in various referenda. Though their opinions were not very different from the opinions of other voters, the large number of indifferent voters on reform issues confirms the judgment of many historians that there was a gulf between the ethos of the typical Progressive and the ethos of the typical immigrant.[7] The *Dziennik Chicagoski's* perceptive judgment that reform was convenient for the English-speaking citizen but inconvenient or irrelevant for the Polish immigrant illustrates the wideness of this gulf.

TABLE 16   PERCENTAGE OF THOSE VOTING FOR HEAD OF TICKET WHO ALSO VOTED
            ON ONE OR MORE PROPOSITIONS: SIX ELECTIONS, 1904-1916

Year	Office at Head of Ticket	No. of Polish Precincts Sampled	% of Poles Voting	% of Voters in City as a Whole Voting
1904	President	20	50.21	76.81
1906	State Treasurer	20	71.87	89.73
1907	Mayor	20	74.65	89.80
1911	Mayor	37	42.78	63.73
1912	President	38	61.31	73.35
1916	President	51	47.67	65.77
Average			58.09	76.53

It should not be assumed, however, that the Polish voting group was necessarily an obstacle to progressive reform. Polish-Americans often voted for progressive candidates, albeit for reasons other than progressivism. If a candidate were a Democrat, possessed a modicum of ethnic savvy, and made his reform proposals concrete, he could be as progressive as he wished and still rely on solid Polish-American support. The Polish vote in local politics was a rigid Democratic vote, but its very rigidity gave the candidate flexibility. He could be either progressive or conservative as circumstances dictated and still depend on Polish support, as Carter Harrison II aptly demonstrated throughout his long career.

And insofar as progressive policies depended on approval in referenda, Polish voters were no obstacle. Many of them simply didn't vote on the referendum ballot; but since only a majority of votes cast, not a majority of all registered voters, was required for approval of most propositions, the indifference of the Polish bloc posed no problem to the reformers. Therefore, the progressive reformers who blamed the immigrant masses for the defeat of reform were simply wrong. Municipal reform failed, whenever it did fail, because of the reformers' lack of political skill and ethnic sensitivity, not because of any innate conservatism of the immigrants.

In Chicago's progressive era battles, the Polish vote was neutral and indifferent. Polish voters pursued other goals in American politics; their votes could be used either for or against reform, depending on the skill and the inclination of the politicians.

Not progressivism, not some abstract ideal of the public intrest, but the progress of Polonia, a concrete ideal of the community's interest, inspired Polish voters. Yet Polonia was not united, and different groups within it had differing ideas on how to further the community's progress.

As we have seen, the church leaders—the Resurrectionists, the *Dziennik Chicagoski,* and the Polish Roman Catholic Union—viewed the Democratic party as the best vehicle for Polonia's progress. The Polish voters generally followed this line, sometimes voting for a Democrat of different nationality rather than a Polish Republican. But the Polish National Alliance campaigned for ethnic solidarity, a vote for one's countrymen (*rodacy*) regardless of party. The Alliance's newspapers hammered on this theme before every election: "We recall to all Polish voters their national duty to give their votes in the first place to Poles. Parties mean nothing."[8]

The Alliance leaders called this policy of ethnic solidarity *Swój Swojego,* which means, literally, "each one for his own." *Swój Swojego* was meant to apply in economics and social life as well as in politics. The nationalistic leaders of the Alliance urged Poles to patronize Polish business establishments, not the Jewish-owned shops along Milwaukee Avenue; to attend only Polish meetings and associations; and to vote only for Poles, not for the Irish, Germans, or other nationalities. *Swój Swojego* was the Polonia ideal in action, a self-sufficient, nationally conscious community acting together to protect its own interests and to further its political goals in Poland and in America.

The Polish socialists, a small but vocal minority, proposed a third alternative to party solidarity or ethnic solidarity—the solidarity of Polish workers with all other members of the working class. The Polish-language organ of the American Socialist party heaped scorn on the churchmen's claim that the Democrats were the workingmen's party:

The so-called Democratic party is of all the parties the most reactionary, the greatest foe of democracy and the working class, the most barbarous, and the most devoted to capitalism, great and small. . . . If we take in hand a little history, we would recall that the Democratic president, Grover Cleveland, sent a federal army to defeat powerful striking workers, and that the governor of the state of New York, Flower, did the same thing with the state militia. . . .
   In Democratic southern states . . . nearly half the workers, both white and black, are deprived of the right to vote. The Democratic governments in the south are capitalist governments just as the Republican governments in the north.

The same paper, with a clear and logical class analysis, tore apart the *Swój Swojego* policy of the Polish National Alliance:

When we go to the store to buy something or other, the simple fact is that we do not want to spend a lot of money, but we want to pay for it as cheaply as possible. The storekeeper, however, wants to take from us as much as possible. The storekeeper cannot be one of "our own," but on the contrary he becomes for us "foreign." A similar relationship exists between the employer and the worker. The employer wants as much profit as possible from the labor of the worker, and the worker wants to have the highest possible wages for his labor. The employer is thus "foreign" to the worker, and the worker is "foreign" to the employer. The employers are "their own" among themselves, and the workers are "their own" among themselves.
   Each candidate of the capitalist parties is a foe of the worker. Each countryman who stands on a capitalist ticket is a foe of his own countrymen. . . . What duty then does the Polish worker have towards his countrymen who are servants of the capitalist exploiters?

The conclusion of such an argument could only be the familiar socialist appeal, "Workers of the world, unite!" Polonia's workers could only progress in unity with all other workers.[9]

Most Polish voters rejected the socialist alternative, not because they lacked class consciousness, but because church leadership and their own religious feelings had convinced them that a vote for the Democrats was the proper way to manifest their working-class unity. Likewise, they rejected the nonpartisan "one for all and all for one" strategy of the Polish Alliance, not because they didn't believe in Polonia, but because they were convinced that the Democratic party was the proper place for Polonia to reside. Working-class and ethnic solidarity were both transformed into party solidarity.

Thus Polonia's capital acted as a Democratic bloc in local politics. Through the Democratic party, Polonia's leaders tried to attain recognition and power—recognition as equals with other Americans, and power to survive both as individuals and as a community.

Before the First World War, Chicago's Polonia attained very little of either recognition or power. This is hardly surprising in light of the short time that most Poles had lived in America. Even the Irish, who have long been regarded as the political geniuses among American immigrants, did not attain political control of any American city for a full thirty years after the great famine of 1848 had sent them in large numbers to the New World.[10] Poles had been engaged in mass migration only since the mid-1890s, so their lack of early political success is not remarkable. But they did establish a beachhead in American politics, a beachhead which they later tried to broaden in a wide-ranging drive for recognition after the First World War.

III National Politics, 1888-1940

Before the First World War, Polish-Americans played only one role in national politics, the role of voter. No American Pole served in the U.S. Congress before 1918, when John C. Kleczka was elected from Milwaukee; and Chicago's Polonia did not elect its first congressman until two years later. The thought of a Polish president, governor, or senator was not even entertained by the first generation of Polonia; until the Wilson administration, no patronage in federal offices throughout the country was available for Polish-Americans. Only when the war thrust the Polish question into prominence, did a Polish-American lobby have any effect on policy matters. Even after the First World War, Polish-Americans' role as officeholders or policymakers at the federal level remained minor.

Throughout the entire half century from 1888 to 1940, Polish voters looked for ethnic sensitivity and a concern for the workingman in national candidates.

They usually found Democratic candidates more sympathetic on both the ethnic and economic issues. Chicago's Polish vote, therefore, was consistently, though not exclusively, Democratic in national politics.

During the war most Polish-American leaders participated in the high politics of Poland's liberation, and American electoral politics received little attention. Wartime issues, however, did affect Polish voters in the presidential elections of 1916 and 1920.

After the war interest in Poland declined remarkably among American Poles, and European issues played almost no part in determining the Polish vote of the 1920s and 30s. Though ethnic issues remained, they involved recognition and awareness of America's Polonia, not of Poland itself. With the coming of the depression, economic concerns eclipsed all other issues in national politics.

9 "Roofs of Silver, Fences of Polish Sausage"

Like most Americans, Polonia's voters showed greater enthusiasm for presidential politics than for local contests. In the years before the First World War (1888–1912), Polish-Americans in Chicago turned out about 30 percent more heavily in presidential elections than they did in mayoral races.[1] And since local bosses probably worked less vigorously to control the immigrant masses in national elections, presidential contests provide a more sensitive barometer of Polish-American opinion than the local machine vote.

This barometer clearly reads Democratic throughout most years of the progressive era, but it also shows more fluctuations than the local vote. These fluctuations indicate that identification with the common man and ethnic sensitivity were the two qualities Polish voters looked for in a presidential candidate.

In the presidential elections of 1888 and 1892, the first in which a small Polish vote appeared in Chicago, Polonia voted overwhelmingly for the Democrat, Grover Cleveland, giving him over 80 percent of its votes. The Polish National Alliance's *Zgoda* argued futilely in favor of the Republicans. The newspaper asserted that the Republicans were *not* a party of prohibition and that the high Republican tariff policy, while it might cause workers to pay slightly higher prices for consumer goods, also guaranteed much higher wages. Polish voters rejected these arguments. Nationally, as locally, they viewed the Democrats as the party of the workers and as opponents of prohibition and intolerance.[2]

In 1896 William Jennings Bryan's nationwide whistle-stop campaign took him through Chicago on three separate occasions, once in midsummer, again on Labor Day, and finally on October 28th, less than a week before the election. The itinerary for his final Chicago visit included a speech at the Union Stock Yards, two mass meetings in the Bohemian neighborhoods, and

TABLE 17   PRESIDENTIAL VOTE IN CHICAGO (IN PERCENTAGES), 1888-1912

Year	No. of Polish Precincts	Polish Vote (City-Wide Vote)			
		Republicans	Democrats	Socialists	Others
1888	3	15.01 (47.89)	84.80 (50.76)		
1892	11	12.84 (42.73)	87.15 (57.26)		
1896	12	28.12 (57.46)	69.43 (41.12)		
1900	12	20.58 (49.90)	78.01 (47.29)		
1904	20	46.15 (57.32)	41.11 (27.13)	10.88 (12.61)	
1908	20	37.44 (54.38)	58.94 (37.92)	2.30 (4.67)	
1912	38	33.13 (17.48)	33.08 (30.79)	12.53 (13.20)	Progressive 20.09 (37.34)
Average		27.61 (46.74)	61.79 (41.75)	8.57 (10.16)	

speeches in three Polish neighborhoods. Bryan, the spokesman of populist farmers from the South and West, knew he needed to link up with urban workers if he were to have any chance of election. This son of the prairies, the very embodiment of rural, Anglo-Saxon America, perceived the importance of urban immigrants to his cause.[3]

Bryan's speech at St. Stanislaus Kostka hall on the night of October 29, 1896, was a remarkable performance. After uttering the usual political pieties about Pulaski and Kosciuszko, he then launched into a lengthy discussion of the monetary question in his usual uncompromising way. "I shall offer no apology," he said, "for discussing in your presence the paramount issue of the campaign." Few of the seven thousand Poles packed in the hall could understand his monetary ramblings. In fact, few understood him at all; for his famous golden voice spoke only in English. But the crowd loved him any-

way; and on election day the Polish voters gave Bryan almost 70 percent of
their votes.[4]

In Illinois and the other industrial states of the northeast, Bryan's attempt to woo the workers was largely a failure. Mark Hanna, the Republican
McKinley's campaign manager, waged a ruthless campaign of propaganda
and intimidation. In many cases employers threatened their workers with loss
of their jobs if Bryan were elected; and Republican newspapers like the
Chicago Tribune thundered: "Whoever votes for Bryan votes for a panic, an
industrial convulsion from the effects of which he cannot escape, no matter
how he earns his living."[5]

In Chicago, the working-class Sixteenth Ward, which in 1892 had given
Cleveland a plurality of over 3,000 votes, went for Bryan by only a scant 421-
vote margin in 1896. Clearly, many Sixteenth Ward voters were scared away
from the populistic Bryan. But the Polish Democratic vote, though it also fell
off from four years previously, still remained impressively large. Whereas
the Sixteenth Ward as a whole cast only 51.52 percent of its votes for the
Democrat, the nine Polish precincts of the ward voted 71.84 percent Democratic.

Bryan was a Democrat, a champion of the common people, and had
visited the Poles personally. In 1896 that sufficed in Polonia's capital.

In 1900 Bryan staged a repeat performance against President McKinley.
This time, while still harping on the monetary question, he focused his attack
on the imperialism and militarism which had appeared during the Spanish-
American War. Again Bryan swung through Chicago on Labor Day and also
a few days before the election. At the packed hall of St. Stanislaus Kostka, he
addressed himself to the paramount issue of imperialism. "My friends,"
Bryan orated, "the Republicans are taking the English system of colonial rule
as a pattern for this country. I believe our forefathers were right in 1776,
and if they were right then the Republicans are wrong now." Bryan said "our
forefathers" as if he were totally unaware that his listeners had different forefathers than he. But again this seeming lack of ethnic awareness made little
difference. Polish voters supported Bryan more heavily than they had four
years previously, giving him 78 percent of their votes.[6]

The *Naród Polski,* organ of the Polish Roman Catholic Union, summed
up Polish feeling about the 1900 campaign:

The Republicans are promising that after their election they will pave the
streets with gold, and the Democrats say that they will cover the roofs of

every house with silver and will build the fences with Polish sausage. The question is, which is better. It seems to us the latter, because after paving the streets with gold, the representatives of the trusts will choose to walk on them, and leave the sidewalks full of holes to the Democrats.[7]

Imperialism was too remote to mention, gold and silver were humorous issues, but the Republicans were the party of the trusts and the Democrats represented honest workmen. Polish-Americans continued to support Bryan on that basis.

Four years later the presidential game altered drastically, and the working-class consciousness of Polonia worked against the Democrats. Conservative William McKinley was assassinated in 1901, and his vice-president, Theodore Roosevelt, succeeded to the presidency. During the next three years, Roosevelt did not depart substantially from McKinley's policies, but he did make a number of unprecedented interventions into the national economy when he thought national welfare demanded it. His most notable acts were mediation of the anthracite coal strike in 1901 and prosecution of the Northern Securities company as an unlawful trust combination. Roosevelt's innate skill at self-publicity parlayed these acts into an image as the great trustbuster and a champion of the people against the corporations.[8]

In the meantime, the Democratic party chieftains had grown tired of losing elections with their own self-proclaimed champion of the people, Bryan, and had determined to present a "safe and sane" Democratic candidate in 1904. "Reorganization" was the Democratic watchword; in the process of reorganizing, the Democrats chose a conservative judge from the New York state supreme court, Alton B. Parker, as their standard-bearer. Parker was virtually unknown outside New York, whereas T.R. was the best known, most popular president since Lincoln.[9]

As one Chicago paper remarked, "Roosevelt himself was the issue," and the electorate predictably responded with a landslide of support for Teddy. In the city of Chicago, Roosevelt increased McKinley's 1900 plurality of about 9,000 votes into a 103,000 vote margin in 1904, carrying every ward of the city in the process. Many dissatisfied Democrats who had followed Bryan bolted to the standard of Roosevelt or else cast a protest vote for the Socialist candidate, Eugene Debs.[10]

Chicago's Polish voters, despite their traditional Democratic allegiance, followed the city-wide and nation-wide trends. The Republican Roosevelt captured a plurality of 46.15 percent of the vote in Polonia's capital, whereas Parker drew only 41.11 percent. The Socialists, despite the usual opposition

from the Catholic church and the Polish nationalist leaders, gained almost
11 percent of the Polish vote, comparable to Debs' 12.5 percent city-wide. In
some Polish precincts around the steel mills of South Chicago, the Democratic vote dipped to 30 percent and the Debs tally rose to nearly 20 percent.

The *Chicago Tribune* analyzed the Roosevelt vote, city-wide, in this
fashion:

Much of Bryan's stock in trade, it must be remembered, was an appeal to the
poor man as against the rich man, and during his two brilliant oratorical
campaigns he was frequently successful in appealing to the suspicion of
organized capital. . . . President Roosevelt's action in settling the coal strike,
his prosecution of the Northern Securities case to a successful issue, and his
apparent readiness to take up the cause of the people as against the
corporations, without regard for the hostility of the trust magnates, naturally
earned for him the support of the very Democratic element which followed
Bryan in 1896 and 1900.

And the *Record-Herald* speculated that Debs's surprising strength was due
to "acceptance by an increasing number of people of socialistic principles,
bitterness in the strife between wage-earners and employers, dissatisfaction
with the platform and the leaders of the Democratic party."[11]

These same factors influenced Polish voters. As members of the working class, they voted much as other American workers did, either for Roosevelt or Debs. The "reorganized" Democrats under Parker could not sell the
fiction that they were the workers' party, as they had under Cleveland and
Bryan. As Mayor Harrison put it:

This election means . . . that the party must stand for something. It means
that the reorganizers must be reorganized. . . . The fact of the matter is that
six months ago the Democratic party stood for definite principles. . . .
It meant something to the people.[12]

After Roosevelt's victory, the Republicans paid more attention to Polish
voters and no longer wrote them off as a sure Democratic bloc. Roosevelt's
letters to other Republicans during his second term show his awareness of
the growing role that Polish-Americans and other Catholic groups could play
in cementing Republican dominance. In May of 1908, Roosevelt's vice-president, Charles W. Fairbanks, accepted an invitation from Father Gordon, the
pastor of St. Stanislaus Kostka, to dedicate a new school building. Father Gordon, a staunch Democrat, was probably thinking only of the prestige an
official visit would bring to Polonia; but the Republicans must have been
aware of the visit's political possibilities.[13]

William Howard Taft, the Republican candidate in 1908, did not draw as well in Polonia's capital as Roosevelt had. But his 37.44 percent of the Polish vote was still far more than the Republicans had won in the 1890s.

In the meantime, however, the Democratic reorganizers were themselves reorganized, and William Jennings Bryan again crusaded at the head of the party. Bryan recaptured a majority of the Polish votes, pulling 58.94 percent of the totals in Polonia's capital. The Polish vote for Debs, the Socialist candidate, plummeted to 2.30 percent.

The three-way presidential campaign of 1912, occasioned by the split of Roosevelt's Progressive party from the Republicans, proved to be the electoral climax of the progressive era on the national scene. This free-for-all contest was also important to Polonia, but for reasons that had nothing to do with progressivism. An indiscretion by the Democratic candidate, Woodrow Wilson, brought the issue of ethnic sensitivity to the fore in 1912.

The indiscretion had been committed by Wilson long before, when he was still Professor Woodrow Wilson at Princeton University. The last volume of Professor Wilson's *History of the American People,* published in five volumes at the turn of the century, dealt, as a matter of course, with the heavy immigration to the United States at the end of the nineteenth century.

Like most contemporary scholars of Anglo-Saxon ancestry, Wilson was uneasy about the decided shift in immigration patterns which became evident in the 1890s. As Wilson put it in his *History*:

Throughout the century men of the sturdy stocks of the North of Europe had made up the main stream of foreign blood which was every year added to the vital working force of the country. . . . But now there came multitudes of men of the lowest class from the south of Italy and men of the meaner sort out of Hungary and Poland, men out of the ranks where there was neither skill nor energy nor any initiative of quick intelligence; and they came in numbers which increased from year to year, as if the countries of the south of Europe were disburdening themselves of the more sordid and hapless elements of their population. . . . The people of the Pacific coast had clamored these many years against the admission of immigrants out of China . . . and yet the Chinese were more to be desired, as workmen if not as citizens, than most of the coarse crew that came crowding in every year at the eastern ports.[14]

This statement was so clearly in accord with what others of Wilson's place and parentage believed that it was little remarked when first published. Early in 1912, however, when Professor Wilson had become Governor Wil-

son of New Jersey and the leading candidate for the Democratic presidential
nomination, foreign-language editors resurrected the statement and publicized it widely as an outrage to the Poles and other "new immigrants." One
journalist for the Polish National Alliance took a philosophical and conde-
scending approach to the outrage:

He [Wilson] is a very learned man, progressive, deserving the support of his
party's voters, in every way, except for one unpleasant episode from the
past. . . . Years ago . . . Professor Wilson made some unflattering statements
about certain groups of recent immigrants in his history of the United
States. . . . There was no bad will in this on the part of the author of the
history. . . . It was a gap in Wilson's education, one of those gaps which a
person educated in Europe often meets in one educated in America.[15]

Other responses were less measured. The volatile Stanley Kunz bluntly
told a Democratic managing committee that he would not support Wilson on
the Democratic ticket and that "no honorable and self-respecting Pole should
give his vote to Wilson, since he has shamefully insulted Poles in his history,
calling them a shady mob, worse than the Chinese." An ad-hoc group of
outraged Polish-Americans put the case just as bluntly, declaring Wilson "an
enemy of European immigration in general, an enemy of the Poles, an enemy
of the Roman Catholic Church, an enemy of the worker and the workers'
unions, an enemy of the noble aspirations of each nation, striving to regain its
independence; in sort, he is an enemy of progress and is a backward looking
person."[16]

On the other hand, the church party in Polonia's capital, which had long
nourished the Polish-Democratic connection, tried to overlook or explain
away Wilson's scholarly indiscretion. During the primary campaign in April,
the Resurrectionist Fathers invited Wilson to speak at St. Stanislaus Kostka;
the candidate readily accepted, much to the scandal of the Polish National
Alliance. The PNA couldn't pass up such a chance to assert its outraged
nationalism and deliver a slap at its old rivals, the Resurrectionists. "For
shame," the PNA paper editoralized, "that Poles, and above all the 'leaders
of the Polish people' are offering their hall for a meeting for such a man as
Wilson. Poles, remember this!"[17]

N. L. Piotrowski, a leading respectable in the church party, soon to be
elected president of the Polish Roman Catholic Union, took it upon himself
to defend Wilson against the ire of the Polish nationalists. Immediately after
the offensive passage in the *History* had been unearthed, Piotrowski wrote
Governor Wilson to warn him of the storm about to break. Wilson's answer-

ing letter of March 12 contained a weak apology and an explanation that, in his *History*, he had been referring only to immigrants imported as contract laborers or those seduced to emigrate by unscrupulous steamship agents, not to Polish immigrants who came to America of their own free will. Piotrowski published this letter in both the English and the Polish press and emphasized that Wilson's feelings toward immigrants were sympathetic. Throughout the campaign, Wilson clung to the distinction set forth in the Piotrowski letter: immigrants who come of their own free will should be welcomed as future Americans, but those induced by steamship agents are often members of that lower class he mentioned in his *History*.[18]

At the same time that Wilson's Anglo-Saxonism was being painfully exposed to the voters, President Taft was making a number of personal appearances which presented him as a model of ethnic sensitivity. On March 10, 1912, during the presidential primary campaigns, Taft visited Chicago and spoke both at a Bohemian church and at the Polish parish of the Immaculate Conception in South Chicago. Father Wojtalewicz, Immaculate Conception's pastor, met the president at a downtown hotel, accompanied him to the Bohemian parish of St. Procopius, then to his own parish school, where the president addressed the school-children. Taft remained about an hour more at the parish rectory, chatting with Polish priests from all over the city.

A simple visit, easily characterized as "nonpolitical" since the president's only speech was to nonvoting schoolchildren! Yet the impact on Chicago's Polonia was great. The Alliance papers declared, on the eve of the primary election: "The visit of President Taft to a Polish school and to Polish children in South Chicago is important in the epoch of present day Polish emigration." An old resident of South Chicago reports that up until the 1940s the chair which President Taft sat in at Immaculate Conception rectory was preserved as a relic by the parish pastor.[19]

In October 1912 President Taft was the featured speaker at the opening of the Polish National Alliance's new college in Cambridge Springs, Pennsylvania. Since Taft was the incumbent president, his appearance was taken as a great honor for Polonia and could be billed as "nonpolitical." But Taft seized the opportunity to disagree with the well-publicized sentiments of his opponent:

I cannot close without some reference to the question of immigration. . . . I am one of those who believe that America is greatly better in her present condition and will have still greater advantage in the future, because of the

infusion into our body, politic and social, of the sturdy peasantry and the
better educated classes who have come to us from the nations of Europe.[20]

In the pages of the Polish press, the contest was largely between Wilson
and Taft; the main issue was immigration and ethnic sensitivity. Theodore
Roosevelt, who as the head of the Progressive party was capturing so much
attention in the rest of the country, was largely ignored or else dismissed as a
power-hungry dynasty builder, breaking the sacred two-term tradition. The
Polish Socialists, ignored or derided by the nationalist and church press, tried
to point out that their candidate, Debs, was evoking considerable comment
in serious English journals. In characterizing the four candidates of 1912,
the Socialists avoided the ethnic issues, concentrating on working class concerns:

Vote for Taft and you will get: Wages as in Lawrence. Pinkertons and
national guard in case of a strike. Injunctions.
Vote for Wilson and you will get: Chinese level of living. Government
of the Democratic bosses. A learned professorial discussion, when you
would rather eat.
Vote for Roosevelt and you will get: "Good" wages, as in the Pittsburgh
steel mills. A federal army, when you would rather have bread. An antitrust
law aimed at unions.
Vote for Debs and you will get: Prosperity and freedom. An administration in the interest of the working class and under its control.[21]

When the votes were counted in 1912, the returns from Polonia's capital were widely different from those in any other election Polish-Americans
had yet participated in. Taft and Wilson finished in a virtual dead heat, the
incumbent capturing 33.13 percent of the Polish vote and the Democratic
challenger, 33.08 percent. This was a drastic falloff in the Polish Democratic
vote; even in 1904, the lackluster Parker had done better. The Taft vote was
roughly the same as his 1908 percentage. Theodore Roosevelt, who had first
broken the Poles' Democratic allegiance in 1904, attracted only about 20
percent of the Polish vote in 1912. Surprisingly, Debs and the Socialists
surged to over 12.5 percent. The Socialist vote was highest in the most
middle-class section of Polonia's capital, the Twenty-seventh Ward on the far
northwest side, and around the stockyards, where Socialist organization had
been increasing since the failure of the packinghouse strike in 1904. In some
precincts of these areas, Debs polled as high as 17 percent and 20 percent of
the Polish vote.[22]

TABLE 18   PRESIDENTIAL VOTE IN CHICAGO (IN PERCENTAGES), 1912

Ward	No. of Polish Precincts	Taft (R)	Wilson (D)	Roosevelt (P)	Debs (S)
4th					
Polish vote	3	27.27	24.98	30.59	12.11
Ward average		18.57	40.83	22.70	16.42
8th					
Polish vote	6	30.86	43.73	15.86	10.59
Ward average		18.53	28.09	35.31	17.32
11th					
Polish vote	3	42.73	34.30	16.64	8.64
Ward average		22.85	36.00	21.80	17.90
16th					
Polish vote	13	35.77	34.80	15.99	11.72
Ward average		29.61	32.43	20.62	16.10
17th					
Polish vote	1	35.37	23.14	26.20	14.84
Ward average		29.01	26.73	28.26	14.97
27th					
Polish vote	3	19.60	24.86	32.84	21.08
Ward average		12.43	22.70	42.80	20.79
28th					
Polish vote	4	37.69	28.60	20.59	12.54
Ward average		17.75	23.83	34.92	22.89
29th					
Polish vote	5	36.38	26.37	24.34	13.93
Ward average		19.10	32.22	27.89	19.44
City-wide					
Polish vote	38	33.13	33.08	20.09	12.53
City average		17.40	30.79	37.34	13.20

In the nationwide balloting for president, Theodore Roosevelt's revolt effectively split the Republican party and ensured Woodrow Wilson's election. But this election of the first Democratic president in sixteen years was accomplished without the support of the hitherto most staunchly Democratic ethnic group, Polish-Americans. Wilson drove away masses of Polish Democrats with his ethnic slur. Many apparently didn't vote at all, since the turnout was lighter than usual in a presidential election.[23] As a result, no candidate clearly commanded the Poles' allegiance in 1912.

The 1912 election points up the sensitivity of Polish voters to their ethnic image, just as the 1904 campaign illustrates the importance of Polonia's common-man, working-class image. Neither church leadership nor party loyalty could overcome the Democrats' failure to provide their usual roofs of silver in 1904 or their fences of Polish sausage in 1912.

10 The Politics of Wartime

When the First World War broke out in August 1914, American politics entered a new era. The progressive crusade for domestic reform took a back seat to foreign policy; and though the U.S. did not enter the war until 1917, many Americans' hopes and fears focused on the European struggle.

Polish-Americans had particular reasons for hope. For over a century, Poles had realized that a general European war, which would find the partitioning powers on opposite sides, was the best hope of freedom for Poland. Some had even dared pray, at the end of their litanies, "For a World War, we beseech Thee, O Lord."[1]

When the conflict at last erupted, leading Poles in Europe disagreed on the strategy they should follow. The Polish Socialist Party (PPS) of Joseph Pilsudski viewed Russia as the real enemy, for Russia held by far the largest portion of Polish territory and had ruled it barbarously and inefficiently. Thus Pilsudski's strategy called for the use of Austria as a tool, and he convinced the Austrian authorities to organize a Polish legion. With this army at his command, Pilsudski fought the battles of the Central Powers, but with Polish independence as the goal.

A group of more conservative Poles, organized as the National Democratic Party (ND) under Roman Dmowski in Russian-occupied Poland, adopted an anti-German and therefore a pro-Russian and pro-Allied position. To the National Democrats, independence was not realistic until national unity had been achieved; and unity could be achieved only through the defeat of Germany and Austria and the addition of their pieces of Poland to the much larger Russian-occupied section. For the great majority of Poles in Eastern Europe, of course, there was no chance to choose sides. Over seven hundred thousand Poles were conscripted by the Russian army to fight against an equal number of their countrymen in the German and Austrian forces.[2]

In America, even before the war broke out, an umbrella organization was founded at Pittsburgh in 1913 to coordinate the support of emigrant Poles for Pilsudski and other would-be liberators. This organization, the Committee of National Defense (*Komitet Obrony Narodowy,* or KON) at first included all the leading Polish-American groups—clerical, nationalist, and socialist; but within a year it was wracked by dissension and abandoned by most of the clerical and nationalist groups. These disagreements and secessions were sometimes related to the pro-Austrian vs. pro-Russian strategy debate in Poland, but more frequently they were due to factional quarrels in the American Polonia. The Polish Roman Catholic Union, for instance, pulled out because of the heavy socialist influence in KON and because the organization was too single-mindedly concerned with Poland, neglecting local considerations in America. KON continued to exist throughout the war, but it was largely a rump group of Polish socialists.[3]

The various groups seceding from KON combined in 1914 to form the Central Relief Committee, and, two years later, the National Department (*Wydział Narodowy*), the Relief Committee's political arm. Both organizations were sympathetic to the National Democratic party in Poland, whereas KON remained loyal to Pilsudski and his Polish Socialist party. The great majority of Poles in America identified with the Relief Committee and the National Department; for both Polonia's church party and the Polish National Alliance were supporting these organizations, and the best-known leaders of Polonia were working for them. John Smulski, the Chicago banker and politician, served as treasurer for the Central Relief Committee, and Bishop Paul Rhode of Chicago, America's first Polish-American bishop, sat on this committee as well. Furthermore, the one Pole known to every American regardless of ancestry, the pianist Ignace J. Paderewski, was sent out by the National Democrats in Poland as their liaison man in the U.S.[4]

Early in 1915 the Central Relief Committee began collecting donations and forwarding them to a clearing house for Polish relief set up by Paderewski in Switzerland. January 24, 1915, was proclaimed Polish Relief Day across the United States; and Chicago's Mayor Harrison, prodded by Polish aldermen, passed a proclamation permitting Polish-Americans to sell tags on the twenty-third and twenty-fourth. These Chicago tag days netted about twenty-five thousand dollars. Almost a quarter of a million dollars were collected nationwide on Relief Day.[5]

In the meantime, Paderewski, unofficial ambassador of a state which didn't exist, succeeded in keeping the "Polish question" before President Wilson and his advisors. Paderewski first met Colonel Edward House, Wilson's closest confidant, in November of 1915 and immediately brought the Texan under his influence. With the help of House, and through the lobbying of the Polish National Department, ably led by John Smulski, Paderewski persuaded Wilson that he represented not only the Poles in Europe but the Polish-American community as well. Using the leverage this position gave him, he convinced Wilson to give Poland's cause special attention in both his "peace without victory" speech of January 1917 and his Fourteen Points peace plan of 1918.[6]

Paderewski also obtained Wilson's permission to recruit Poles in America into a separate Polish army to fight on the western front. The American draft law of May, 1917, applied to Poles of American citizenship who had not been born in the enemy countries of Austria or Germany. All other Poles in America, as well as those from countries such as Canada and Australia which did not have a conscription program, were eligible to serve in the new Polish Army. About twenty thousand volunteered from North America and were trained at Niagara-on-the-Lake in Canada, finally arriving on the western front in June 1918. A far greater number of American Poles, about a hundred thousand, saw service in the U.S. Army, either as volunteers or conscripts. In Chicago's Polonia the federal authorities had little trouble recruiting. At the draft board set up in the Polish Roman Catholic Union building, seventeen hundred men enlisted in the first three weeks. A settlement-house worker whose home had been turned into a draft board reported that many of the Poles were unhappy about going, having left Europe, in part, to escape conscription; but all of them told him, "I go if you need me."[7]

Thus, throughout the war years, the politics of Polish liberation and, secondarily, the internal politics of rival Polonia organizations came to the fore. Many Polish-American newspapers printed little else but the news from Europe, with American politics and other local news receiving scant attention. Yet American elections run on an inexorable schedule, and these wartime elections could not be ignored altogether. Nor could the tensions and hostilities of wartime be kept out of electoral politics. Hopes for Poland and suspicions of Old World enemies joined the usual concerns of Polish voters in the elections of the war and immediate postwar period.

In the national elections of 1916, anti-German sentiment proved to be a formidable handicap to the Republican party. Since 1914 German-Americans had perceived that President Wilson's policy of neutrality tended—in effect, if not in intention—to favor the British and their allies. Thus the Germans were expected to support the Republican party in 1916, and some Republicans feared being labeled the "German party."

Charles Evans Hughes, the Republican candidate for president, attempted to dodge the sensitive German issue during the campaign and made no outright appeals for German support. Theodore Roosevelt, on the other hand, stumped the country for Hughes, delivering fiery anti-German speeches which eroded some of the support the Germans might naturally have given the Republicans. Yet, for many Americans, the suspicion that Hughes was the German candidate remained.[8]

American Poles were particularly susceptible to this suspicion. The Polish National Alliance found itself torn between its usual Republican leanings and its fierce anti-German, Polish nationalist sentiments. The Alliance's daily paper attempted to show that Hughes was "an unwilling and accidental candidate of the German-Americans" and that "the Republican party is not the German party." It made its usual efforts to expose the hollowness of Democratic election promises, dismissing the Wilsonian appeal to labor groups as so much "Democratic bluff." In the end the Alliance paper refrained from openly endorsing either presidential candidate, and it cautioned that "no one should vote for Wilson only because the Germans are against him today."[9]

Yet throughout the presidential campaign, the Alliance paper often fed the prevailing anti-German hysteria. *Dziennik Zwiazkowy* painted a picture of insidious German maneuvering at the Republican convention in June:

Everywhere German-Americans are running about, putting the word German before American. . . . In discussions at the convention it is often heard reported, "The Germans are supporting him," or "The Germans have told him what they want," or "The Germans have conceded this or that."

The paper later reported:

The Germans are calling out, all over the country, the length and breadth of America, for a solid front against Wilson. In the van of this punitive expedition against Wilson, stands the German Alliance of North America, following in all its activities the pernicious directives from Berlin.

Thus the Polish Alliance denounced the German Alliance, and vice versa. The war and American politics were rending the fragile ethnic fabric of American society.[10]

Wilson and the Democrats, however, enjoyed other advantages in Polonia besides the fierce anti-Germanism of the Poles. Since his abysmal showing among Polish voters in 1912, due to the anti-immigrant bias of his historical writings, Wilson had been listening to his political advisors and had begun to upgrade his ethnic image. When an immigration bill containing a literacy test, aimed frankly at exclusion of many illiterate southern and eastern European immigrants, reached his desk in 1915, Wilson vetoed it. When the House again passed a similar bill in 1916, Wilson used his political powers to stall approval in the Senate. Polonia coupled these presidential actions with the fact that Wilson had made the first appointments of Polish-Americans to federal patronage positions and concluded that "the Democrats, as the party of the people, always are sympathetic to immigration." Wilson also sent strongly worded appeals to the warring powers for American relief supplies to be allowed into a ravaged Poland to alleviate suffering and prevent starvation. Though these pleas were unsuccessful, Polish-American leaders were satisfied that Wilson had done all he could.[11]

Wilson's growth in ethnic sensitivity was shown in his 1916 campaign speeches. In October he invited Americans of foreign birth to interpret for him and the American people the issues of Europe, stating that "America is the only country that understands the other countries of the world," because so many of her citizens can act as interpreters. In a speech at the Chicago stockyards before almost twenty thousand people, many of them newly naturalized Poles and other eastern Europeans, the President orated:

It is not demanded and expected of men or women becoming citizens of the United States that they discard their ties with the nation of their Fatherland. . . . It is not necessary even to mention to you that this nation is composed of every nation of the earth, among them there is none which does not possess great traditions and a great history which should be retained.

Though Wilson, in this same speech, tactfully reminded his immigrant listeners of their duties to learn English, to study the laws of the land, and to try to understand the national spirit of America, the sympathetic tone of his remarks was clear.[12]

Besides the specifically ethnic reasons for supporting Wilson, the general appeals to peace and progressivism which Wilson was making across the nation resounded through Polonia as well. Despite the high stakes involved for Poland, American Poles were none too eager to see their adopted homeland drawn into the general war; thus the Democrats' oft-repeated slogan, "He kept us out of war," was attractive. The dominant feeling in Polonia was summed up pointedly by two cartoons in the Polish Roman Catholic

Union's national journal. One cartoon contrasted a happy, prosperous family scene, entitled "America with Wilson," with a starving, emaciated refugee mother and child—"Europe without Wilson." The other sketch presented a stately President Wilson at Ellis Island welcoming an immigrant family with open arms. Tying the two themes together, the paper stated simply: "Our President has kept open to all immigrants the door to this country of happiness, freedom, and prosperity."[13]

Clinging to this vision of a free, open, and prosperous America under the leadership of their traditional Democratic friends, and spurred by the darker passion of anti-German suspicion, Polish-Americans in Chicago voted overwhelmingly for Woodrow Wilson. Polish resentment against Wilson, manifested so strongly in 1912, disappeared completely in 1916. Polonia's capital voted almost three to one for the Democrats at both the national and state levels. In every ward of the city where Polish-Americans voted in this election, they gave Wilson at least two-thirds of their votes.[14]

The Polish vote in Chicago, overwhelmingly Democratic as it was, proved to be of no significance for Wilson's reelection, since Hughes carried the city and the state for the Republicans. There are some indications, however, that Polish-American votes did help Wilson win his narrow pluralities in Ohio, North Dakota, and Missouri.[15] In any case, Polonia's heavy vote for Wilson marked a return to Democratic loyalties in national politics after the confused election of 1912. Anti-German sentiment reinforced the usual ethnic and economic concerns in bringing this about.

Woodrow Wilson's image in the minds and hearts of Polish-Americans continued its spectacular rise after the election of 1916. The president proved unable to keep the nation out of war, but, when war came, he declared unequivocally that one of the American war aims was "an independent Polish state . . . which should include the territories inhabited by indisputable Polish populations . . . assured a free and secure access to the sea." No other Allied leader stated Poland's case so explicitly; and when the war ended, Wilson continued to insist on an independent and viable Polish state at the treaty conference. Though Poles and Polish-Americans were not altogether satisfied with the Versailles accord, they had gained far more than most of the other eastern European nations and had little reason to be unhappy with Wilson's wartime leadership.[16]

Thus when President Wilson returned from the treaty negotiations in France, he was enthusiastically greeted by a large delegation from the American Polonia, headed by the presidents of both the Polish National Alliance

TABLE 19   PRESIDENTIAL VOTE IN CHICAGO (IN PERCENTAGES), 1916

Ward	No. of Polish Precincts	Wilson (D)	Hughes (R)	Benson (Soc)
4th				
Polish vote	5	74.33	24.89	0.76
Ward average		67.84	29.98	2.07
8th				
Polish vote	8	81.73	17.17	1.38
Ward average		47.59	47.68	4.20
11th				
Polish vote	3	71.25	27.10	1.63
Ward average		58.76	36.17	4.79
12th				
Polish vote	1	66.26	32.53	1.19
Ward average		62.68	31.26	5.85
16th				
Polish vote	17	79.46	19.45	1.17
Ward average		72.23	24.83	2.79
17th				
Polish vote	2	67.67	30.14	1.89
Ward average		59.16	38.44	2.30
27th				
Polish vote	5	70.27	26.74	2.71
Ward average		39.51	53.26	6.76
28th				
Polish vote	6	72.09	25.44	2.46
Ward average		47.67	45.73	6.29
29th				
Polish vote	4	53.93	43.31	2.75
Ward average		53.33	42.77	3.67
City-wide				
Polish vote	51	74.34	24.04	1.64
City average		46.23	49.65	3.78

and the Polish Roman Catholic Union. One Chicago Polish paper avowed its faith in a safe future for Poland because it had as its most powerful protector President Woodrow Wilson, who was "already an immortal." Another leading Polish-American paper placed prominently on its masthead a quotation from Wilson's "peace without victory" speech—"Men of state everywhere agree that there must exist a united, independent, and self-governing Poland"; this appeared next to Abraham Lincoln's famous phrase, "Government of the people, by the people, for the people, shall not perish from the earth." The politics of wartime had made him whom Polonia spurned as a waspish chauvinist eight years previously into an immortal, in the mold of Lincoln.[17]

Unfortunately for the Democrats, this immortality was not transferable to another presidential candidate on the Democratic ticket; for in 1920 Polonia felt the tides of "normalcy" which were sweeping the nation and gave Warren Harding almost as much electoral support as they gave the Democrat, James Cox. But Cox and the Democrats tried. The ever-Democratic *Dziennik Chicagoski* was filled with appeals to vote for Cox "to show approval in this way for the official actions of President Wilson," as well as reminders that the Democratic party "has an historic tie with Poland." Other newspapers in Chicago's Polonia echoed these sentiments; even the Republican John Smulski, who endorsed Harding and Coolidge, was unable to hide his admiration for Wilson, a president he had worked with personally as head of the Polish National Department. Smulski wrote, in his endorsement of the Republicans:

I will not omit the fact here . . . that the Polish nation retains a deep regard and gratitude for President Wilson who dedicated his knowledge and influence to the liberating of the Polish nation. We, Polish citizens who belong to the Republican party, while giving President Wilson every credit for his marvelous help, nonetheless realize that he is not a candidate.[18]

The Polish National Alliance, however, retaining its strong Republican leanings, endorsed Harding and chose to play on the intense Polish-American interest in Poland in a more abrasive fashion, by denouncing Wilson and the Versailles treaty-makers as tools of the "Jewish internationalists."

This "Jewish issue" in the Polish community was a complex one. The immediate cause of ill will against the Jews was the Minorities Treaty which the Allied Powers had imposed on Poland and other new states in eastern Europe. On her eastern frontiers, Poland had sizable groups of Jewish, Russian, and Ukrainian minorities that many Westerners felt might be discriminated against by the new Polish government. When rumors of pogroms against the Jewish populace of Galicia reached American ears, Wilson appointed a committee of notables, including the well-known Jewish banker, Henry Morgenthau, Sr., to investigate. The committee found no evidence of pogroms, but it did recommend strong guarantees for Jewish and other minorities in Poland. The Allies imposed these guarantees unilaterally in the Minorities Treaty, with no corresponding safeguards for minority Poles in Germany or Russia.

To the Polish National Alliance in America, these actions were "humiliating invasions upon the internal affairs of Poland through the granting of special privileges for the Jews." Since Harding seemed to be against the League of Nations, which was to be the guarantor of the Minorities Treaty, *Dziennik Zwiazkowy* used the Jewish-minority issue as one justification for its support of Harding. In this view, Wilson became a weak tool of powerful interests and Harding "the next in a line of great and wise [Republican] presidents." For good measure, the Alliance paper printed a letter from "an old citizen" charging that the *Dziennik Chicagoski* [supporting Cox] "teems with Jewish advertisements" and "always supports Jews and even bitter foes of Poland and Poles."[19]

Polish hostilities toward Jews had deeper roots than just the incidents of wartime. In the prewar Russian Empire, the large Jewish population had been restricted to an area called the Jewish Pale, which included much of the Polish territory occupied by Russia. Within this Pale, Jews, who had previously acted as commercial middlemen under the Polish kings, took up positions as shopkeepers, innkeepers, tradesmen, and moneylenders. Thus, throughout much of partitioned Poland, Polish-Jewish relations consisted of Polish peasants bargaining for goods or money with Jewish shopkeepers and moneylenders. Such an economic relation led often to ill feelings and a pervasive sentiment among the peasants that they were being exploited by the Jews.[20]

In America, Poles and Jews often ended up in a similar economic relationship. Whereas the peasant Poles generally took up industrial work in the New World, the Jews frequently continued in occupations similar to those they had practiced in the Pale. Thus the business streets of Polonia were lined with many shops and stores owned by immigrant Jews, and the Poles again found themselves dealing day by day with Jewish shopkeepers and moneylenders. Very early this caused resentment. In 1895 one Polish newspaper called for an increased Polish effort to establish and patronize their own businesses since "the Jews, the leeches of Polish society, have monopolized business in this section of town." Youth gangs in Polonia exploited this resentment, and pitched battles were often fought in the parks and other borderlands between Polish and Jewish neighborhoods.[21]

This hostility might have eroded in the New World had the tensions of war and postwar not reinforced it. The prominence of many Jews in the Russian and American Communist parties caused many Poles to identify Bolshevism and Judaism during the days of the red scare. Not only the Polish National Alliance, but other Polish leaders fell prey to this hysteria. The Polish Roman Catholic Union's organ even gave credence and publicity to Henry Ford's anti-Semitic ravings in the *Dearborn Independent*. When the Minorities Treaty issue arose, the Polish Alliance seized on it as yet another evidence of insidious Jewish influence. This anti-Semitic scare in Polonia was the last abrasive legacy of the politics of wartime.[22]

When the ballots were counted in 1920, Chicago's Polonia was found to have given the Democrats the barest majority—50.45 percent of their votes. This majority, in fact, reflected the comfortable margins which Democratic bosses were able to turn out in the two most heavily Polish areas, the Sixteenth and the Eighth Wards. In every other ward where Polish-Americans voted, Harding actually ran slightly ahead of Cox. Though their vote was far more Democratic than that of any other group in this year of the Harding landslide, Polish-Americans' loyalty to the Democrats was eroded.[23]

The old ethnic tie with the Democrats and the near deification of Wilson for aiding Poland tugged Polonia toward its traditional friends. But the sharp anti-Jewish sentiment unleashed by postwar issues pulled in the other direction. Even more important, postwar economic conditions in the U.S., deteriorating rapidly since late 1919, undermined confidence in the Democrats. In a vague way, many Polish voters shared the general American yearning for "normalcy" and economic recovery as symbolized by the Republicans. The editor of *Dziennik Chicagoski* concluded:

In general, it is quite evident; the vote was very unintelligent. . . .Our countrymen in this respect were little better or worse than the rest of the American citizenry. When we write about unintelligent voting, we mean this characteristic of the results, the lack of any rational motive for voting one way or the other. We have spoken with some of our countrymen about this . . . and almost without exception we have met with this response: with an unaccountable, unreasonable aversion to the party in power and with a desire for change. Enough of the Democrats—let's have a change.

The Polish daily in South Chicago grimly challenged the Republicans to carry out their mandate for normalcy and change. "The Republicans said that if they were elected, everything would get better, since they would normalize the standard of living. We are waiting. . . ."[24]

TABLE 20   PRESIDENTIAL VOTE IN CHICAGO (IN PERCENTAGES), 1920

Ward	No. of Polish Precincts	Cox (D)	Harding (R)	Debs (Soc)
4th				
Polish vote	5	43.22	52.61	3.41
Ward average		40.76	54.04	4.39
8th				
Polish vote	9	64.55	30.95	3.99
Ward average		29.12	64.08	5.38
11th				
Polish vote	6	43.46	53.45	3.07
Ward average		27.36	62.85	9.19
12th				
Polish vote	3	41.47	47.13	10.64
Ward average		31.05	51.86	16.01
16th				
Polish vote	18	62.99	34.37	2.40
Ward average		53.44	39.94	6.22
17th				
Polish vote	3	43.61	52.06	4.22
Ward average		47.18	48.48	3.93
27th				
Polish vote	9	39.19	52.75	6.89
Ward average		21.01	68.66	8.93
28th				
Polish vote	11	44.44	47.19	7.19
Ward average		20.83	69.53	8.40
29th				
Polish vote	3	30.59	63.50	5.70
Ward average		27.22	63.94	7.59
City-wide				
Polish vote	67	50.45	44.22	4.74
City average		23.21	69.96	6.08

11 Ethnic and Economic Heroes

In presidential elections Chicago's Polonia had traditionally voted for candidates with an image of ethnic awareness and concern for the ordinary workingman. By the 1920s, however, each of these two main issues, the ethnic and the economic, had become more complex and had assumed a double aspect. With the rise of a free Poland from the ashes of war, ethnic awareness could be defined either as concern for the state of Poland or concern for group needs in the American Polonia. Economic awareness could mean advocacy of the workingman and the underdog; or, with the growth of a middle-class consciousness in Polonia, it could be a general trumpeting of prosperity for the whole economy.

Polish Republicans had long tried to broaden out the economic issue, arguing as early as 1888 that the high Republican tariff, though it might cause slightly higher prices, would ensure prosperity, high wages, and employment for all. The "full dinner pail" was often invoked but to little avail in Polonia. So long as Polish-Americans were at the bottom of the economic ladder, Republican prosperity had little meaning for them.[1]

The situation changed slowly and subtly, however, as more of Polonia's residents left the working class for small shops and for white-collar jobs. In 1916 Woodrow Wilson's appeal to "peace and prosperity" showed that a generalized slogan of well-being for the whole economy could be as useful as a specific play to the workers. In 1920 Republicans made many such generalized promises. The Polish Alliance's organ, staunchly backing Harding, printed frequent advertisements proclaiming: "Assure prosperity for the whole country, work for all, decent wages, and a lower cost of living." But at the same time, the paper carefully supplemented this general appeal with a specific defense of Senator Harding's labor record, avowing that Harding's newspaper office in Marion, Ohio, was 100 percent unionized. This twofold

understanding of the economic issue remained important in Polonia throughout the two decades of the postwar period.[2]

The issue of ethnic awareness also wore a double face in the twenties and
thirties. Both parties tried to identify their cause with that of the new state of
Poland; and they both dredged up the names of "heroes" from the wartime
period who had "saved" Poland from tyranny, starvation, communism, or
anarchy. They found, however, that the politics of Poland were diminishing
in effectiveness, and that voters in Polonia's capital were more interested in
the progress of their ethnic group in America. Thus, awareness of or identification with Polonia proved more important to politicians in the period between the world wars than awareness of or service to Poland.

In 1924 it took considerable stretching of the imagination to view the Democratic hopeful as the workingman's candidate. The Democrats, having nearly
destroyed themselves at their convention by reaching a deadlock between Al
Smith and William Gibbs McAdoo after 103 ballots, turned to John W.
Davis, a wealthy Wall Street lawyer and former ambassador to Great Britain.
The party tried to impart some common-man flavor to the ticket by nominat-
ing Charles W. Bryan, the Great Commoner's younger brother, for vice-
president. The ever-faithful *Dziennik Chicagoski* also tried to establish labor
credentials for Davis, pointing out that "Mr. Davis was not only one of the
authors of the Clayton Act (passed by a Democratic Congress), but he rose
several times to its defense in the discussions in the House of Representatives." But the imaginations of many Polish voters were not that pliable; so
just as in 1904, when the Democrat Parker was in no sense a man of the
people, the Democratic percentage in Polonia's capital fell below 50 percent
in 1924 (47.87 percent in 1924; 41.11 percent in 1904).[3]

But unlike in 1904, the Republican incumbent was no Roosevelt. Calvin
Coolidge had shown his attitude toward labor as governor of Massachusetts,
when he sent in state troops to break the Boston police strike of 1919. He had
done little since then to show an interest in labor. Thus, in 1924 working-
class interest focused on the third party effort of Robert M. La Follette's
Progressive party. The Progressives had fashioned a jerry-built organization,
not really a party at all, but simply a vehicle for La Follette's last stand. Yet
the old reformer, endorsed by the remnants of Debs's Socialists and by some
labor leaders, stirred up a good deal of excitement in farm and labor areas,
including Polonia's capital.

All of Chicago's Polish papers (except the Socialist *Dziennik Ludowy*)

TABLE 21   PRESIDENTIAL VOTE IN CHICAGO (IN PERCENTAGES), 1916-1936

Year	No. of Polish Precincts	Polish Vote (City-wide Vote)		
		Republicans	Democrats	Others
1916	51	24.04 (43.31)	74.34 (53.93)	
1920	64	44.22 (69.96)	50.45 (23.21)	
1924	48	37.43 (59.86)	47.87 (21.96)	Progressive 14.41 (17.95)
1928	61	19.74 (50.40)	79.95 (48.70)	
1932	90	15.13 (39.40)	83.29 (57.20)	
1936	87	11.08 (32.10)	87.65 (65.00)	
Average		25.27 (49.17)	70.59 (45.00)	

denounced La Follette's party vigorously and often. This was a sign that he was catching fire, for these papers usually ignored the socialists and other radical reformers. The Alliance paper generously avowed, "We do not believe the unsubstantiated rumors that the third party movement is financed from Moscow;" but it added, "The economic views of Senator La Follette are dangerous for this country. He is a proponent of a certain system which has been tried in the European countries" [what delicate red-baiting!]. For good measure, the editors mentioned that "Senator La Follette has never tried to get close to the Poles, he has never spoken out on the Polish question, he always takes the side of Germany and defends only the German point of view."

Dziennik Chicagoski dismissed La Follette's class appeals in phrases that could have come from any of the business organs of the 1920s:

Where is this capitalism of which Mr. LaFollette so often speaks? It is obvious today to everyone that the giant firms are not in the hands of a few capitalists, but in the hands of all their stockholders, drawn from among the workers and the poorer classes of our society. Everyone has more or less of an interest in them. Thousands of American workers have entered today into the ranks of the capitalists.

The South Chicago Polish paper was less subtle in its analysis of the Progressive-Socialist alliance: "Practically the whole world knows that the Jews direct socialism, Jews who through socialism are striving to stir up in various countries ferment and social unrest which always results in harm to Christian society and in profit and gain for the Jews."[4]

La Follette's only defender in the Polish press was the struggling *Dziennik Ludowy*, soon to cease publication for lack of support. But apparently the candidate's message that he was the only authentic opponent of the "powers of the monopolies" with their "paralyzing hold on the political and economic life of the citizens" got through to some Polish voters. The Progressive candidate polled 14.41 percent of the overall vote in Chicago's Polonia, and as high as 18 or 19 percent in two Polish wards. Though not necessarily impressive in itself and slightly less than La Follette's strength city-wide (18 percent), 14 percent of the Poles was more than any Socialist-backed candidate had ever drawn before; as a third-party showing, it was second only to Theodore Roosevelt's total in 1912.[5]

The Republican Coolidge, though lacking labor or working-class appeal, did have a tight hold on the second aspect of the economic issue, overall prosperity—the famous "Republican prosperity" of the 1920s. The Republicans asked the nation to "keep cool with Coolidge," and they concentrated their attacks on the boat-rocking radicalism of La Follette. The Polish Alliance organ echoed this approach, presenting Coolidge as the happy medium between La Follette's "bolshevism of the left wing" and the Ku Klux Klan's "bolshevism of the right wing" (the Republican platform was silent on the Klan issue). "The Republican platform . . . is a program for creative national work which will give a guarantee of maintaining balance," this paper announced to its readers. When Coolidge was reelected, the editors rejoiced, "since for the next four years we are all assured of work and prosperity in the whole country." Prosperity is an effective issue for any incumbent, and Coolidge did reasonably well with it in Polonia, winning about 37 percent of Chicago's Polish vote. Though this was better than usual for a Republican, it was still less than either Harding or Theodore Roosevelt had done.[6]

Polish Democrats, knowing their candidate lacked appeal on the twofold economic issue, worked hard to create an ethnic platform for Davis. Late in October, the candidate made the prescribed pilgrimage to Polish Downtown in Chicago for a speech at the Polish Roman Catholic Union hall. The *Dzien-*

nik Chicagoski tried to build up anticipation for the visit, stating that "the election of Mr. Davis for president could in the future decide the immigration question. . . . He is the only candidate who has come out for modification of the present immigration restriction." The Democratic paper in South Chicago also presented Davis as a man "who had declared war on the Klan," an organization which "plays a similar role in America to that played by the Fascists in Italy."

Davis, however, who was not emphasizing either of these two sensitive issues in his campaign, delivered a weak and rather routine "ethnic" speech to the Chicago Poles. After an introduction in Polish by a local Democrat, the candidate rose to say: "I must admit to you that I do not understand any foreign language. . . . Nevertheless, I understood one word of the introduction, the name of Woodrow Wilson. He was a proponent of the idea of personal freedom and of national freedom." Obviously let down after its glowing buildup for the Democrat, *Dziennik Chicagoski* simply commented the next day: "Mr. Davis said little about immigration, but did say that everyone must have an equal right to enter the U.S."[7]

Coolidge had no ghosts from World War I to invoke on his side and was vulnerable on the immigration restriction issue. A Democratic ad in the Polish papers pointed this out:

That Coolidge completely agrees with the pro-English politics of [Secretary of State] Hughes is proven by the fact that he signed the so-called immigration law, which admits to America—
   five Englishmen to every German.
   fifteen Englishmen to every Italian.
   twenty-four Englishmen to every Pole.[8]

Senator La Follette, knowing well that Slavic citizens counted his vote against the declaration of war in 1917 a sign of pro-Germanism, sent his vice-presidential candidate, Burton K. Wheeler, to Polish Downtown a week after Davis's visit. Wheeler carried with him an "open letter from Senator Robert M. La Follette to the citizens of Polish origin" which attempted to face some of the ethnic concerns of the Poles:

I am a decided and unequivocal opponent of every secret organization, such as the Ku Klux Klan. I also firmly state that every prohibition imposed upon any nationality in the use of its mother tongue will be opposed with all my might. I am of the opinion that the state must have a control on immigration. I am, however, decidedly opposed to the limitation of immigration on the basis of race.

La Follette concluded, however, by attempting to transcend the ethnic issues. "The most important question for every citizen is the matter of bringing to an end the power of the monopolies."[9]

In 1924 no one candidate epitomized all the concerns of Polonia; and the Polish vote, therefore, fragmented accordingly. John W. Davis's Democratic affiliation, buttressed by a hastily fabricated labor and immigration record, and crowned by the invocation of Woodrow Wilson, gave him a slight edge, with 47.87 percent of the Polish vote. Coolidge's solid appeal to national prosperity netted him 37.43 percent whereas Senator La Follette's championing of the workingman drew one out of every seven Polish voters away from the two major parties. Coolidge, however, won the election; and even the *Dziennik Chicagoski* called it a "national triumph," more elated that La Follette and the Socialists had been defeated than depressed at the loss of its own Democratic candidate.[10]

In 1928 the prime concerns of Polonia divided more symmetrically between the two major candidates. Herbert Hoover held down the general issues of economic prosperity and friendship to Poland; whereas Alfred E. Smith embodied the more specific labor and ethnic concerns in his own person—a common man from an immigrant milieu, a Catholic, a "foreigner,"a "wet." Smith's appeal proved more immediate, easier to identify with, than Hoover's Olympian stance as master organizer of the economy and friend of Poland.

Herbert Hoover was even more justified than Coolidge had been in running on a platform of "Republican prosperity"; as Secretary of Commerce throughout the 1920s, he had played a larger role in shaping economic policies than the strict-constructionist presidents had. Polish Republicans fairly glowed when they sang Hoover's praises and trumpeted his qualifications:

The candidacy of Hoover is supported by the wide ranks of the American nation, which represent the healthy element in every class. . . .

For the first time in the history of the United States a great national party has nominated for the highest office in the land, not some political leader, but an outstanding engineer and an already renowned international administrator. Mr. Hoover has a record and public reputation which in every case can measure up to the record and good reputation of the Democratic candidate—and in some cases is better, especially in regards to experience and training and preparation for holding such a high office as the presidency of this republic.[11]

Furthermore, if ethnic appeal to Poles were based solely on service to the cause of Poland in Europe, Herbert Hoover had a better record for making such an appeal than any other living man. Hoover had led an American Food Mission to Poland immediately after the Armistice in Europe. Using the leverage of American economic aid, he had united the Paderewski and Pilsudski factions in the new state, thus forging a united Polish government for the peace talks. Subsequent food relief, under Hoover's direction, literally saved thousands of lives in Poland and no doubt saved the Polish government in Warsaw from collapse.[12]

In the immediate postwar election of 1920, when Hoover's reputation as a relief organizer was at its zenith and both parties were unofficially considering him a possible candidate, the Polish National Alliance openly championed him as the best possible Republican standard-bearer. Eight years later, when Hoover's nomination seemed certain, some of Polonia's respectables in politics, such as Anthony Czarnecki from the Republicans and N. L. Piotrowski of the Democrats, called together nonpartisan businessmen's and citizens' committees to promote Hoover's cause. Even Ignace Paderewski, the Polish pianist and wartime political leader, spoke out from retirement on Hoover's behalf, avowing that the former relief administrator had given Poland "bread, strength, and internal peace" in its hour of greatest need. A front-page cartoon in *Dziennik Zwiazkowy* eloquently summed up the "Hoover, Savior of Poland" appeal. Herbert Hoover appeared strangling a wolf, named "Hunger," with one hand, while delivering a basket of food to a woman and four emaciated children with the other. The caption read: "He who saved millions from starvation."[13]

The Democrats had a difficult time countering Hoover's image as administrator of continuing prosperity, though they emphasized Smith's experience in the "second most important public office in America," the governorship of New York. One Polish paper went so far as to proclaim Al Smith a man "who recalls in energy, Roosevelt; in political wisdom, Wilson; in political ability, Cleveland [sic]; and other great presidents of the United States such as the immortal Abraham Lincoln." This paragon could not, however, even in Democratic propaganda, match Hoover's record of service to the Republic of Poland. But Woodrow Wilson could! So the ghost of Wilson was paraded around once again. Democratic advertisements proclaimed, "Not Hoover, but President Wilson and the American people saved the children of Poland from hunger. . . . Alfred E. Smith is the successor of Woodrow Wilson, to whom Poland is thankful."[14] The European side of the ethnic issue degenerated into a game of "Will the real Savior of Poland please stand up?"

While Poland was being rhetorically saved in the pages of the Polish press, the voters in Polonia's capital were looking at what the two candidates, particularly the Democrat, symbolized in the American context. Even *Dziennik Zwiazkowy,* amid all its praise for Hoover, took time to admit that "the complete victory won by the governor of New York at the Democratic convention in Houston has particular significance. . . . The tradition up to this time that the candidate for president must be only a Protestant has fallen." Not only was Al Smith a Roman Catholic; he also hailed from New York's preeminent immigrant quarter, the Lower East Side, and had himself been a workingman in a fish market. Smith vigorously opposed the most visible symbol of native-American intolerance—prohibition—and defended the "personal liberty" which Polish-Americans prized. In short, the question of who saved Poland had become irrelevant to Polonia's voters; but whether an immigrant workingman who belonged to the church of Rome and opposed the "bigots, professional reformers, and anti-saloon league hypocrites" could get ahead in America was vitally important. As one Polish editor put it:

The present election for president of the United States belongs to the most important elections in the history of this country. What is at stake is the victory of religious tolerance, the victory of personal freedom and all the great principles which the Constitution of the United States guarantees us. Governor Smith has dared to come forward in defense of these principles.[15]

Chicago's Polish voters turned out massive majorities in defense of these principles. Whereas Al Smith was narrowly defeated in the city as a whole, Polish voters marked nearly 80 percent of their ballots for him. Neither Hoover's authentic record of service to Poland nor his promises of general prosperity availed him anything against Polish-American identification with Al Smith, the common man, ethnic, Catholic, and wet candidate of the Poles' traditional party.[16]

Though Hoover's reliance on Republican prosperity had not been effective in Polonia, it proved decisive in his victory throughout the country. The onset of economic depression in 1929, however, showed the hollowness and fragility of this vaunted prosperity and brought the economic issue to the fore in terms of life or death, food or hunger, work or charity. By 1932 nearly 750,000 men were unemployed in Chicago. Residents of Polonia's capital were, perhaps, no worse off than their neighbors; but they had so recently begun to climb to economic success and security that the threat of the depression to wipe out these gains was a particularly bitter blow.[17]

The depression was not simply a working-class issue, for it affected all strata of society. But the inept actions of Hoover's administration in extending aid to large institutions while refusing direct aid to farmers, the unemployed, and the World War veterans added a bitter edge of class outrage to the feelings of ordinary men in Polonia as elsewhere. The Polish Alliance paper asked, at the time of the Veterans' March on Washington:

The government recently voted millions to aid the reconstruction of finance. . . . Will it also appropriate millions for work for the veterans who . . . are only asking for what is owing them?

When the administration responded by unleashing the military on the bonus marchers, and the Republican convention mechanically endorsed the person and policies of Hoover, all the newspapers of Polonia stated, as if they had rehearsed the phrase together, "All eyes are turned toward Chicago and the Democratic National convention." All the hopes of Polonia for the economic issue—hopes for a return of general prosperity, for a more sympathetic deal for the ordinary worker, and for badly needed aid and public works—united on the Democratic party.[18]

When the Democrats convened, the eventual nominee was by no means certain. Al Smith, Franklin Roosevelt, and John Nance Garner were the leading candidates, and Governor Albert Ritchie of Maryland was mentioned as a possible compromise candidate. In the back of some minds was the deadlocked convention of 1924. If such a deadlock happened again, the Democrats might destroy their golden chance and with it the hopes of millions who were disgusted with Hoover's administration.[19]

The previous election had shown decisively that Poland was no longer of much concern to Polish-American voters, and the depression crisis at home was likely to further erase any thoughts of the old country. Yet, for those who still cared for such things, the Polish press pointed out that Governor Ritchie of Maryland was the best candidate from Poland's point of view. Ritchie had lobbied vigorously in Wilson's administration for increased aid to Poland in the immediate postwar period. In gratitude, the new Polish state had awarded him its highest honor, the Order of Polonia Restituta. This was not likely to be of much importance at the convention; but an older ethnic issue of immediate import, prohibition, was.[20]

The Chicago convention, of course, settled on Franklin Delano Roosevelt as the Democratic candidate and wrote into its brief platform promises of federal aid to state relief efforts, increased public works, and other vaguely worded economic aids as well as a strong wet-plank on prohibition. Polonia had no reason to be enthusiastic over Roosevelt, as it had been over Smith. *Dziennik Chicagoski* commented: "It could be argued that Roosevelt was not the most able or the strongest of the candidates considered by the Democrats; but he is far from the least also." Yet the Democrats had not destroyed themselves in a divisive convention, they had promised relief from depression (however vaguely), they had opposed the hated prohibition law; and, of course, Hoover was a known evil. Thus, all the active concerns of Polonia in 1932 united around Franklin Roosevelt. One Polish writer summed up the sentiment: "On November 8, an overwhelming majority of the great American nation will declare itself for Franklin D. Roosevelt . . . for the Republican administration must bear the blame for the situation of terrible depression which prevails in this whole country."[21]

In 1932 Polonia's interests were not divided among several candidates as they had been in the 1920s. Poland's cause was long forgotten, and Roosevelt seemed sound on the one ethnic issue which still retained meaning, prohibition. The promised New Deal of the Democrats gathered together hopes of general economic improvement and sensitivity to the "forgotten man" at the bottom of the economic pyramid. Thus, Polonia's capital voted, not yet with much enthusiasm but in great hope, as one voice, giving Franklin Roosevelt 83.29 percent of its votes.

The great majority of Polonia's citizens did not feel let down by Roosevelt's New Deal. Relief and works programs gave lifesaving aid to many, and federal home-loan insurance helped numerous Polish-Americans save their homes. Perhaps one simple letter to a local Chicago Democrat can speak for the thousands who found immediate help from Roosevelt's "alphabet agencies:" "Thank you very much for your troubles. I have received work on WPA again, for which I am every greatful [sic] to you." The Republicans were helpless against the New Deal's satisfaction of direct economic needs. In their desperation, they denounced the federal government's encroachments on the freedom of the individual. Polonia had always had a lively sense of personal liberty; but in the depression crisis the issue rang hollow. *Dziennik Zwiazkowy* remarked in 1936:

It is true that everyone wants to be free and does not wish the government to dictate to him what he can do, and does not want it to put its head into everything. But a certain control is necessary and must be exercised in order to fight unemployment.

The Republican nominee, in his approaches and his comments about American freedom, takes the point of view of the great corporations and people like the DuPonts and the Fords.[22]

The Republicans could not find a base or any organized support in Polonia. The president of the Polish National Alliance campaigned for Landon in 1936, but when he proclaimed in one speech that he "was speaking in the name of a Chicago Polonia, 650,000 strong [sic]," the *Dziennik Chicagoski* asked on its front page, "Since when?" Even the Alliance's newspaper abandoned the Republicans and its own organization's president. After forty years of opposing the Democratic leanings of the Polish Roman Catholic Union and the Resurrectionist press, forty years of advocacy for the Republicans with occasional retreats into nonpartisanship, the *Dziennik Zwiazkowy's* conversion is striking. The rest of the story is best told in that paper's own words:

In reality there is only one question before the country at this time: Whether to continue the New Deal and reelect the Democratic party, or to return to the old system with the Republican party. . . . The old order or the new order—that's the question.

After the country's voters answered that question in 1936, the newspaper exulted:

Victory!
President Roosevelt and the New Deal have emerged victorious from the national election.
There has never been such a victory in the history of America!
President Roosevelt is a Leader and a Hero of the nation. The mass of the people love him and worship him.[23]

In Polonia's capital the "mass of the people" did indeed love Franklin Roosevelt; 87.65 percent of them voted for his reelection.

The era which had begun with much trumpeting of heroes who had supposedly saved Poland from starvation ended with near unanimous acclaim for a new hero who had saved America from starvation, want, and a failing leadership.

IV The Rise of the Chicago Democratic Machine

Chicago politics before the First World War had been the age of Harrison. The Carter Harrisons, father and son, used personal charisma to build a following and stay in office. Yet, though a Harrison reigned as mayor more often than not, he did not control the politics and politicians of Chicago. The Harrison performance was a juggling act, a balancing of rival factions and bosses, not the rule of a disciplined machine.

When the juggler faltered in 1915, it was the Republicans' moment of opportunity. William Hale Thompson, another flamboyant performer, began his own act and made the moment his. The Thompson era, which lasted until 1931, had all the trappings of a carnival sideshow, playing on center stage. Big Bill postured, bellowed, ranted, and raved, giving Chicago the most eccentric politics and the worst government in its history. But in the end, it proved to be only a sideshow. For during the Thompson years, Roger Sullivan and his successors to the chairmanship of the Cook County Democratic Committee, George Brennan and Anton Cermak, were slowly building the regular Democratic organization into a powerful machine.

When Thompson's corruption and incompetence in the early years of the

depression proved too much even for Chicago, Tony Cermak and the Democrats took over. Thompson dominated an era, but he ruined the Republican party in Chicago. The Democratic machine, first led to victory by Cermak, has, under his Irish successors Edward Kelly and Richard Daley, tightly controlled Chicago politics ever since.

Thompson's era also presented opportunities for the Republicans to break the traditional Polish-Democratic connection. Chicago's Polonia wavered in its allegiance during the Thompson years, trying to pick its way through the emotional appeals Thompson tossed off in bewildering variety. The tensions of wartime and then the abrasive ethnic issues of the 1920s posed challenges to Polish voters. Some were drawn by Thompson's appeals; the majority stayed with their Democratic friends. Thompson only toyed with ethnic issues and did not make the most of his moment. When the Thompson era ended, Polonia's Democratic loyalty still stood, confirmed and strengthened by the rise of the Czech leader, Cermak.

Polonia's capital entered the era of Democratic dominance as an important component of the machine. Not all Chicago Poles were happy with the situation; many felt the machine took them for granted. Nevertheless, the Polish-Democratic connection, which first emerged in the time of Harrison, Kiol-bassa, and Kunz, persisted, stronger than ever, in the years of Cermak, Kelly, and Szymczak.

12 Big Bill the Boisterous

Many citizens of Chicago were unhappy with Carter Harrison and the Democrats in 1915. As we have seen, Harrison was soundly defeated in the Democratic party primary by Robert Sweitzer, in part because of the unpopularity of Harrison's anti-vice crusade. But Sweitzer could not capitalize on the voters' desire for a change since he had numerous handicaps of his own.

Sweitzer's political mentor was the long-time Democratic boss, Roger Sullivan. For almost twenty years Sullivan had been welding together whatever elements of the Democratic party were not loyal to Carter Harrison. But Sullivan, never a popular figure, was at a low point of public esteem in 1915. He was still known as the "boss of the gas ring," even twenty years after the Ogden Gas affair. The public sentiment against bosses of any kind that had harassed Carter Harrison in his last years as mayor was still running strong.[1]

Besides the albatross of Sullivan, Sweitzer also bore the burden of his Roman Catholic religion. Many Protestants had long resented Carter Harrison's practice of recognizing new ethnic and religious groups through appointments to the Board of Education. During his five terms as mayor, Harrison had made seventy-seven appointments to the Board of Education. Five of these appointees were Polish-Catholics, and other Catholic immigrant groups obtained even greater recognition. To many Protestants, who looked upon the public schools as their own, this Catholic representation on the board was an insidious influence. They were ready to vote against any further increase of Catholic influence in the city.[2]

The accidental circumstance of his last name brought a further weight of prejudice down upon Sweitzer, as anti-German sentiment in wartime was on the rise. That this Germanophobia fell upon Sweitzer was cruelly ironic, for he was actually of Irish parentage. His Irish-American father, however, had died young; and his mother married a man named Sweitzer, who adopted the

children and gave them his name. But Sweitzer himself may have been partly
responsible for the storm of anti-German feeling which broke around him.
Late in the campaign, someone, supposedly from the Sweitzer camp, distributed handbills bearing the pictures of Kaiser Wilhelm and Emperor
Franz Joseph of Austria. Beneath the pictures, Gothic lettering stated that a
vote for Sweitzer would aid the Fatherland and the brave German soldiers
fighting in the trenches. Such a poster was not yet treasonous or disloyal, for
the U.S. was still a neutral nation. Yet it was so clearly incendiary that most
likely Sweitzer's enemies, rather than his followers, were actually responsible
for it. In any case, the Republicans made good use of this "Our Fatherland"
poster, reprinting it and flooding the Polish, Bohemian, and other anti-German areas with it.[3]

The Fatherland poster and Sweitzer's German name had a particularly
strong impact in Chicago's Polonia. Poles in Europe, of course, had long
hated the Germans, who had partitioned their country, seized much of the
best farmland in occupied Poland, and ruthlessly suppressed the Polish language and culture. Immigrants carried this hatred of the Germans to America.
An old Polish saying was often repeated in Polonia: "As long as the world
is going to be a world, a German will never be a brother to a Pole." Some of
this hostility eroded in the New World, but the rising tide of anti-German
sentiment throughout the U.S. in wartime reinforced it. The Poles, through
one of their representatives on the school board, agitated for the end of German language classes in the public schools and for the renaming of Bismarck
School on the North Side. A Polish newspaper even called on all Polish
schoolchildren to tear out page 154 of the common spelling book, where a
picture of Kaiser Wilhelm was reproduced.[4]

The Polish National Alliance, always a leader in stirring up nationalist
sentiment among the Poles, constantly emphasized the Germanness of
Sweitzer. The Alliance's daily paper published a large reproduction of the
"Our Fatherland" poster, just before election day, and commented:

> The Germans wish to make the election of the Mayor of Chicago a
> matter of nationality politics, since they are openly declaring that Germans
> must, through the election of their candidate as Mayor of Chicago, prove that
> the name of German is not so defiled as the American press would wish it to
> be. It is fortunate that Sweitzer will not reach the City Hall so easily, for the
> people of Chicago will not buy the Catholicism of Sweitzer and Poles will
> stand as one man for W. H. Thompson, the Republican candidate for
> Mayor of Chicago.[5]

With Sweitzer handicapped among the Poles and other Slavs by his Ger-

man name, among the WASP middle class by his Catholic religion, and in the
city as a whole by his boss label, the mayoralty fell to the Republican, William
Hale Thompson.

After the departure of the former Republican boss, William Lorimer,
into obscurity, Fred Lundin, a patent medicine salesman who had served
Lorimer in politics, picked up the pieces of the Lorimer machine and began
cultivating Bill Thompson as a fresh face. Former mayor Busse, who might
have challenged Lundin and Thompson's bid for power, had died unex-
pectedly in 1913; and Charles Deneen, who led a large faction of respectable
Republicans, had been soundly defeated in the governorship race of 1912.
Deneen put up a candidate against Thompson in the 1915 Republican primary, Judge Harry Olson of the Chicago Municipal Court; but Olson was a
lackluster politician and Thompson defeated him by a narrow margin for the
nomination.[6]

Thompson came from an old Chicago family and had fallen heir to his
father's real estate fortune. Not needing to work for a living, Big Bill went
west as a young man, seeking adventure as a cowboy. Upon his father's death,
he returned to Chicago to claim his inheritance and then briefly dabbled in
politics as a Lorimer candidate for alderman and county commissioner. But
Thompson was dumped from the Republican slate in 1904 in a factional
fight, and he quickly lost interest in politics. For the next decade he devoted
himself to his real love, sports, distinguishing himself as a yachtsman and
water-polo player and helping to organize the Illinois Athletic Club. In
short, when Fred Lundin began grooming him for the mayoralty at the age
of forty-five, Bill Thompson was a tall, athletically inclined, but politically in-
experienced, playboy.[7]

Thompson, however, brought two political assets with him to his first
important campaign. One was his bluff good nature and likability, coupled
with a knack for delivering rip-roaring speeches. These features gave Thompson the freshness and personal appeal which proved so important in this
election. The other asset was a great popularity among the growing number of
Negroes in the South Side's Black Belt. Thompson's appeal to Negroes went
back to his aldermanic days, when he had served the largely Negro Second
Ward in the city council. Partly from conviction and partly from political
calculation, Big Bill always treated the black men of Chicago as equals and
catered to the Negro community's leaders. His solid strength in the Negro
wards was one of the deciding factors in his narrow victory over Olson in the
primary.[8]

In the mayoral election all the seething sentiment against Sweitzer and

Sullivan, against the Catholics and the Germans, worked in Thompson's favor. A secret Protestant organization called the Guardians of Liberty sprang up and disseminated anti-Catholic propaganda, while Lundin made maximum use of the ill-fated Fatherland poster. The growing middle class of clerks, skilled workers, and shopkeepers, seeing themselves as little people squeezed between the big business interests on the one side and immigrant machines on the other, backed Thompson as a new man, unattached to any industrial organization or foreign machine. Advocates of the "wide open town," chafing under the Harrison-imposed vice crackdown, sided with Big Bill, whose "liberal" views were well known. At the same time, staid old ladies and prominent ministers supported Thompson, the Anglo-Saxon Protestant, as a counterweight to the "immoral and insidious" Catholic influence.[9]

Big Bill used to the utmost his ability to rouse a crowd, playing on the accumulated grievances of many groups as well as the growing passions of wartime. Election eve witnessed a wild, twelve-hour demonstration in Chicago's Loop. A parade of Thompson supporters with calliopes, fireworks, and animals paralyzed downtown traffic, while fistfights and near riots erupted nearby in side streets and back alleys. The respectable newspapers of the city saw little difference between the candidates' qualifications, and they viewed the injection of religion and other divisive issues into the campaign as an aberration. Actually, though Chicago didn't know it yet, the city was about to enter the Thompson era, with public violence, bitter campaign fights, and ethnic and religious slander the political norm rather than the exception. On April 5, 1915, William Hale Thompson defeated Robert Sweitzer by a landslide margin of nearly 150,000 votes. For twelve of the next sixteen years, he was to serve as Chicago's mayor.[10]

Chicago's Polonia played its small part in producing this swing to the Republican Thompson. Sweitzer captured only 51.53 percent of the Polish vote, whereas Carter Harrison and other Democrats had consistently rolled up 65 to 70 percent of that vote in the previous decades. The only reason why Sweitzer did even this well in Polonia was that Stanley Kunz, a loyal Sullivan-Sweitzer man, was able to produce a comfortable Democratic majority in the Sixteenth Ward. In many other areas of the city where Polish-Americans voted, Thompson won a majority.

Disappointment over the defeat of Carter Harrison in the primary as well as strong anti-German sentiment must have played a part in the weak support Polonia gave the Democrats. In the Twenty-ninth Ward around the

TABLE 22   ELECTION RETURNS (IN PERCENTAGES): MAYOR, 1915

Ward	No. of Polish Precincts	Sweitzer (D)	Thompson (R)	Stedman (Soc)
4th				
Polish vote	3	53.04	45.03	1.84
Ward average		58.94	38.87	1.98
8th				
Polish vote	6	55.53	42.21	2.09
Ward average		34.79	6.77	3.16
11th				
Polish vote	3	46.97	51.59	1.42
Ward average		42.57	53.82	3.42
12th				
Polish vote	1	29.82	67.91	2.25
Ward average		34.66	60.29	4.90
16th				
Polish vote	16	66.92	31.42	1.57
Ward average		57.13	40.10	2.60
17th				
Polish vote	2	52.75	44.08	3.15
Ward average		49.72	46.98	2.97
27th				
Polish vote	5	38.52	55.91	5.46
Ward average		26.02	65.62	7.62
28th				
Polish vote	8	38.41	58.41	3.42
Ward average		30.82	63.89	4.94
29th				
Polish vote	3	27.58	69.54	2.79
Ward average		40.24	56.35	3.20
City-wide				
Polish vote	47	51.53	45.90	2.53
City average		37.19	59.04	3.62

stockyards, the revenge of Harrson was most marked. Here the Polish precincts, under the direction of ward boss Thomas Carey, a Harrison lieutenant,
gave Sweitzer only 27.58 percent of their votes. On the far northwest side
in the Twenty-seventh and Twenty-eighth wards, Sweitzer percentages were
also very low. Polish-Americans in these areas voted much like their middle-
class Republican neighbors.[11]

The election of 1915 was a political upheaval long in the making. Thompson was the right man at the right time to capitalize on a number of grievances against the Democrats. The growing fear of everything German added an extra element of wartime bitterness to the campaign and helped pry many normally Democratic Polish votes away from Thompson's opponent.

The Thompson era soon got into full swing. Big Bill had initially pleased the respectable Protestants in his following by cracking down on saloons which operated illegally on Sunday or after hours. But the rigid enforcement didn't last, and Thompson's police quietly allowed saloonkeepers to have their way. The vice dens which Carter Harrison had previously closed began reappearing in the Levee district. A running feud then began between State's Attorney Maclay Hoyne, a protégé of Harrison's, who tried to continue the cleanup campaign, and Mayor Thompson, who virtually abandoned it. The slow progress in the city's civil service evaporated overnight as Thompson found innumerable means of circumventing the civil service law. Rumors circulated concerning outrageous fees paid to "experts" brought in as consultants on various street-widening and bridge-building projects.[12]

Thompson soon became embroiled in the politics of wartime. Fred Lundin, Thompson's political mentor, convinced the mayor to grab for national attention by opposing American involvement in the war. Thompson did so with vehemence. Despite his own Anglo-Saxon background, he took special delight in denouncing Great Britain and Britain's war. His intemperate statements soon earned him a host of Germanophobe nicknames such as Kaiser Bill, Burgomaster Bill, and Wilhelm der Grosse. As the war came to an end and his own reelection battle approached in early 1919, Thompson shocked the nation by refusing to greet Marshal Foch when his triumphal tour of America brought him to Chicago. In order to appeal to the Irish as well as the German vote, Thompson also declared himself unequivocally in favor of home rule and independence for Ireland, no matter how irrelevant the issue was for the governance of Chicago.[13]

Plenty of opponents to Thompson appeared in 1919; too many, as it turned out. Judge Harry Olson and Professor Charles Merriam, both former seekers of the mayoralty, jumped into the Republican primary, neatly dividing the good-government vote between them and allowing Thompson a narrow renomination victory. Robert Sweitzer was again the Sullivan candidate on the regular Democratic ticket; but many dissatisfied Democrats called on Carter Harrison, then serving in France with the Red Cross, to return and run an independent race. When Harrison refused, his former assistant, State's Attorney Hoyne, leaped into the battle as an independent.[14]

The ranks of labor were also restless in these confused postwar months, and in December of 1918 the Chicago Federation of Labor issued a call for the formation of a local Labor Party to contest the election. The labor ranks demanded municipal ownership of all public utilities, the recognition of union labor, and the eight-hour day in all city departments. The new party's ticket was an ethnically balanced one, consisting of John Fitzpatrick, long-time head of the CFL, for mayor; a Swedish house-painter for city clerk; and John Kikulski, a Polish union leader from the stockyards, for city treasurer. Thus, with the addition of the usual Socialist candidate, the 1919 election shaped up as a five-way race.[15]

As in the primary, the divided opposition to Thompson proved to be its own undoing. Hoyne cut sharply into the Republican vote, but Hoyne and Fitzpatrick also gathered in many ex-Harrisonites and other discontented Democrats. The result was that Mayor Thompson slipped through to reelection with only 37 percent of the city's vote while the other four candidates divided the remainder. Big Bill's solid Negro bloc of votes and whatever Irish and German votes he picked up with his rantings provided the mayor's eleven-thousand-vote margin over Sweitzer, the nearest contender.

Voters in Chicago's Polonia found themselves in a dilemma in this first postwar election. They were still cool to the Sullivan-Sweitzer combine that controlled the Democratic ticket; and Carter Harrison's cablegrams from France in support of Hoyne, by resurrecting the "Our Fatherland" poster from 1915, helped turn the coldness into an icy chill. On the other hand, most Polish voters wouldn't think of supporting Thompson as some had done four years previously; with wartime memories fresh, he was still Kaiser Bill to them. The *Dziennik Zwiazkowy,* which had boasted of its support for the victorious Thompson just after his first election in 1915, was completely silent on American politics in 1919, publishing no political ads and not even mentioning the local elections. Other Polish papers endorsed Sweitzer, rather unenthusiastically; for after all he was a Democrat and the strongest alternative to Kaiser Bill. The Polish socialist press ridiculed the quandary of the major Polish dailies:

> The Polish papers in Chicago are supporting the candidacy of Sweitzer ... because he alone can cleanse Chicago from the horrible stain of being a pro-German city, which was imprinted upon it by Thompson.
> The people read this and no one believes it. Chicago at this moment

need not worry about doing something about its pro-Germanism. . . . It needs action against corruption, establishment of honest, knowledgeable, financial administration, and a restoration among police of respect for the civil rights of citizens and a restoration of public trust.

However, the Polish papers do not wish to write about these things.[16]

This socialist analysis was clear-eyed, for the German issue was certainly a red herring. Yet the issue must have had some effect. Thompson's vote plummeted to 13 percent in Chicago's Polonia; and Sweitzer polled 54 percent, just two percentage points higher than in 1915. A sizeable minority of Polish votes went to either Fitzpatrick, the labor candidate (16.15 percent), or Hoyne, the independent (14.58 percent).

Hoyne's Polish vote total was highest in the Twenty-ninth Ward, near the stockyards, where ward boss Thomas Carey was loyal to Harrison and his friends. The labor vote was also comparatively high in the two wards near the stockyards, the Fourth and the Twenty-ninth, where the influence of John Kikulski, labor candidate for treasurer, obviously had some effect. In the more middle-class reaches of the Twenty-seventh and Twenty-eighth wards, Polish-Americans actually voted more independently than their neighbors.[17]

Clearly the Polish vote in this election was an aberration. In a confused, five-way race, with wartime issues making both major-party candidates unattractive, Polonia's capital fragmented its vote. Still, the majority remained Democrats.

In 1923 politics returned to a more familiar mold in Polonia's capital. War and Thompsonism had disrupted the Polish voting pattern, greatly reducing the Democratic vote in 1915 and 1919. But the passions of wartime finally cooled; and, in 1923, Bill Thompson temporarily left the scene.

Rumors of graft and scandal, particularly in the construction of new school buildings, had run rampant during Thompson's second term. The new Republican state's attorney, Robert E. Crowe, a factional opponent of Thompson's, hauled Fred Lundin into court with boxes of records linking him to the school scandals. Lundin was eventually acquitted by a jury, but the Thompson-Lundin partnership came to an end. When all the anti-Thompson factions in the Republican party united on one candidate for mayor, Arthur Lueder, a respectable businessman then serving as postmaster, Big Bill knew enough to call it quits.[18]

The political situation favored the Democrats in 1923. Bill Thompson's eight-year rule had shifted the onus of boss rule to the Republican party; and

TABLE 23   ELECTION RETURNS (IN PERCENTAGES): MAYOR, 1919

Ward	No. of Polish Precincts	Sweitzer (D)	Thompson (R)	Collins (Soc)	Fitzpatrick (Lab)	Hoyne (Ind)
4th	5					
Polish vote		33.86	14.00	0.99	27.57	23.85
Ward average		47.74	23.52	1.50	14.12	12.93
8th	9					
Polish vote		60.41	11.19	0.95	14.10	13.36
Ward average		33.88	38.64	1.65	12.90	12.62
11th	3					
Polish vote		64.35	17.99	1.21	8.59	7.83
Ward average		44.65	32.59	4.21	9.72	8.54
12th	1					
Polish vote		38.65	23.31	2.14	17.17	18.09
Ward average		47.36	25.54	5.90	12.29	12.99
16th	15					
Polish vote		63.55	13.85	1.11	12.12	9.04
Ward average		54.27	19.86	2.19	13.28	10.05
17th	2					
Polish vote		53.53	20.57	3.35	8.80	13.73
Ward average		52.03	26.10	1.73	9.79	10.15
27th	5					
Polish vote		42.43	12.51	2.22	23.05	19.65
Ward average		24.99	41.05	5.08	11.48	17.06
28th	6					
Polish vote		56.52	8.21	1.12	20.19	13.53
Ward average		33.34	36.62	4.53	13.77	11.39
29th	4					
Polish vote		33.39	18.76	2.50	18.74	26.33
Ward average		36.07	33.04	3.35	16.06	11.24
City-wide						
50 Polish precincts		53.80	13.48	1.41	16.15	14.58
City average		34.48	37.61	3.48	8.10	16.05

TABLE 24   ELECTION RETURNS (IN PERCENTAGES): MAYOR, 1911-1935

Year	No. of Polish Precincts	Polish Vote (City-Wide Vote)		
		Republican	Democratic	Other
1911	37	Merriam 24.40 (43.80)	Harrison 68.91 (48.52)	
1915	47	Thompson 45.90 (59.04)	Sweitzer 51.53 (37.19)	
1919	50	Thompson 13.48 (37.61)	Sweitzer 53.80 (34.48)	(3 others) 32.14 (27.63)
1923	48	Lueder 12.43 (39.77)	Dever 83.47 (54.47)	
1927	61	Thompson 42.20 (51.58)	Dever 54.07 (43.27)	
1931	61	Thompson 23.20 (41.50)	Cermak 76.80 (58.40)	
1935	87	Wetten 8.08 (15.80)	Kelly 84.84 (75.70)	
Average		24.20 (41.30)	67.63 (50.29)	

George E. Brennan, Roger Sullivan's successor as Democratic leader, shrewdly capitalized on the public's weariness of bossism by slating Judge William E. Dever to make the race for mayor. Dever had been elected alderman five times early in the century by Graham Taylor's reform club in the Seventeenth Ward, and then had served on the bench with distinction since 1912.

Dever championed all the standard reform issues—municipal ownership of traction lines, a drive against vice and organized crime, and a thorough housecleaning at City Hall. All factions of the Democratic party, from Carter Harrison to Bob Sweitzer, united behind Dever, as did many Republican independents such as Charles E. Merriam, Raymond Robins, and Harold Ickes. The newspapers conceded that Dever and Lueder were equally honest

and capable and that the city was thus faced with an unusually happy electoral choice. But the bad reputation which Thompsonism had given the
Republican party and the smooth, efficient precinct work of Brennan's
Democrats easily tipped the scales. Dever won handily by over a hundred
thousand votes.[19]

Among the Polish voters there were no issues of particular interest in
this election. The Republican Lueder was of German descent; and the post
office, under his administration and that of previous postmasters, was well
known as a German patronage preserve. But the rabid anti-Germanism of
wartime had passed, and none of the Polish papers mentioned Lueder's nationality. After the uncertain results of the last two mayoral races, Chicago's
Polish voters returned decisively to the Democratic allegiance of the Harrison years, giving Dever over 83 percent of their votes.[20]

Even more clearly than Harrison's triumph in 1911, this election illustrates the neutrality of Polonia's voters on matters of progressive reform.
Dever, the reform candidate, was Polonia's choice even though he spoke in
the remote accents of good government and efficiency and made no special
appeals to the ethnic group. He enjoyed Polish support simply because he was
a Democrat and had done nothing to alienate Polonia.

Mayor Dever lived up to his reform label during his four-year term at
City Hall. He failed, as many other mayors had failed before him, to obtain
municipal ownership of the traction lines; but he did effect the promised
cleanup of government workers, installing many prominent "goo-goos" and
settlement-house workers in city departments. His police chief put the heat
on organized crime, forcing Johnny Torrio and Al Capone to find a new
haven in Cicero, Illinois, just outside the western limits of Chicago. The
mayor also made an honest attempt to enforce the prohibition laws, which
had been so openly flouted under Thompson.[21]

This latter aspect of reform proved to be Dever's undoing among
Polish-Americans and other ethnic groups. The liquor question had always
been a sensitive issue in Polonia, and any hint of prohibitionism in a candidate
could be easily played up by an ethnically aware opponent, as Charles Merriam had discovered against Carter Harrison in 1911. Polish opposition to
blue laws did not diminish after prohibition became the law of the land.
When Chicago held a special referendum in 1919 to allow an expression of
opinion on the Volstead Act, Polish voters overwhelmingly rejected the act,
as did most other ethnic groups.[22]

George Brennan, the Democratic boss, made no secret of the local party's unalterable hostility to prohibition. In 1926 a delegation representing the main ethnic components of the party (Stanley Kunz, Jacob Arvey, Anton Cermak, and George Brennan) journeyed to Washington to advocate modification of the Volstead Act at Senate hearings on the question. But William Dever, though personally not a prohibitionist, believed with judicial certainty that respect for the law outweighed political expediency; thus he tried to enforce the Volstead Act.[23]

More than a love of beer and liquor was involved in Polish opposition to this enforcement. Dever's police grew overzealous in their drive against crime and booze, and many a city policeman broke into private homes in working-class neighborhoods looking for bootleg liquor. Ethnic opposition to blue laws had always presented itself as a movement for "personal liberty" and "local self-government." This was not only a public relations euphemism but also an accurate reflection of the way European ethnics viewed the issue. Many a European had come to America looking for liberty, for the right to live his own way. So the fight against prohibition was more than a matter of thirst; it was also a fight for an ideal of America.

In the atmosphere fostered by 100 percent Americanizers during the war and the Ku Klux Klan in the 20s, this fight took on added urgency. One Polish paper commented:

The whole prohibition campaign, and every tendency to forbid even the sale and use of tobacco and cigarettes, as well as the chauvinist urge to forbid the teaching of children in any language besides English or any religion besides Protestantism, all this is an echo of the former Puritan laws brought to America from England by English emigrants.

In other words, the whole constellation of intolerant acts which characterized the 1920s was un-American, brought to the New World by English Puritans and revived by their Anglophile descendants. In their fight against the Volstead Act, and against all 100 percenters, Polish-Americans felt they were fighting for their vision of America, an ideal of liberty. In opposing Mayor Dever's police raids, they were defending the liberty and security of their own homes.[24]

This hostility to Dever on the personal liberty issue was exacerbated by none other than Big Bill Thompson, who reentered the political wars as Republican mayoralty candidate in 1927. Thompson's 1927 race is best remembered as his "America First" campaign, in which he appealed to the Irish Democrats by yelling "I wanta make the King of England keep his snout out of America. . . . America first, and last, and always! That's the issue of this campaign!" But Thompson also roared around the city proclaiming that he was "as wet as the Atlantic ocean" and that he would "fire every policeman who enters a home in search of liquor." Outraged at Dever's police, Polish-Americans at Thompson rallies responded with cries of "hurray for beer and Big Bill." It's possible that Polish voters made a vague connection between Big Bill's rantings against the king of England and his opposition to the crusading puritans and police. If English Puritans were responsible for prohibition and attacks on liberty and if Thompson hated both the English and the prohibitionists, then America First meant that Big Bill shared the Poles' vision of American liberty.[25]

Thompson played for the Polish vote in other ways as well. At a meeting of Polish voters, calling themselves the William H. Thompson Polish Club, Big Bill harangued:

It used to be said to me that Poles vote the Democratic ticket with massive majorities. Now I don't think this is true. If the Poles give me 50,000 votes on election day, you'll be able to call City Hall the Capitol of Poland.

This was Thompson's stock speech for the normally Democratic ethnic groups; and the Polish Alliance paper remarked wryly that "if Thompson promises any more capitols to particular nationalities, the present city hall will surely have to be rebuilt or else several additional floors will have to be added." Still, Polonia was becoming more conscious of its underrepresentation in city government; Thompson's broad hint at greater ethnic recognition was tempting. Dever, with his reform image in mind, had made many appointments of nonpartisan and independent individuals to his administration, neglecting the regular practice of ethnic recognition. Immediately after Dever's election, the leading Polish Democrats had sent the mayor a list of Polish-Americans whom they deemed qualified for office; but Dever did not appoint any of them to a major city position. Polonia was, therefore, ready to rise to Thompson's bait in 1927.[26]

The Democrats fought back desperately against Thompson's ploys. The mayor met the personal-liberty issue head-on in his speeches: "It has been charged that I have given the police orders or will give them orders, if I am reelected, to invade and enter people's homes and unlawfully to search for and seize liquor, home brew and wine. This is utterly false." Boss Brennan, in an attempt to counter the widespread disaffection among Polish voters, slated Miecieslaus S. (Matt) Szymczak, a young professor at DePaul University and a second-generation Polish-American, to run for city treasurer. Szymczak

was a political protégé of the Czech leader, county board president Anton
Cermak; and the two of them campaigned hard for the regular ticket in
Slavic areas. The Democrats, who, except for Dever, were all notorious wets,
tried to impugn Thompson's sincerity on the liquor issue, pointing out that in
1915 the ex-mayor had rigidly enforced the saloon-closing ordinances and
that as recently as 1926 he had campaigned for anti-saloon candidates in the
congressional and state elections. Others tried to defend Dever, highlighting
his 1926 appearance before the Senate hearings on prohibition.[27]

But the Democrats' efforts to lose the prohibitionist label among ethnic
voters were unsuccessful, and Thompson returned to City Hall with an eighty-
thousand-vote margin. Both English and foreign-language papers ascribed
Dever's defeat to defections by Polish, German, Czech, and Italian voters,
objecting to the mayor's enforcement tactics. Dever actually retained a majority of Polish votes (54.07 percent), but it was a greatly reduced majority
compared to 1923 (83.47 percent). Thompson's 42.20 percent of the Polish
vote about equalled the percentage he had polled in 1915 when strong anti-
German sentiment had been working in his favor. Furthermore, Polish voters
split their tickets in large numbers to show their rejection of Dever. While
only 54 percent voted Democratic on the mayoralty line, 81.46 percent voted
for their fellow countryman, Szymczak, on the Democratic line for city treasurer, nearly salvaging a victory for Szymczak out of the party wreckage.[28]

Other divisive issues, besides prohibition, had bubbled to the top of the
political pot in 1927; but they did not seem to affect the Polish vote. Supporters of both Thompson and Dever made veiled use of the religious issue
but, if this had been a factor in Polonia, the voters would have been more
solid for the Catholic Dever than they were. In their desperation, the Democrats also tried to pit one ethnic group against another in order to cut into
Thompson's support. One Polish paper rather feebly revived the wartime
anti-German feelings, reminding its readers that "in the time of the World
War, Thompson openly worked and spoke out for the Germans. Kaiser
Wilhelm was his ideal." This issue, however, was dead; and the newspaper
heard no echoes of its sentiments in Polonia.

Other Democrats tried to turn Thompson's staunch Negro support
against him by stirring up racial feelings. When Thompson, on one of his
campaign junkets into the Black Belt, was photographed kissing a black child,
Democratic headquarters immediately distributed cartoons parodying this
event. One of these cartoons turned up on the front page of *Dziennik
Chicagoski*. This paper published several other cartoons during the campaign

linking Thompson with "black bootleggers," South Side "gambling dens," and "race riots." It also repeated some gossip that Negroes were trying to buy homes in Polish neighborhoods and attempting to purchase land for a Negro cemetery on the northwest side.[29]

But the racial issue failed to strike fire in Polonia. Polish hostility to other ethnic groups was strongest when a grievance inherited from the old country was reinforced by the American experience. Thus, the Old World suspicion of Jews and hatred of Germans lingered in the New World, since Poles first settled in German neighborhoods and continued to rub elbows with Jews on the business streets. When wartime hysteria sparked these old passions, they flamed into a roaring blaze. But Poles had brought with them from Europe no attitude at all toward Negroes, who had not existed in the old milieu. Whatever racial prejudice they did show was largely an acquired trait, an ironic indicator of Americanization.

Most references to Negroes in the Polish press were American stereotypes about the black man's laziness and his love of a crap game. Even as well-educated a man as John Smulski once referred to the Negro crapshooters in a campaign speech for Charles Merriam in 1911. But this use of stereotypes was seldom orchestrated into a direct attack on Negroes.[30]

The Poles in Chicago, furthermore, had little contact with blacks, and thus there were few occasions for friction to develop. Polish Downtown and the entire northwest side were far removed from the black areas of the city, as was the large Polish communiy of South Chicago. The only areas of Polonia near the Black Belt were Bridgeport and the yards district on the South Side; but in the 1920s the railroad tracks and other natural boundaries kept these communities insulated from their neighbors, and the Black Belt expanded straight south at the expense of largely Irish neighborhoods. The 1919 race riot in Chicago certainly roused the South Side Poles, for several of the pitched battles of this riot occurred in Bridgeport and other nearby Polish areas. But, fortunately for Bill Thompson, the riot occurred shortly after his reelection in 1919; and he did not run again for mayor until eight years later. By 1927 Poles who might have been frightened by the rioting blacks had apparently forgotten the incident. In the Polish wards closest to the Black Belt, Poles tended to vote just as strongly for Thompson, the Negro's champion, as did their countrymen elsewhere in the city. The outstanding fact in this election is that Thompson did well in Polonia, despite all the Democrats' attempts to smear him.[31]

Bill Thompson's career and the Democratic responses to him roiled the political waters with a whole series of ethnic crosscurrents. Polish voters were unaffected by some of them, such as the racial issue; but they reacted strongly to others. Germanophobia reduced Sweitzer's Polish support in 1915 and cooled Polonia on both major parties in 1919. William Dever, though supported by Polonia in 1923 as an inoffensive Democrat, broke a cardinal rule of ethnic politics when he tried to enforce the Volstead Act. Prohibition and personal liberty were issues of prime importance to Polish-Americans. When Thompson used them against Dever in 1927, he didn't destroy the Polish-Democratic majority, but he did reduce it greatly.

The 1920s were filled with ethnic issues—prohibition, the Klan, immigration restriction, the desire of new ethnic groups for recognition. Bill Thompson's inroads into the Polish vote show that the Polish-Democratic connection could have been broken by shrewd use of these issues. But Thompson's approach was scattershot. In his last term as mayor, he destroyed his potential ethnic support, his party, and his personal hold on the electorate. The Democratic machine was ready to take over.

13 The End of the Republican Alternative

Big Bill's third term as mayor was even more corrupt and crime-ridden than his first two. The prohibition laws were openly flouted by police and gangsters alike. Al Capone made a national reputation for bootlegging and violence, with the ill-concealed cooperation of City Hall. When the depression struck in 1929, many Chicagoans saw it as the last straw. Economic disaster would have threatened any mayor's position, but Thompson's reputation had become so unsavory that depression seemed a fitting denouement to his reign.

Thompson made no attempt to fulfill his ethnic promises. City Hall did not become the "capitol of Poland" or of any other nationality. In fact, Thompson alienated Polonia by slating Polish candidates only for minor offices or in contests where they had no chance of winning. Anti-Thompson elements in the Republican party were even less sensitive to ethnic candidates. A Better Government Association official told one Polish office-seeker there were three things wrong with his candidacy: his name, his nationality, and his religion.[1]

In the meantime, a leadership change in the Democratic party drew ethnic attention away from Thompson and the Republicans. Upon the death of George Brennan in 1928, Anton Cermak, the Czech boss, succeeded to Brennan's leadership of the Cook County Democrats. Cermak, born in Bohemia under the Austro-Hungarian Empire but brought to the United States as a child, had grown up in the coal mining district of Southern Illinois. After coming to Chicago in 1889, he had risen in the Democratic party, using the West Side Czech community and a city-wide anti-prohibition organization as twin power bases. Throughout the 1920s, he served as president of the Cook County Board, the chief administrative post in the county government. When he became leader of the Cook County Democrats, he was the first from a "new immigrant" group to attain a position of real power in local politics. Under the circumstances, a swing back to the Democrats by Polish-Americans and other ethnics seemed likely when Cermak announced his candidacy for mayor in 1931.[2]

Thompson made the ethnic swing to the Democrats inevitable by reversing his position of four years earlier and running for reelection as the pure Anglo-Saxon candidate opposing the Slavic tide. He tastelessly dubbed Cermak "pushcart Tony"; and he constantly asked his campaign audiences, "Tony Cermak? What kind of a name is that for a World's Fair mayor?" (The Century of Progress exhibition was scheduled for 1933 and was considered an opportunity for national publicity for the successful mayoral candidate.) To make certain that Poles were just as offended as Czechs, Big Bill dragged in the names of two of Cermak's Polish lieutenants, declaring the Democratic "double play combination" to be "Szymczak to Zintak to Cermak." The Democrats, too, reversed their position of 1927, denouncing Thompson's use of ethnic rivalries and posing as the party of "true Americanism," that is, the party of harmony among and tolerance for all groups.[3]

Cermak need hardly have campaigned among the Slavic groups. Everyone of Chicago's Polish newspapers united behind his candidacy. Even the Polish Alliance's organ, a former Thompson supporter, editorialized:

We must vigorously push forward our own interests at this crucial moment when two elements, the Slavic and the Anglo-Saxon are contending. . . . Go to the polls and cast your vote for Anton J. Cermak. . . . Citizens of Polish origin must remember that in voting for Cermak they are voting for their own interests, for the due recognition of Poles, and for an increase in their participation in the government of the city.[4]

Cermak's real feat in this election was his successful appeal to Republican independents who were disgusted by the open crime, corruption, and vulgarity of the Thompson regime. Cermak was fortunate in his opponent. Big Bill made it easy for the immigrant boss to look respectable. The arch-Republican *Chicago Tribune* excoriated Thompson in language it usually reserved for Democrats or communists:

For Chicago Thompson has meant filth, corruption, obscenity, idiocy, and bankruptcy. He has given the city an international reputation for moronic buffoonery, barbaric crime, triumphant hoodlumism, unchecked graft, and a dejected citizenship. . . . He made Chicago a byword for the collapse of American civilization.[5]

With such an opponent to run against, and with his own carefully cultivated reputation as an efficient "master administrator" in the county board presidency, Cermak successfully revived the old alliance of the Carter Harrison and William Dever years—machine Democrats, ethnic groups, and dissident respectables from the Republican ranks. The Democrat Cermak became Chicago's first mayor of Slavic descent by the comfortable margin of almost two hundred thousand votes, picking up 76.80 percent of the Polish vote in the process. Cermak had not slated a Polish-American to run on the ticket with him, but he had promised Polonia an important position in his administration, if he was elected. True to his word, he appointed his protégé, M.S. Szymczak, as city controller.

Ethnic identification, disillusionment with Thompson's hollow promises, and a return to party loyalty clearly explain the Polish swing to Cermak. It is easy to overemphasize Cermak's importance in solidifying the Polish vote for the Democrats. Though Cermak's nationality certainly aroused much enthusiasm and a feeling of bloodkinship among Poles, nearly any Democratic candidate would have won back the lost Polish votes of 1927. Thompson had discredited himself in his last term and would not have been able to use the prohibition issue effectively, since any conceivable Democratic candidate in 1931 would have been dripping wet. It is worth noting, furthermore, that the Irishman Dever had drawn even better in Polonia in 1923 than the Slavic Cermak did in 1931 (83.47 to 76.80 percent) and that Carter Harrison II had consistently done nearly as well over the span of five elections (a 71.86 percent average in five elections).[6]

Cermak's candidacy, on the other hand, came at a time of rising ethnic awareness among all the Slavs in Chicago; so he was certainly the strongest possible candidate among the Poles and related groups. In any case, Polish voters had been Democratic for decades; only unusual circumstances during the Thompson era had sometimes diminished (though never destroyed) the Democratic pluralities in Polonia. The year 1931 saw Thompson's final exit and a reassertion of Democratic strength among Poles and other Slavs.

Cermak's career was cut short in 1933 by an assassin's bullet which missed its intended target, President-elect Franklin Roosevelt. Cermak's tragic death ensured his heroic standing in Polonia. Had he lived, squabbling over patronage and recognition would surely have broken out; for despite the appointment of Szymczak and others, Polonia made no dramatic gains in political power in the city. In fact, Cermak was aware of this problem. Among the other purposes of his ill-fated journey to Miami to meet Roosevelt was a desire to secure federal appointments for Szymczak and for another prominent Polish-American, Judge Edmund K. Jarecki. Besides, how-

ever brotherly the Poles may have felt with the Czechs while opposing the
WASP enemy, the substantial differences among Slavic groups would naturally have reemerged once a Czech was in power. But, as it turned out,
Cermak was cut down prematurely, and Polonia remembered only the best
about him. *Dziennik Zwiazkowy* editorialized, while Cermak hovered between life and death in a Miami hospital, "The Chicago Polonia awaits with
fear and trembling the news from Miami, knowing that even though it
might have wished more from Cermak, it will probably be worse without
him."[7]

The warning proved accurate; for in the maneuvers following Cermak's
death, old-line Irish leaders seized control. Patrick A. Nash, a seventy-year-
old ward leader with a lifetime in politics, gave continuity to the machine as
the new county chairman of the party. In the choice of a new mayor, public
confidence and avoidance of political turmoil were the prime considerations;
for the shock of the assassination, the bitterness of the depression, and the
approach of the World's Fair all dictated a consensus strategy. A special law,
therefore, was obtained from the state legislature permitting the city council to dispense with the usual special election and appoint the new mayor
instead. Despite the irregularity of this measure, the procedure met with
widespread approval. The Democratic council then appointed Edward J.
Kelly, president of the South Parks Board and chief engineer for the Sanitary
District, to fill out Cermak's unexpired term.

As a consensus choice for World's Fair mayor, Kelly was ideal. The fair
was to be held in parkland under the South Parks Board's jurisdiction, and
thus the new mayor had been intimately involved in its planning. His career
as an engineer and administrator, furthermore, gave him the proper image
as the man to face Chicago's problems; whereas his party regularity and
political shrewdness indicated that he and Pat Nash might be able to keep
the Democrats' ethnic coalition together. The English-language newspapers
greeted Kelly's appointment with general satisfaction; and the Polish press
raised no significant protest, proclaiming that it would judge him by his
actions.[8]

Mayor Kelly's actions provided satisfaction all around. The Century
of Progress exhibition was a splendid success, the mayor's administration
made some progress in rescuing the city from economic depression and organized crime, and the Kelly-Nash combination completed the work of
Brennan and Cermak in building a strong Democratic machine. By 1935,
when the next regular mayoral election was scheduled, there was no alternative to a triumphant reelection of Ed Kelly.

The Republican party, shattered by Big Bill Thompson's vile reputation, simply ceased to exist as a viable institution in local politics. Ethnic and
working-class voters had been moving to the Democrats for decades; now even
the business and upper classes, impressed by Cermak's and Kelly's attempts
at an efficient administration, saw no reason to stay with a sinking Republican
ship. Thus, in one of the quietest elections in anyone's memory, Mayor Kelly
was reelected over token Republican opposition by more than six hundred
thousand votes. Kelly was later reelected twice more, and his two Democratic
successors have held Chicago's mayoralty down to the present day.[9]

At first glance, Polonia's capital seems to have been as satisfied with the city
government in 1935 as the rest of Chicago. In the general election between
Kelly and his weak Republican opponent, 84.84 percent of the Polish voters
supported Kelly. Only Carter Harrison the elder, forty years before in 1893,
had ever garnered a greater percentage of Polish votes; and that was in a
considerably smaller Polonia. A look at the Democratic primary results, however, reveals that a sizable minority of Polish voters were not satisfied.
    The primary, like the election which followed, was an extremely quiet
and uneventful one in most of Chicago. On the Sunday before the balloting,
the *Tribune* stated that "there has been no campaign, either Democratic or
Republican. The spirit of contest has been entirely lacking." On primary day,
despite a late February snowstorm, the machine's heelers turned out a record
total for Mayor Kelly, whose main opponent received only forty thousand
votes, or about 7 percent of those cast.[10]
    Among Polonia's voters, however, Kelly's opponent, Martin Powroznik,
picked up over a third of the votes (34.34 percent). Who was Martin Powroznik, and what did his relative strength in Polonia signify? First of all,
Powroznik was a Polish-American; so much of his sizable minority total can
be explained as simply a vote for a countryman. But there was more to it
than that.
    In the prosperous times just before the depression, Martin Powroznik
had been a successful real estate developer on the northwest side. Having
worked in a munitions factory during the World War, he applied the mass
production techniques he had learned there to the business of home building
in the 1920s. Buying up low-priced vacant land beyond the "frontier" of
settlement and transportation on the northwest side, he built over one thousand homes in the 1920s. By sponsoring local improvement clubs and by
offering an annual hundred-dollar prize for the best garden in each development, Powroznik encouraged the buyers of his homes to help improve their

raw subdivision environment. He gained his first experience of political action
by leading his home buyers in agitation for the extension of city streetcar or
bus lines to his new developments. This campaign was successful in 1930,
when the city extended feeder bus lines into the furthest reaches of the northwest side.[11]

The onset of depression brought difficult times to actual and prospective
homeowners of the northwest side Polonia, endangering Powroznik's business. The homeowners sought tax relief to help them save their homes; and
late in 1931, the county judge, Edmund K. Jarecki, came to their aid by
invalidating the entire 1928 and 1929 county tax assessment. As in most
American cities, valuable downtown property was scandalously underassessed
while small homeowners bore the brunt of taxation. In explaining his decision, Judge Jarecki stated: "The public has lost all confidence in the present
setup of the taxing machinery in Cook County. They have seen examples of
complete and absolute discrimination for a favored few." The state supreme
court, however, overruled Judge Jarecki, and the 1928–29 tax rolls remained
intact. The homeowners also pressured the politicians for a mortgage foreclosure moratorium. The state legislature passed such a law, but Governor
Henry Horner vetoed it in July 1933.[12]

Frustrated on both these fronts, Powroznik and others organized in
1933 the United Home Owners of Illinois, a taxpayers' lobby composed
mainly of Polish-Americans from the northwest side. The homeowners
directed their fire on the county assessor's office. The county's Board of Tax
Appeals finally took a hard look at the assessment rolls in early 1934 and
ordered the 1932 rolls reduced 15 percent across the board. These cuts were
later extended to 1933 and 1934. When the county assessor refused to carry
out the board's order, Judge Jarecki again acted, issuing a court order to com-
pel compliance. The Hearst newspapers in Chicago, which had joined the fight
on the side of the "little fellow" in Cook County, estimated that this decision
saved four hundred thousand small homeowners six million dollars in taxes.[13]

Powroznik's United Home Owners, claiming twenty thousand members
with real estate equities of twenty million dollars, continued to protest the
very real threat of foreclosures and denounced the maladministration of the
Federal Home Owners' Loan Corporation in the area. When in 1935 the
Kelly-Nash machine overlooked Polish candidates in slating for the top city
offices, Powroznik combined ethnic resentment with the still smoldering
fears of the homeowners and ran his own slate in the primary.

In the two years since Powroznik's United Home Owners had been organized, however, the HOLC home loan program had finally begun to take effect. The homeowners' fears were no longer strong enough to base an entire campaign on them. Powroznik, therefore, emphasized the issue which had first brought him into politics, transportation. He called for the replacement of streetcars with motor buses, for a five-cent fare, and for public ownership of transportation by the city.

In all the Polish wards except one, the insurgent slate pulled at least 25 percent of the vote, with highs of 46.59 and 43.69 percent in the heavily Polish and homeowning Thirty-third and Thirty-fifth wards (Avondale and Cragin). Most of Powroznik's forty thousand votes must have been cast by Polish-Americans, for he drew practically no support at all outside the "Polish corridors" of the city. After the primary, Powroznik had a conference in the mayor's office to make his peace; and a few weeks later both Kelly and Powroznik addressed a mass meeting of small homeowners to ratify the reconciliation. Polonia, of course, had little choice in the general election and closed ranks behind Kelly; but Powroznik and a few others were not truly reconciled. In 1936 he managed the unsuccessful campaign of another Polish real estate agent for Illinois secretary of state on the Union Progressive ticket.[14]

This short-lived revolt of Polish homeowners in Chicago was not an isolated phenomenon during the depression. Taxpayers' or ratepayers' associations in middle-class areas banded homeowners together in many cities to protect their homes and their hard-won middle-class status. The United Home Owners of Illinois was more ethnically based than some other groups, but Polonia had strong reasons for outrage. Besides their general dissatisfaction with a lack of recognition in city government, Polish-Americans also had a strong homeowning drive which the depression was frustrating.[15]

As early as 1886, American observers noted the Chicago Pole's strong urge to buy land and a home of his own. A study of Polish homeowners in the thirties indicated that it took, on the average, eighteen years' residence in the city for a Pole to buy his first home. This means that, on the eve of the depression, the great bulk of prewar Polish immigrants would already own a home or else be on the verge of buying one. One set of estimates indicates that in 1928 over thirty-three thousand Polish families were homeowners. Most of these homes were in the rapidly expanding "bungalow belts" on the northwest and southwest sides of the city. Block after block of nearly uniform brick bungalows on small, neatly kept lots advanced into the surrounding Chicago prairie. Ownership of property brought feelings of pride, security, and status

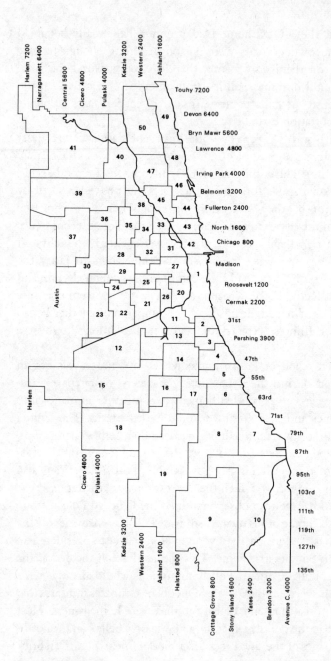

Map 5. Chicago ward boundaries,
1931–1941

TABLE 25   DEMOCRATIC PRIMARY ELECTION RETURNS
            (IN PERCENTAGES): MAYOR, 1935

Ward	No. of Polish Precincts	Kelly	Powroznik
7th			
Polish vote	7	65.30	33.64
Ward average		87.25	8.62
10th			
Polish vote	7	60.41	37.57
Ward average		80.71	15.89
11th			
Polish vote	8	72.89	26.40
Ward average		89.86	9.14
12th			
Polish vote	3	59.58	37.77
Ward average		68.64	27.13
13th			
Polish vote	4	86.86	12.67
Ward average		90.74	6.00
14th			
Polish vote	4	69.75	29.58
Ward average		88.05	10.58
21st			
Polish vote	5	74.20	25.14
Ward average		81.70	14.76
22nd			
Polish vote	2	59.82	38.80
Ward average		85.15	11.81
26th			
Polish vote	10	69.55	29.81
Ward average		76.61	22.54
32nd			
Polish vote	14	65.52	33.39
Ward average		69.87	28.41
33rd			
Polish vote	8	51.99	46.59
Ward average		69.20	26.54
35th			
Polish vote	15	54.78	43.69
Ward average		64.26	32.40
City-wide			
Polish vote	87	64.45	34.34
City average		88.83	7.39

to Polonia; and the meticulous upkeep of these houses and lawns reflected the sense of pride. Any threat to this new security was bitterly resisted by the bungalow dwellers, and Powroznik's United Home Owners was one manifestation of such resistance.[16]

Much later, during the prosperity of the post–World War II period, taxpayers' associations often underwent a revival. The threat which these later groups fought was not usually foreclosure but social change, defined differently by circumstances in each city. In Chicago in the fifties and sixties, the social change which small homeowners feared most was racial "invasion" of a stable neighborhood. Many ad-hoc groups of taxpayers have organized in recent years to resist racial change, and Polish-Americans on the northwest and southwest sides have often been prominent in them. Like the earlier groups fighting the assessor and the creditor, these groups have entered politics, many of them affiliating with George Wallace's American Independent party or else backing local candidates to city council and legislature. In Polonia's capital, Powroznik's group in the thirties can be seen as a forerunner of this recent movement. In the depression the homeowners' movement spoke of economic threat and ethnic assertiveness, whereas today the rhetoric stresses racial fear and ethnic assertiveness. But the two insurgencies manifest the same underlying principle, the "bungalow mentality"—defense of property as a symbol of security and status for the group and the individual in America.

Thus the bungalow mentality first surfaced as a leading issue in Polonia's capital in Martin Powroznik's quixotic challenge to Mayor Kelly. It was basically a new incarnation of the personal-liberty issue, stripped of its associations with liquor and prohibition. Defense of the bungalow was seen as defense of a basic American liberty.[17]

The new issue, however, could only be fought out within the Democratic party. Polonia's capital had been solidly Democratic since the days of Carter Harrison I; but during the age of Harrison and especially in the Thompson era, the Republicans were still a possible alternative if the Democrats ignored an issue of fundamental importance to Polonia. Thus many Polish voters defected to the Republicans on the personal-liberty issue in 1927. But when Thompson destroyed this alternative and the Democratic machine consolidated its hold on Chicago, Polish-American dissent could only manifest itself in intraparty quarreling and in party primaries.

The depression threat to the small homeowner in the early thirties aroused significant dissent among Polish Democrats, but the threat was too vague and unfocused and could not be tied specifically to the leaders of the machine. So Martin Powroznik's challenge within the party foundered in 1935.

An even more fundamental issue, the desire for ethnic recognition, caused greater dissent among Polish Democrats and posed a potentially grave challenge to the machine. In fact, this issue underlay so much of the political history of Polish-Americans from the First World War on that it merits extensive, separate treatment. But as we shall see in the following chapters, the Democrats weathered this storm as well, and Polonia's capital remained an integral part of the Democratic machine in Chicago.

V Polish-American Power: Hopes and Realities

The period between the two world wars was the most critical phase in Polonia's history, the period of hyphenated Americanism. Nativist demands for Americanization put external pressures on Polish-Americans; but the most important pressure was generated within Polonia itself, in the self-image of Polish-Americans.

Before the First World War, the Polonia newspapers had always identified its readers as "We Poles" (*My Polacy*), "Poles in America." The majority in Polonia were not yet American citizens, took no part in American politics, and thought of themselves still as transatlantic citizens of Poland. But at the end of the war, with Poland liberated from the partitioning powers, most inhabitants of Polonia realized that they no longer wished to return to their homeland. They had established roots in the New World, their children were becoming Americans in fact as well as in name, and the pressures of 100 percent Americanism were forcing them to define their loyalties. So, for the majority, Poland became merely a nostalgic memory. Naturalization proceeded rapidly, Polonia's participation in politics increased, and the term "Polish-American" replaced "Poles in America."

The hyphenated term accurately reflected both the status and the self-image of Polonia in the interwar period. Polish-Americans were suspended in a state of maximum tension between a Polish past they had largely rejected and an American future they were not yet able to grasp fully. The passage of time, the gradual dying-off of the immigrant generation, and rapid material advance in America largely resolved the tension after the Second World War and made Polonia's residents, for the most part, simply "Americans of Polish descent." But during the interwar period, a divided self-image was fundamental to Polish-American life.

American politics in Polonia had reflected this divided self-image even before the First World War. Ethnic politics is always a function of hyphenization. Participants in politics before the First World War had been Polish-Americans before their time, and practitioners of ethnic politics after the Second World War were Polish-American survivals. But during the interwar period, nearly all of Polonia was Polish-American.

Polonia politics was dominated by the struggle to find a place for this hyphenated group in the American system. "Recognition" became the political watchword. Like black Americans today, Polish-Americans in the twenties and thirties sought recognition and acceptance of their collective power and importance in America. But this very desire for recognition implied that they still saw themselves as distinct from the American mass. This distinctness proved a disadvantage in pluralist politics, making it difficult to build alliances with other groups.

The drive for recognition, the attempt to attain acceptance and yet retain distinctiveness, the search for an appropriate means of achieving Polish-American power form the scenario of American politics in Polonia's capital between the two world wars. Polish-Americans gained some recognition but very little power. A lack of skillful political brokers who could form coalitions with other groups constituted their major limitation in American politics.

14 A Changing Polonia

By the end of the First World War, Chicago's Polonia had become a sizable part of America's second city, counting 318,338 residents (first- and second-generation) in a city of 2,700,000 (11.8 percent of this total). Among the foreign-born, Poland's 137,611 formed the largest single group in the city.[1]

In the postwar years, Polonia continued to expand along the lines established earlier in the century. On the northwest side, many moved straight west from Polish Downtown to the Cragin community, around St. Stanislaus Bishop and Martyr Church. By 1930 they formed roughly a quarter of that neighborhood's population. Many others migrated along the Milwaukee Avenue corridor, filling one-third of Avondale's population by 1930 and then fanning out in smaller clusters into the new neighborhoods on the far northwest. Seven Polish parishes had already been established before 1918 in Cragin, Avondale, and the neighborhoods beyond; in the postwar period, Polish Catholics founded only one additional church in this area, St. Thecla, in Norwood Park, Chicago's farthest northwest corner.

On the West Side, the area around the old church of St. Adalbert continued to fill with Polish settlers; and migration westward to the city limits, along with the Czechs and Italians, continued. On the far southern fringe of the city, another of Polonia's original communities, the South Chicago steel district, became about 40 percent Polish by the 1920s. Poles then spread out to the smaller manufacturing and residential districts of the booming Calumet area immediately south and west of the steel mills.

The one area of Polonia not pioneered before the war lay on the southwest side of the city, at the far end of the Archer Avenue corridor. Polish settlers had expanded out from Bridgeport and the yards district into McKinley Park and Brighton Park, but settlement had halted at the Santa Fe railroad tracks, running north and south between Kedzie and Crawford avenues. Be-

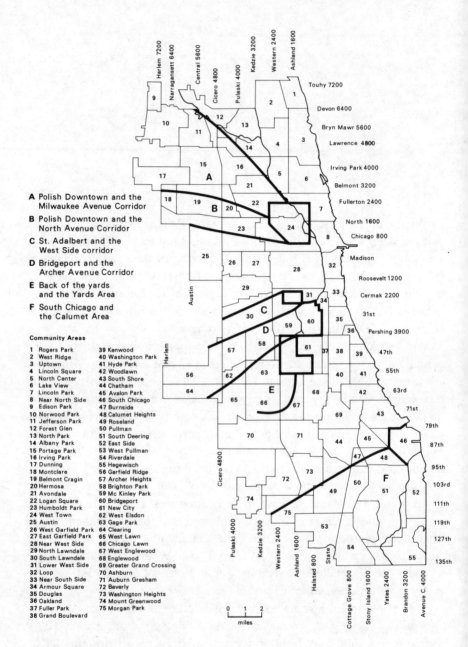

A Polish Downtown and the
Milwaukee Avenue Corridor

B Polish Downtown and the
North Avenue Corridor

C St. Adalbert and the
West Side corridor

D Bridgeport and the
Archer Avenue Corridor

E Back of the yards
and the Yards Area

F South Chicago and
the Calumet Area

Community Areas

1 Rogers Park	39 Kenwood
2 West Ridge	40 Washington Park
3 Uptown	41 Hyde Park
4 Lincoln Square	42 Woodlawn
5 North Center	43 South Shore
6 Lake View	44 Chatham
7 Lincoln Park	45 Avalon Park
8 Near North Side	46 South Chicago
9 Edison Park	47 Burnside
10 Norwood Park	48 Calumet Heights
11 Jefferson Park	49 Roseland
12 Forest Glen	50 Pullman
13 North Park	51 South Deering
14 Albany Park	52 East Side
15 Portage Park	53 West Pullman
16 Irving Park	54 Riverdale
17 Dunning	55 Hegewisch
18 Montclare	56 Garfield Ridge
19 Belmont Cragin	57 Archer Heights
20 Hermosa	58 Brighton Park
21 Avondale	59 Mc Kinley Park
22 Logan Square	60 Bridgeport
23 Humboldt Park	61 New City
24 West Town	62 West Elsdon
25 Austin	63 Gage Park
26 West Garfield Park	64 Clearing
27 East Garfield Park	65 West Lawn
28 Near West Side	66 Chicago Lawn
29 North Lawndale	67 West Englewood
30 South Lawndale	68 Englewood
31 Lower West Side	69 Greater Grand Crossing
32 Loop	70 Ashburn
33 Near South Side	71 Auburn Gresham
34 Armour Square	72 Beverly
35 Douglas	73 Washington Heights
36 Oakland	74 Mount Greenwood
37 Fuller Park	75 Morgan Park
38 Grand Boulevard	

Map 6. Polish residential boundaries in
Chicago, 1930

TABLE 26   POPULATION OF CHICAGO's POLISH NEIGHBORHOODS, 1930

Community Name and Community Area Number	Total Population	Estimated Polish Population and % of Total	Other Prominent Nationalities, %
Bridgeport (60)	53,553	14,878 (28)	Lithuanian, 17
Brighton Park-McKinley Park (58, 59)	68,584	24,998 (36)	Lithuanian, 13 German, 11
South Chicago-Hegewisch (46, 55)	64,573	27,646 (43)	German, 5 Swedish, 4
Back of the Yards (61)	87,103	29,130 (33)	German, 8 Irish, 10 Czech, 10 Lithuanian, 6
St. Adalbert's (31)	66,198	20,517 (31)	Czech, 22 Yugoslav, 9 Lithuanian, 9
Far Southwest Side (56, 57, 62)	17,031	7,191 (42)	Czech, 9 Italian, 9 Lithuanian, 5
Polish Downtown (24)	187,292	91,697 (49)	Italian, 10 Russian (Jewish), 9
Far Northwest Side (9, 10, 11, 12, 13, 14, 15, 16, 17, 18, 19, 20, 21, 22)	516,495	89,707 (17)	German, 18 Russian (Jewish), 6 Swedish, 5
City-wide	3,376,438	401,316 (12)	German, 11 Scandinavian, 7 Italian, 5 Russian (Jewish), 5 Irish, 5 Czech, 4 Lithuanian, 2

Source: Ernest W. Burgess and Charles Newcomb, Census Data of the City of Chicago, 1930 (Chicago: University of Chicago Press, 1933), pp. 626-35.

yond lay open prairie, broken only by frequent railroad tracks. After the war, Chicago's population pushed new residential subdivisions into this area. Its remoteness caused the first settlers, including about two hundred Polish families, to nickname it "The Sticks." In a few years, others pushed even farther west to the vicinity of the city's new Midway Airport. By 1930 the area west of the Santa Fe tracks, virtually empty a decade earlier, contained 17,031 people, including 7,191 Poles (42 percent of the total).

This extension of the Archer corridor and the population growth elsewhere in the city caused the last parish-building boom in Chicago's Polonia. Altogether seven new Polish parishes were established, and one old church in Polish Downtown was transferred from the Germans to the Poles and renamed St. Szczepan. This brought the total number of Polish parishes in the city to forty-four and largely completed the physical expansion of Polonia. The five original Polish villages in Chicago had opened out into six definable but open-ended geographical regions: the Milwaukee Avenue corridor, the North Avenue corridor (through Humbodlt Park and Cragin), the west side corridor (between the Sanitary Canal and the Burlington tracks), the Archer Avenue corridor, the yards district, and the Calumet area. Certainly some Polish-Americans moved outside these corridors; but when they did, they did not form Polish parishes, and they were, for the most part, no longer a part of Polonia in any meaningful sense. By 1930 Chicago's Poles numbered 401,316; and over 80 percent of them lived within the six major corridors of Polonia. The Polish residential index of dissimilarity by community areas was still a relatively high .55.[2]

As Polonia expanded, its citizens developed a greater economic and emotional stake in Chicago. Although the majority of Chicago Poles were still common laborers or salaried workers, in the prosperous 1920s over ten thousand Polish-Americans owned business or commercial establishments. Taken as a whole, Polonia's business worth in Chicago was estimated in 1928 as $29 million, the value of its church and school buildings stood at nearly $25 million, and 33,767 Polish families had sunk $389 million into private homes.[3]

Before the First World War, many American Poles had said that if only Poland were free and independent they would return in an instant. At the end of the war, the instant arrived. The Polish National Alliance, which had long worked for Poland's liberation and had contended all the while that America's Polonia was merely the "fourth province of Poland," changed its

position when the Polish state was finally established. The Alliance proclaimed to its members the need for a choice:

Until there was a Polish homeland, we had to defend ourselves with hands
and feet against those who wished to denationalize us wherever they might be.
Today, however, a Polish homeland exists. Thus every one of us must
presently decide whether he wishes to return to Poland and thus remain a
Pole, or whether he wishes to live out his life in the land of Washington and
thus not only become, heart and soul, an American, but also raise his children
in this spirit, for their own good. There is no middle ground.[4]

Few chose Poland. In the four years immediately after the war, approximately ninety-six thousand Poles out of the millions in America re-
emigrated to the Republic of Poland. Many were disillusioned upon arrival,
finding, not the Poland of their dreams, but a poor country, ravaged by war,
disease, starvation, and internal dissension. Some consciously sought to
"Americanize" the new Poland by introducing American machinery, building
techniques, and technical know-how. One group of returning emigrants
summed up the mood in homely fashion, "We will put in every house an
American bath tub." But the great majority stayed in America, and even
some who had returned in the postwar flush of excitement eventually emigrated once again to the New World.[5]

Polonia's leaders began adjusting to the new realities of the postwar
period and trying to work out a new self-image for the community. Increasingly, the term "Polish-Americans" replaced "We Poles" in the press. Despite the PNA's brave call for a choice between Poland and America, many still
felt that some middle ground was necessary. John Smulski, in a speech "On
the Position of the Polish Community in the USA" at the Polish Emigration
Congress in 1925, tried to sketch out his idea of the proper relations between
Poland and its migrants:

England, a small country, which contains within its borders no more
inhabitants than Poland, is probably the most powerful nation in the world
and the British nation dominates the world because its people are conscious
of their heritage and have respect for their blood. The emigrants of Great
Britain are its strength. Its sons are in every corner of the world, giving
allegiance to the government under whose jurisdiction they live, but remem-
bering their origin and understanding and conscientiously paying back what
they owe their nation.[6]

This loose and inaccurate historical analogy proved of little use, and the
problem of Polonia's self-definition remained.

A survey taken in Buffalo in the 1920s indicates that the younger generation was well ahead of its elders in accepting a new self-image. Only 7 percent of the second generation surveyed considered themselves Poles, 39 percent Polish-Americans, and 54 percent simply Americans. The same survey found that 100 percent of those asked could identify George Washington and Abraham Lincoln but only 86 percent knew who Kosciuszko was. While a mere 52.6 percent could identify Joseph Pilsudski, at that time president of Poland, 80.6 percent recognized the name of Babe Ruth.[7]

But if Polonia had turned away from Poland (its youth more clearly than its elders) and if the Polonia leaders were unable to clarify theoretically their new position in America, the institutions of a distinct Polish-American community still existed. The major older organizations like the Polish National Alliance and the Polish Roman Catholic Union remained strong and active. The PNA's naturalization and Americanization classes experienced a great vogue immediately after the war and remained one of the main activities of the local member associations for many years. Yet there was ambiguity and uncertainty in the old-line organizations' actions. While stressing the need for Americanization to its own members, the PNA still spoke out forcefully that it was "unalterably opposed to forced Americanization," and that "every such move in that direction will receive the treatment it deserves." Still proclaiming the need to bring up children as good Americans, both the PNA and the PRCU painfully felt the necessity of instilling some appreciation of their Polish heritage in the younger generation. Thus, the PRCU instituted a special youth department in 1928 to recruit the younger residents of Polonia, and the PNA set up a Polish Boy Scout organization and arranged trips to Poland for outstanding scouts.[8]

Three Polish daily papers survived the decade of the 1920s with healthy circulations, but they found it necessary to print more features in English and to present "American" innovations like comic strips and a sports page. The Polish parochial schools reached their high point both in number of schools and in students enrolled in 1930, and many Polish high schools were also founded in the twenties and thirties. Similarly, the Congregation of the Resurrection, Polonia's leading religious order, enjoyed its greatest boom in religious vocations in the 1930s. Although Poland had been left behind, Polish-American institutions were trying to adapt and, for the time being, were still flourishing.[9]

Polonia even fashioned a wide range of new organizations to accommodate the changes in community life. Professional groups, growing more numerous in the twenties and thirties, formed their own associations, such as the Polish Lawyers' Society and the Polish Teachers' Club; and some educated citizens gathered together in cultural societies like the Polish Arts Club and the Polish-American Historical Society. Numerous ad-hoc groups sprang up for various kinds of group defense or advancement. Martin Powroznik's United Home Owners is a good example; but businessmen, government employees, and others occasionally organized in this way as well.[10]

One organization, the Chicago Society, illustrates particularly well both the aspirations and the frustrations of Polonia at this time. The Chicago Society was originally founded in 1912 as a local affiliate of the Polish National Alliance; but, in the early twenties, its leaders broke off from the PNA and attempted to make the society an independent organization of Polish-American professional men. The society envisioned two broad goals for itself: enhancement of ethnic solidarity and the winning of greater recognition for outstanding Polish-Americans. In many ways it was carrying on the traditional work of Polish-American organizations, attempting to realize the Polonia ideal by drawing together the fragmented Polish communities in Chicago. It even sent out organizers to other major cities with large Polish populations. They established Cleveland, Milwaukee, Buffalo, and Detroit societies on the same model, hoping to encourage large, active cells throughout Polonia.

But in its emphasis on professional people, its complete divorce from church influence, and its breach from the established PNA affiliation, the Chicago Society was clearly trying to chart a new course. The society published its own weekly newspaper, containing commentary on current business, social, and political affairs, and eventually built its own hall on Humboldt Boulevard, which was also used by other cultural and professional groups founded in the twenties. The society's membership reached a high point of five hundred, including many of the most influential Chicago Poles.

A former president of the society, in reminiscing about its history, stated that the numerous Negro organizations of the present day which are striving for black power and recognition remind him of the early militance of his organization. However, Polish-Americans did not attain the degree of unity that blacks have been forced to maintain. The Chicago Society was unsuccessful in wielding any influence in the city as a whole, and it eventually reestablished a tie with the PNA and became just another local member association of that organization.[11]

Race prejudice exerts an external pressure which reinforces the black ideal of strength in unity. It excludes blacks from the larger American society, but it can have the side effect of strengthening black pride and helping define the black self-image. However, the nativist ideology of 100 percent Americanism in the 1920s could dissipate as well as strengthen the comparable Polonia ideal of strength in unity; for it held out the path of assimilation as an alternative to group power. Thus the Polonia ideal was never fully realized. Just when the Polish-American community's potential for leadership and solidarity was greatest, in the interwar period, it began dissolving into the surrounding American society. The Polish press was full of denunciations of professional people who abandoned Polonia, joining city-wide, nonethnic professional associations instead of the Chicago Society or the Polish Lawyers' Society.

The Chicago Society itself felt the tensions of a divided self-image, of a suspension between two cultures, of an ambivalence between the desires for acceptance and for distinctiveness. Founded to unite professionals with a sense of Polish identity, it held its meetings initially in Chicago's Loop at the Masonic Temple, raising many Polish eyebrows and perhaps alienating some potential members. At election eve dinners, organized to inform leading Polish-Americans, the table fare was invariably corned beef and cabbage, not *kielbasa z kapusta*.

The Chicago Society typified the dilemma of Polonia's capital in the crucial years of rapid change between the World Wars. Expanding in size, wealth, and attachment to America, Polonia's capital wished to unify and strengthen itself to wield power and influence in the city. But the Chicago Society and the other leaders of Polonia's capital never decided whether to seek power as *Polish*-Americans or as Polish-*Americans*. In this unresolved dilemma lay the further failure of Polish-American politics and of group power in Chicago.

15 The Drive for Recognition

Polonia's turning away from the old country at the end of World War I, when the politics of Poland had finally borne fruit, meant a consequently increased interest in American politics. The church party of PRCU, *Dziennik Chicagoski,* and the Resurrectionist Fathers had always participated actively in politics, but now even the PNA realized it could no longer remain aloof. One of the Alliance's annual congresses declared:

In regard to politics in this country the Alliance is a sleeping giant and its ostrich position . . . is calling forth in important American circles the impression of passivity and indifference in very important matters. . . . These congresses have decided that the PNA ought to take part in the political life of this country.[1]

The most important result of increased political interest was a drive for greater recognition of Polish-Americans in politics. The urge to get ahead in the political arena, of course, was not a new one. Even before the war, the Polish press had frequently called for more representatives on the city council and in other political bodies. There is no identifiable point in time when the recognition drive was "proclaimed." But with the change in attitudes toward Poland and America after 1918, progress in American politics became more urgent. At election times in the twenties and thirties, Chicago's Polish press was filled with evidence of a heightened drive for recognition. Polonia had finally made up its mind that it was coming inside American society, and politics was one doorway that now needed to be swung wide open.[2]

The drive for recognition became more organized in the postwar period than it had been previously. Not only did the Polish press keep hammering on the theme, but delegations of Polish politicians made annual pilgrimages to the Democratic leader's office, demanding more representation on the ticket. Stanley Kunz, never the retiring type, practically terrorized the county central committee into slating additional Polish candidates. And in the early 1930s, a city-wide organization of Polish-American Democrats came into being to act as an ethnic lobby within the party. Though most of the efforts of the recognition drive were focused on the Democrats, the Thompson Republicans in the 1920s gave Polish-Americans more attention than any previous Republicans had, thus temporarily drawing some Polish voters out of the Democratic fold. Certainly Thompson's pledge to make "City Hall the capitol of Poland" in the 1927 election attracted many of the recognition-conscious.

The drive for greater recognition was not confined to politics. Practically as soon as Polish Catholics had begun to organize parishes in America, they had begun agitating for representation in the local hierarchy of the Catholic church. In 1908 the first Polish-American bishop, Paul Rhode from South Chicago, was appointed an auxiliary of the Chicago archdiocese; but this milestone hardly satisfied Polonia. During and after the First World War, George Cardinal Mundelein, Chicago's strong-willed bishop, little interested in Polish-Americans and hostile to ethnic parishes in general, so irritated Chicago's Polish priests that in 1917 they organized the Polish Clergy Association. Under Reverend Louis Grudzinski of St. John of God Parish, this association pushed for greater consideration of Polish Catholic interests.[3]

Polish-Americans sought success in many other fields as well and exulted whenever one of their own became famous. The Polish press never failed to feature the triumphs of actress Pola Negri in Hollywood or the gridiron heroics of Bronco Nagurski at the University of Minnesota. But the Polish drive for recognition was focused mainly on the Democratic party and the Catholic church, for those were the two dominant insitutions in the America which most Poles were trying to enter. In Chicago, both were run by the Irish, with a little help from the Germans. To be accepted in Chicago, the citizens of Polonia's capital needed participation in and recognition by the leadership of both these institutions.

In politics, the recognition drive attempted to provide two types of satisfaction for Polonia's citizens. One was psychological, a sense of pride and prestige, a feeling of belonging, of being an insider, of having influence; the other was economic—politics meant jobs. Prestige came, for the most part, from gaining elective office or significant appointive postion (high-level patronage); whereas the vast number of clerical and laboring jobs in government bureaus (low-level patronage) provided the bulk of economic rewards. Above all, the final goal of politics was the gaining of power; so the ultimate aim of the recognition drive was to wield political influence in Polonia's interest.

At the end of the First World War, Chicago's Polonia had some reason to take pride in the range of elective offices which Polish-Americans had attained. A list of political "firsts" would read like this: first Polish alderman, A. J. Kowalski, 1888; first state senator, Stanley Kunz, 1902; first city-wide office, Peter Kiolbassa, treasurer, 1891; first state-wide office, John Smulski, treasurer, 1906; first judge, Joseph S. LaBuy, 1912. There was no reason for complacency, however; most of these attainments had been short-lived. In 1919 no Polish-American held a significant city, state, or county office; there were still only two Polish judges in Chicago; and few Polish candidates were slated to run for office by either party.

Particularly galling was the lack of a Polish representative in Congress. Polonia's capital felt humiliated when, in 1918, Milwaukee's much smaller Polish community elected America's first Polish-American congressman, John C. Kleczka. Thus in 1920 attention focused on the congressional races in the Eighth District, where Stanley Kunz, the Sixteenth Ward alderman and longtime Democratic boss, was running, and the Fourth District, around the stockyards, where the Polish candidate was John Golombiewski, a former Republican alderman. The *Dziennik Zwiazkowy* berated Polonia for the "political immaturity" which had denied it a congressional representative previously and exhorted it to "storm a new outpost."[4]

By any ordinary political standard, Polonia's capital should have had a congressman long before. The northwest side's Eighth District contained almost the whole of Polish Downtown, and Poles were the dominant group in the constituency. In at least two other districts, around the stockyards and on the West Side, Polish voters formed a sizable minority. As early as 1904 Stanley Kunz had staked out the Eighth District seat as his own; and since the district was heavily Polish and heavily Democratic, he would have had little trouble getting elected under normal circumstances. When Kunz was involved, however, circumstances were seldom normal.

The Eighth District seat had already been claimed by another Democrat early in 1904, none other than Preston Harrison, the mayor's brother. When Harrison first announced his candidacy, Kunz, who at the time was Sixteenth Ward alderman as well as a state senator, was expected to back him. But in June, senator-alderman Kunz decided to challenge Harrison and try to add a third title to his name. A long-simmering resentment at what he con-

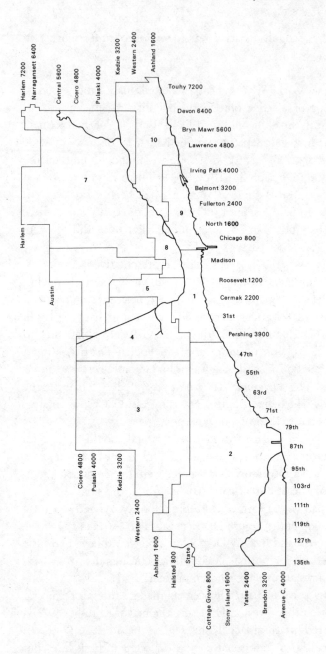

Map 7. Congressional districts in Chicago,
1920

sidered lack of attention from Mayor Harrison, as well as a desire to prove his strength to reformers and journalists who were constantly attacking him, were the probable motives behind his challenge. There were as yet no direct primaries in Illinois where Kunz could test his strength, though; and at the district convention which made the party nominations, the Harrison forces crushed Kunz by almost a two-to-one margin. Stanley took his revenge in the general election by throwing the contest to Preston Harrison's Republican opponent. More than 50 percent of the district's Polish votes went Republican at Kunz's instigation, and thus this normally Democratic district defeated Harrison by over seven thousand votes.[5]

Two years later, Kunz and Preston Harrison went at it again, with a similar, but reverse, result. Kunz organized his supporters at the convention and defeated Harrison for the nomination, but then it was the Harrisons' turn to knife their own party's candidate. Kunz ran strongly in all the Polish precincts, but enough votes were turned over to the opposition in the rest of the district to defeat him by a hairline margin of eighty-five votes. The Republican incumbent enjoyed a second term, representing the cannibalistic Democrats in the Eighth District.[6]

In the next election year both Preston Harrison and Stanley Kunz withdrew from the battle, and the Democrats put up an Irishman, Thomas Gallagher, for the congressional seat. Polish hopes of representation switched to the Republicans, who, under the influence of Governor Deneen and his friend John Smulski, nominated Philip Ksycki, an officer of the Polish National Alliance. The Alliance papers, naturally, campaigned hard for Ksycki, observing just before election day:

It would certainly be a bad joke, if, in a Polish district, we elected an Irishman. The Irish already have in Congress around one hundred of their countrymen, and we do not have one. The first Polish bishop in America and the first Polish congressman [Paul Rhode had just been named bishop]—what an honor for the whole Polish people this year.

But the Eighth District continued to be a bad joke for Polonia. Gallagher won by more than one thousand votes. Polish-Americans gave a majority of their votes to Ksycki, but they did not defect from their ordinary party allegiance in the massive numbers necessary to elect him.[7]

With a Democrat in the congressional seat, Stanley Kunz's chances diminished, for the incumbent gained regular party backing for reelection in the following years. Still, Kunz continued trying for the seat, runnng in the direct primaries which were instituted after 1910; but factionalism continued to dog his attempts. For instance, in 1914, Kunz challenged Gallagher but was himself opposed by John Czekala, a Polish Harrisonite. In this three-way battle, the Polish vote split down the middle and Gallagher was re-nominated, even though the combined vote of the two Polish candidates was more than his. Such factionalism kept the Poles back even when Kunz was not involved. In the 1916 primary, Gallagher again won over a divided field, this time made up of six candidates, including two Poles, Z. H. Kadów and N. L. Piotrowski. The combined vote of the two Polish candidates exceeded Gallagher's total, but to no avail.[8]

In other districts, luck was no better. In the Fifth District on the West Side, A. J. Sabath, the Jewish leader of the Eleventh Ward, had firmly en-sconced himself in the congressional seat which he was to hold until 1950. Though Sabath gave the Poles comparatively full participation in his ward organization, all hope of going to Congress in that district was gone. In the stockyards area of the Fourth District, John Golombiewski made repeated tries for Congress, but he was hindered by his Republican affiliation, the Poles' minority position, and his own lackluster record. By the last years of the second decade, Polish newspapers were lamenting that no Polish-American was yet in Congress to speak up for Poland and Polonia during the momentous war years.[9]

The reasons for the failure of Polonia's capital to elect a congressman throughout these years are instructive, for they apply to other Polish-American political efforts as well. Paradoxically, both factionalism and a bloc vote hindered the congressional drive. The bloc Democratic tendencies of Polonia made the election of Philip Ksycki or John Golombiewski or any other Polish Republican extremely difficult. Polish voters would switch parties in an important election but usually not in sufficient numbers to make a difference. But if the Polish vote was too monolithic from the Republicans' point of view, for Polish Democrats it was often too fragmented. When an important office was at stake, several Poles would jump into the fray on the Democratic side instead of uniting on a single Polish candidate. The ethnic solidarity which most Polonia leaders either advocated fervently or at least paid lip service to was often lacking.[10]

Finally, in 1920 Chicago's Polonia elected a congressman, and another first could be added to the recognition list. Though Golombiewski lost again in the Fourth District, Stanley Kunz won the long coveted Eighth District seat. The local Democrats were so demoralized by the death of Roger Sullivan and the gloomy national political prospects that no one but Kunz challenged

Thomas Gallagher in the party primary that year. Kunz won the two-way race easily; then with the full strength of the party and the Polish community for once united behind him, he also won in the general election, practically the only Democratic victor in the whole city that year of the Republican landslide. A few years before, Polonia might have wanted a representative in Washington to deal with weighty matters of state concerning Poland's place in the new Europe; but by 1920 Kunz's election had mainly symbolic value. In any case, the new congressman was more interested in furthering the recognition drive back home than in attending to dull routine in Washington.

One of the victims of the 1920 landslide, Judge Edmund K. Jarecki, defeated for reelection to the municipal court bench, soon proved to be the vehicle for the next big recognition drive by Polonia's capital. Early in 1922, when the Democratic leaders met to arrange that year's county ticket, many Polish politicians began talking themselves up for new offices. A situation presented itself in the committee which allowed them some success. Roger Sullivan's successor as head of the county Democrats, George E. Brennan, did not yet have a firm grip on the organization. Michael Igoe, James Dailey, and several other Irish rivals were fighting many of his choices for the slate. At this juncture Tony Cermak, Stanley Kunz, A. J. Sabath, and other non-Irish Democrats saw a chance to hold back their support as the balance of power between the two Irish factions, thus winning greater representation for their own groups on the ticket. Cermak emerged as candidate for county board president, a position which he won and held throughout the twenties and used as a power base for his later rise to leadership of the whole organization. Kunz nailed down the post of county judge for Edmund Jarecki and five other lesser positions for Polish candidates.[11]

A few years later, in the 1927 city elections, Boss Brennan, by then well aware of the voting strength of Polonia and worried about Thompson's appeals to the ethnic groups, gladly agreed to Polish demands for a candidate on the ticket. He slated M.S. Szymczak, the bright young economics professor who was active in business and politics, for city treasurer. Though Szymczak went down with the Dever ticket, he ran ahead of the mayor; and politicians nearly fell over themselves trying to make a place for him.

Bill Thompson, in a calculated move to detach the popular professor from the Democrats, offered him the post of assistant treasurer in his administration; but Szymczak refused. A year later, he was back on the Democratic ticket, where he was elected chief clerk of the superior court. Another county-wide office had been gained for Polonia, less prestigious than the judgeship,

but rich in patronage and potential influence. When Szymczak resigned this
post to join Mayor Cermak's cabinet in 1931, another Polish Democrat,
Frank Zintak, succeeded him. Other Polish-Americans in the next decade
carved out niches for themselves in various medium-level positions in the
county and the state.[12]

While Polish candidates were seeking prestige in elective offices, a
growing supply of low-level patronage offered basic economic satisfactions
to many individuals and, to some extent, a feeling of power and prestige for
the whole community.

Chicago had had a supposedly comprehensive civil service law since
1895, but numerous loopholes existed. Two parallel personnel systems
coexisted in Chicago government. As one city worker remarked to an investigator, "There are two ways to get into city service—by examination or
through ward organization." Many Polish-Americans obtained city jobs
through the second method. The ward boss or precinct captain was nearly
always willing to help a job-seeker, whereas the examination procedure was
slow, forbidding, and difficult for a new American to understand.[13]

In 1915, the last year for which complete city personnel records are
available, only five city departments had more than token numbers of Polish
workers employed: the Board of Election Commissioners, the city attorney's
office, the Bureau of Streets of the Department of Public Works, and the
municipal court clerk's and bailiff's offices.

By far the greatest number of Polish workers for the city in 1915 were
employed by the Department of Public Works, but very few had positions
in the more specialized divisions of the department. For instance, only two
Polish workers were listed as elevator operators, two as construction workers,
and ten as bridge-tenders. Most worked as common laborers for the Bureau
of Streets, hired in work gangs in the individual wards where local bosses
had complete control over the labor flow. The Eighth Ward (South Chicago)
labor force was more than 30 percent Polish, and the workers of the Eleventh
and Twenty-eighth wards (St. Adalbert's and Avondale) were about 35
percent Polish. The Sixteenth Ward in the heart of Polish Downtown employed thirty-three Polish workers in a labor force of fifty-seven, including
three Polish section foremen. The ward superintendent and ward clerk, however, were Irish.[14]

On the eve of the First World War, therefore, Polish-Americans formed
only a small part of Chicago's patronage army. As the recognition drive
gained momentum, however, patronage followed along with it. Whenever a

Polish candidate won an eléctive or high appointive office, he brought many of his countrymen along with him. Judge Jarecki made the Board of Election Commissioners under his jurisdiction a Polish "preserve." When Matt Szymczak gained the post of superior court clerk in 1928, the Polish language became a common sound in the court's corridors. Julius Smietanka, appointed Chicago's internal revenue collector by President Wilson in 1917, brought a number of Polish-Americans into federal service. Republican Anthony Czarnecki was appointed Chicago customs collector by Calvin Coolidge in 1926, thus opening up that bureau to his countrymen. Under Czarnecki and a Polish Democratic successor appointed by the Roosevelt administration, it became well-known that a Polish-American seeking a job in the burgeoning federal bureaucracy would do well to visit the customs house. In 1933, Chicago Polish-Americans in the federal service were numerous enough to form their own organization, called the "Polish Associated Federal Employees."[15]

As Polonia became an increasingly important part of the Democratic machine in the 1930s, Democratic officeholders of other nationalities began hiring Polish-Americans in large numbers. In 1932, for instance, Clayton F. Smith, the county recorder of deeds, employed more Polish-Americans than Frank Zintak did at the superior court; and the sanitary district had almost as many Polish workers as the Board of Election Commissioners.[16]

Incomplete data from Chicago's Civil Service Commission indicate that as many Polish-Americans entered the city's classified service in the 1920s as had done so in the two previous decades combined. Government hiring then dropped off in the depression years, but Polish-Americans entered the civil service in a flood after the Second World War. Although civil service jobs were theoretically immune from political influence, the growing number of Polish voters was by no means an irrelevant factor in obtaining such jobs for Polonia.[17]

The main significance of low-level patronage and civil service jobs was economic. Hundreds of Polish-Americans found jobs, and often careers, in city, county, state, and federal bureaus. After 1920 many Democratic patronage positions were nearly as secure as civil service positions since the Democratic machine had begun its rise to absolute power in Chicago. When Leonard White of the University of Chicago studied the city service in the 1920s, he was impressed with its stability. Most workers told him they had sought jobs from the city because of security. Apparently most of them found it, for White noticed many inefficient or incompetent employees who would never have been carried on the payroll of a corporation. The willingness of party bosses to dole out government jobs to needy voters and the security and stability of these jobs made the patronage machine a surrogate welfare system for many.[18]

Yet the patronage system also had psychological effects on Polonia's residents. An increase in the number of Polish workers in city bureaus gave Polonia some of the same sense of satisfaction and feeling of belonging that the attainment of prestigious offices did. Increasingly, politicians were becoming aware of this; in the 1930s political candidates advertising in the Polish papers began to list the numbers of Polish-Americans who worked for them. There was, apparently, some prestige in numbers.

More subtly, a patronage worker from Polonia or elsewhere, even if he were only a street sweeper or a paper-pusher, felt a dignity which a welfare recipient or even a laborer in a private company lacked. The jobholder put on a white shirt and a tie, or perhaps a uniform, and reported every day to City Hall, the County Building, or the local ward office. No matter how unimportant his job, even if it were make-work, *he* worked for the boss. This psychological plus was important to many in Polonia at the time and even has ramifications today. Now, when welfare systems proliferate and patronage jobs are on the decline, Negroes and Puerto Ricans on welfare are numerous and highly visible. Second- or third-generation Polish-Americans, even those whose uncles or parents may have worked on patronage jobs that were tantamount to welfare, like to pride themselves on the fact that *their* group made it on its own. In fact, no group made it completely on its own. But in the heyday of the political machine, patronage jobs disguised the welfare aid from government, made it more personal and more satisfying, and gave an ego boost to Polish-Americans and other ethnic groups.

Polonia's capital made definite gains during the interwar period in the attainment of both elective and appointive offices. But a fundamental weakness of the recognition drive was its preoccupation with symbolic victories. Polonia leaders spent much time and effort trying to use the power of government to arrange greeting committees for visiting dignitaries from Poland, to appropriate money for statues of Polish heroes, and to declare official days of mourning for prominent Polish-Americans upon their death. The Polish newspapers and leading Polonia organizations continuously, but unsuccessfully, petitioned Congress to declare an annual Casimir Pulaski day. In 1936, on the motion of a Polish alderman, May 3, the anniversary of Poland's ill-fated 1791 constitution, was officially recognized as Polish Constitution Day in Chicago and the mayor's presence was required for a celebration. Ever since then, May 3 has been a gala day in Polonia's capital, marked by a parade and rally at the Kosciuszko statue in Humboldt Park on the northwest side. Not only has the mayor always attended, but in recent years Democratic bigwigs have come from Washington—Robert Kennedy in 1961, Lyndon Johnson in 1963, and Edmund Muskie in 1971.[19]

A seemingly harmless attempt to gain symbolic recognition by renaming a street turned into what might be called the "great Pulaski Road controversy." The naming of streets in Chicago has often had political ramifications. Countless streets were named for various American heroes, and even "foreign" notables were not neglected. For instance, a prominent downtown street became Balbo Drive in the 1920s, after one of Mussolini's supporters, General Italo Balbo. Consequently, recognition-conscious Polonia began a movement to rename a major Chicago street after General Casimir Pulaski. When Anton Cermak became mayor, he seemed favorable to the idea, but nothing was done about it. After Cermak's death, Mrs. A. Emily Napieralski, former president of the Polish Women's Alliance, then serving as civil service commissioner for Cook County, took up leadership of the agitation. She and other Polish leaders demanded that Crawford Avenue, a long north-south street five miles west of the Loop, should be renamed Pulaski Road.

Mayor Kelly, never one to pass up a cheap means of currying favor with the voters, presented a recommendation for the name change to the city council on October 25, 1933, but controversy ensued. Crawford Avenue was a major business street, and many merchants disliked the trouble and expense of changing their stationery and advertisements to the new name. They probably feared that the "foreignness" of the Pulaski Road address might be detrimental to business. So petitions were signed by property owners on Crawford protesting the proposed change. The city council committee responsible for streets and alleys recommended the renaming anyway; but a minority of the committee filed a dissenting report in which these members, though declaring themselves "heartily in accord with the desire to honor General Casimir Pulaski," suggested "as a substitute, that the name of Augusta Boulevard be changed to Pulaski Boulevard." Augusta had few business establishments along it, and it ran through largely immigrant districts, including Polish Downtown. The original proposal won out, however; and on December 12, 1933, Crawford Avenue officially became Pulaski Road.[20]

Yet, amazingly, the issue did not subside. The Crawfordites continued gathering petitions and bombarded Mayor Kelly with protests. Rumors circulated that as much as thirty thousand dollars had been raised as an anti-Pulaski war chest. In reply Polonia formed a committee with the sonorous title "United Societies in Defense of Pulaski Road," which emphasized in its propaganda, not the "Polishness" of Pulaski, but his "Americanness" as a Revolutionary War hero. Mayor Kelly stood firm and the name change was final; though, interestingly, to this day the street is still named Crawford Avenue in the suburbs and then changes abruptly to Pulaski Road at the city limits.[21]

The whole matter seems, today, silly in the extreme; but to Polonia, the fact of such bitter opposition to the name change only reinforced the feeling of rejection, of being outsiders in Chicago, and led to renewed resolve to fight for recognition. Polonia's residents were still self-conscious and often insecure; they knew their image was a negative one in the American mind.

A fund-raising pamphlet from the Gads Hill settlement house near St. Adalbert's church made clear just how negative this image was. The pamphlet, directed to possible business donors, was entitled "Does Stanley Brankowski Work for You?"; and it featured a large picture of a stereotyped "Polak" with a strong back and a dull look in his eyes. The settlement workers stated:

You are familiar with the Stanley Brankowski type. You, your executive division and efficiency men have no doubt found him a perplexing problem. . . . Perhaps you have solved the Stanley problem; but here is the big thought that is worthy of recognition. In three or four years Stanley will direct his children to your employment department. . . . Remember, the environment that has probably effected an influence over these children is centered in some filthy alley. . . . In your community there is a successful organization that is salvaging and enlightening the younger generation. [The Gads Hill Center, naturally.][22]

Symbolic victories, then, like Pulaski Road and Polish Constitution Day were attempts to overcome or compensate for the negative "Stanley" image, to show the power and importance of the Polish community. They were largely hollow victories, however; for they only served to emphasize the group's separateness in Chicago. Anton Cermak had used his leadership of the United Societies for Local Self-Government, an anti-prohibition lobby, as a stepping-stone to power; for it brought him into coalition with many other Chicago ethnic groups. Polonia's United Societies in Defense of Pulaski Road, on the contrary, closed the group in on itself and won it no allies.

Such symbolic victories also deflected Polonia's attention from the basic structure of political power in the Democratic party. The real winner of the Pulaski road controversy was Mayor Kelly. His firm stance in favor of the name change permitted him to act as the Poles' champion without expending any significant political or financial capital and without making any major concession to Polish Democrats in the party organization. Irish ward leaders must have chuckled heartily when Mayor Kelly showed that Polonia could be bought off so cheaply. Polonia's major organizations were quite capable of fighting symbolic publicity battles in the press, but they were unequipped for the more significant forms of political infighting and power-brokering.

For a group that provided so many consistently Democratic votes, Polish Chicago was woefully weak in the basic positions of influence on the Democratic county committee—the ward and township committeemen. The two wards of Polish Downtown had generally had Polish committeemen since the early days of the century, but in 1920 these were still the only two such wards in the city. The weakness of the Polish position in the party was vividly illustrated in 1923 when a major redistricting of the city's wards (declared by ordinance July 22, 1921, but not put into effect until 1923) was accomplished. Chicago was carved into fifty wards with one alderman each, in place of the former thirty-five wards each with two aldermen. This meant that the total number of aldermen had to be reduced from seventy to fifty. Ward leaders sacrificed several Polish aldermen in the process.

South Chicago fared the worst. Not only did it lose its Polish alderman, but the Polish community in the neighborhood was split evenly between two new wards, ensuring that Polish voters could dominate neither ward. As a result of this gerrymander, South Chicago was left without a Polish alderman for the next two decades. In several other areas of the city, an incumbent Polish alderman relinquished his seat to a non-Polish colleague. On the balance sheet of council reorganization in 1923, Chicago's Polonia lost four aldermanic seats and picked up one, reducing their overall representation from seven to four. The lack of strong voices at the ward-committeeman level made the difference.

This ward redistricting did have one beneficial effect for Polonia. The old Twenty-seventh Ward which had covered the entire northwest side was divided into several smaller wards; and in the Cragin district, Leo Winiecke, a veteran Polish Democrat, slipped into the committeeman's post for one of these new wards. Then in 1930, Frank Zintak succeeded a deceased Irish boss in Brighton Park's Twelfth Ward on the South Side, giving Polonia four members on the party committee. For the rest of the 1930s, except for a

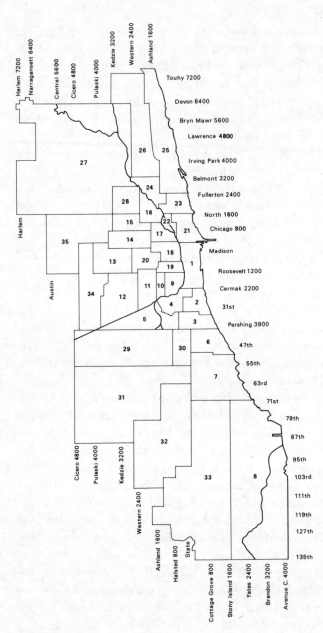

Map 8. Chicago ward boundaries before
the 1921 redistricting

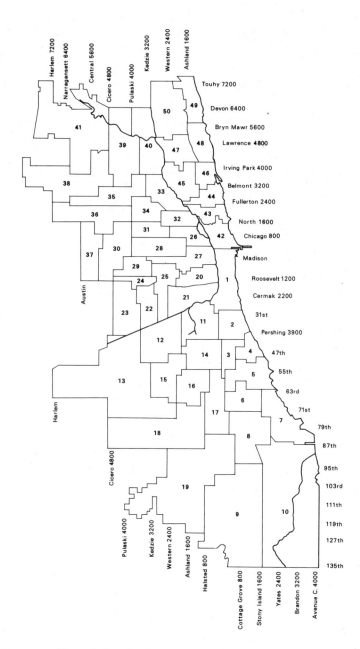

Map 9. Chicago ward boundaries after
the 1921 redistricting

few brief months when a fifth committeeman joined them, the Polish ward leaders numbered just four.[23]

Of the non-Polish leaders in Polish districts, Clayton F. Smith, A. J. Sabath, and Anton Cermak were the most responsive. In the various city and county offices which Smith held during the twenties and thirties, he always appointed Polish-American assistants; and he kept a Polish alderman on the job throughout the period. Sabath and Cermak doled out patronage to Polish-Americans roughly proportional to their strength in the wards; but since the Czechs generally outnumbered them in these areas, Polish politicians remained subordinate. The Irish leaders in Bridgeport, the yards district, and South Chicago kept tight control of their wards; Polonia made only slight gains in those areas of the South Side.

In sum, by the middle of the interwar period, the Polish recognition drive had enjoyed some success. Kunz had gone to Congress; and in 1930 he was joined by a second Polish congressman, Leonard Schuetz, from the Seventh Illinois District, the rapidly growing middle-class area on the northwest side. Edmund Jarecki was firmly ensconced in the county judgeship, and Szymczak had begun to make a name for himself. Anton Cermak's election as mayor in 1931 brought a kind of reflected glory to all Slavic nationalities in the city, and two of Cermak's top city appointments went to Polish politicians. Numerous Polish-Americans held patronage or civil service jobs at all levels of government. Polonia's capital also won several symbolic victories, such as the renaming of Pulaski Road and the proclamation of Polish Constitution Day. But if these gains brought a feeling of pride and prestige to Polonia, the basic power arrangements in the Democratic party had altered little in its favor. Only four of the twelve wards where Poles lived in sizable numbers had Polish ward bosses; in the rest they had to rely on Jewish, Czech, Irish, or WASP leaders for recognition and advancement.

16 Organizing the Recognition Drive

The recognition drive in Polonia's capital achieved its highest organizational expression with the founding of the Polish-American Democratic Organization (PADO) in 1932. PADO attempted in the political realm what the Chicago Society was essaying in intellectual and professional life, to unite Polonia into a powerful, centralized association.

Organizations of Polish Democrats were practically as old as Polonia itself. Democratic clubs sprang up in nearly every precinct of Polonia's capital at election times to work for the party candidates and to give the voters a sense of identification with the party. As early as 1893 Stanley Kunz had seen the need to draw all these clubs into a permanent organization. Thus a Polish-American Central Committee was organized to , "1) Join all Polish Democratic Clubs in Chicago and Cook County into one political unit, 2) To bring about the recognition that the Poles rightly deserve and to raise the Poles' political significance in general." This group was later joined by a similar one called the Polish Democratic League of the State of Illinois; but neither association had the financial means, the personnel, or the power to overcome the persistent localism and occasional factionalism of Polonia's capital. Both organizations continued to exist on paper down to the 1930s, and at election times, some politicians issued statements in the organizations' names. But neither was an effective political instrument.[1]

Then in 1932 Polonia's capital found the leadership it needed to forge a central political body of some permanence and strength. Matt Szymczak, serving at the time as city controller under Mayor Cermak, founded the Polish-American Democratic Organization with the help of other Democratic politicians and businessmen.

The purposes of the organization were: to "arouse greater political interest among citizens of Polish extraction," to channel this interest into the

189

Democratic party, and to "obtain proper political representation and recognition" from the party. In short, PADO intended to campaign on behalf of the Democrats among Polonia's citizens and then fight on behalf of those citizens within the Democratic councils. Szymczak and his followers felt that a centralized political body of Polish-Americans could do this more effectively than either the individual ward leaders or the old-line Polonia organizations like PNA or PRCU. In addition, PADO intended to rationalize and centralize the random services which most precinct captains and ward leaders were called upon to deliver. Thus the organization attempted to render assistance on a case-work basis "to those with relief problems . . . , to those seeking medical care at county, city or state institutions, and to those with citizenship papers problems." The deepening depression in 1932 made a strong organization necessary, to deal with immediate needs; and the national campaign of Franklin Roosevelt, which seemed to promise a Democratic victory in November, made a Polish-American political presence desirable, to ensure that Polonia was not left out of the division of spoils.[2]

An executive committee, which included all leading Polish Democrats in Chicago, was quickly assembled under the chairmanship of Judge Peter Schwaba, and, after the national elections were over, a permanent slate of officers was elected. The first officers of PADO were as follows: president, Max A. Drezmal; secretary, Frank Zintak; treasurer, Bernard L. Majewski; assistant treasurer, William W. Link (Linkowski); chairman of the board of directors, Peter H. Schwaba. Throughout these early days of the organization, however, the real leader was Matt Szymczak. As managing director, he supervised the day-to-day activities of the organization.[3]

PADO threw itself wholeheartedly into the 1932 election campaign. A suite of rooms was rented at the Sherman Hotel in downtown Chicago, speakers addressed ward meetings and made radio broadcasts, and campaign literature was sent to all Polish newspapers and organizations throughout the country. Democratic leaders in all forty-eight states were contacted concerning the number and status of Polish-American citizens within their states. Ten of the replies were sufficiently favorable for PADO to send out speakers to address Polish audiences in those states. A letter was sent out on PADO stationery to Governor Roosevelt, informing him that:

A Polish American National Democratic Organization has been formed for the purpose of promoting your candidacy. . . . We assure you that your efforts to effect economic and governmental reforms shall receive the whole-hearted support and cooperation of the overwhelming majority of our Polish-American citizens.

To make certain that Roosevelt's response had the best possible effect in Polonia, Szymczak had a short reply drafted for the governor's use and sent along with the original letter. Roosevelt altered it slightly and then duly issued it over his signature.[4]

On the night of the election, Szymczak requested his Polish contacts in the major states of the American Polonia to wire him an estimate of their state's Polish vote for Roosevelt. Szymczak and PADO were aiming for a 95 percent Polish-Democratic vote in order to make a convincing show of strength. The incoming telegrams showed that they didn't fall far short.[5]

Financing this campaign had been a constant struggle, for the PADO organizers wanted to be financially independent of the local party apparatus. They would have liked to receive some money from the Democratic National Committee, but none was forthcoming. The campaign finally cost them $6283.38; and on the eve of the election they had managed to raise $4136. The deficit had to be made up by pledges from individual members.[6]

With the national election over, PADO tried to keep up its contacts with Polish-American leaders throughout the country. In the next presidential year, 1936, it obtained recognition from the Democratic National Committee as the official campaign body among Polish-Americans, was severed from the jurisdiction of Congressman A. J. Sabath's Nationalities Division within the party, and was authorized to campaign in several states other than Illinois. But PADO was not equipped to function well nationally, and before the 1940 election members were still clamoring for a more perfect Democratic instrument to unite all of the American Polonia.[7]

Between presidential years PADO functioned largely as a local organization. The officers established a headquarters in a downtown office building a few doors from City Hall, and the full membership gathered for meetings four times yearly. Before every local election the organization determined which offices should be staked out for Polonia and sent to the Democratic leaders a list of Polish-Americans qualified for these posts. It didn't always get every office it sought, but it tried especially hard to ensure the permanence of any gains it did make. After five years of existence, it boasted (inaccurately) that no elective office held by a Polish-American had been lost to another nationality group.

PADO worked very much within the party system, and at no time did it threaten to bolt the party if its demands were not met. As the president of PADO told one meeting:

The organization cooperates with all the powers that be, and obtains recognition by convincing them that we are entitled to it in all departments of public offices. We shall obtain even more positions than we now have if our people will cooperate with our organizations and with the press, working together as one, loyally and with logic.

This was the old *Dziennik Chicagoski* strategy of ethnic solidarity within party solidarity; although it compromised the group's militance as an ethnic lobby, it created less tension within the organization than might be expected. PADO members were all regular politicians. They had been so sold on the virtues of regularity that few questioned the tactic.[8]

Between elections PADO was kept busy as a service organization. It regularly screened all Polish-Americans seeking jobs in the patronage army. Whenever a job-seeker came to the group's attention, it prepared a dossier for him, listing his qualifications, experience, and family data, as well as the position and salary sought. This file was then sent to the mayor, the individual's ward committeeman, and the immediate superior in the bureau where the desired job was. PADO hoped that its recommendation would carry more weight than that of a personal patron. During the depression years a wide variety of people came seeking work, not only unemployed laborers and clerks, but even some prominent citizens of Polonia as well. At the end of 1932, the president of the PRCU asked PADO to try and get him a job as a tax appraiser or an assistant in the state attorney general's office. One PADO dossier which went routinely to the committeeman of the Twenty-sixth Ward for approval was the job application of the Twenty-sixth Ward committeeman, himself out of work. During the four-year period from 1933 to 1936, the organization handled 3,348 cases of persons seeking work. Not all of these were political job-seekers. Some were referred to private companies, and many were placed on WPA or National Youth Administration projects. PADO estimated that it had about 50 percent success in finding work for applicants.

Even more of Polonia's residents came seeking assistance with relief problems—5,875 such cases in the same four-year period. Many of these people found it impossible to communicate with welfare administrators, due to the language barrier, or found the forms to be filled out simply mystifying. PADO's staff helped such individuals negotiate the halls of bureaucracy, and they also checked out specific complaints of unfair treatment directly with caseworkers or district welfare supervisors. A sampling of letters received by PADO in the mid-30s indicates the kinds of services it was able to provide:

Jan. 29, 1934—Just dropping you a few lines to inform you that we are again receiving charity, with the letter I got from you several weeks ago. . . .

Sept. 14, 1935—I just want to express my appreciation to you and your secretary for the way you have helped me to have my gas service restored. I regret very much that I cannot come and personally thank you both but my age does not permit such a long walk and I lack street car fare.

April 22, 1936—I am dropping you a few lines to let you know that I reiceved great success thrue you people that I really repay some how I phone you people in the morning and about one hour later one of the case workers she come over to see me and notified me and left me some blue ticket that I will be working in a short time only I have to wait for a letter where I will be placed I just cried from gladdness so really I should thank you for this. . . . [sic]

PADO supplemented the overtaxed practical services of the ward boss during the depression years. As a downtown organization, it was less immediate and personal than the boss; but with its semiprofessional staff, it was better equipped to deal with the growing tangle of government agencies in the New Deal years. And its services were completely gratis; for, unlike the boss, it was not in a position to pressure the applicant for a vote.[9]

During PADO's first year of existence, Matt Szymczak supervised this welter of political and practical activity. He was constantly bombarded by letters and phone calls from Polonia's citizens with ideas on how to forward the recognition drive as well as with personal appeals for aid. Since he was serving as city controller and committeeman of the newly-formed Thirty-eighth Ward as well, his duties as managing director of PADO must have been a burdensome addition. He also had to resist efforts to use his name and his office for dubious purposes. For instance, a Polish-American journalist asked for some city controller's stationery to use for his dispatches to several papers, "as it makes an impression on the out-of-town newspapers." The request was refused.

In the wake of PADO's concerted effort for Roosevelt in 1932, many Polish-Americans began agitating for a Polish appointee to his cabinet; and Szymczak's name was the one most often mentioned. Others within the organization admitted, more realistically, "cabinet jobs are a dream" and attempted to obtain appointments of various Polish-Americans to lesser offices in federal bureaus. Finally, in June 1933, the prestigious federal appointment which Polonia hoped for was granted. M. S. Szymczak was named a member of the Federal Reserve Board of Governors, not quite a cabinet post, but a higher position than any Polish-American had yet attained in the United States. Polish newspapers universally rejoiced at the honor; they should, perhaps, have paused to reflect that PADO was thus losing its most effective or-

ganizer and Polonia's capital its most promising American politician. Szymczak's absence was felt almost immediately, for the Democratic organization
appointed a WASP banker, Robert Upham, to succeed him as controller and
an Irishman, P. J. Cullerton, to take his place as Thirty-eighth Ward leader.[10]

Frank Zintak, the Brighton Park ward boss, succeeded Szymczak as managing director of PADO; but he lacked the reputation and the extrapolitical
contacts of his predecessor. His effectiveness was further undermined around
election time in 1936, when a financial scandal developed in his superior
court clerk's office. A widespread series of investigations, following the dis-
covery of a half-million dollar shortage in county treasurer Robert Sweitzer's
office, turned up ten other county officers, including Zintak, with financial ir-
regularities. The sum of $22,560 was missing from escrow accounts in Zin-
tak's keeping. The prosecutor charged that the money had been used as a
political "slush fund" to pay campaign expenses, but the defendant claimed
he used the money for salary advances to clerks and judges during the payless
paydays of the depression. PADO stuck by its managing director, helped raise
$25,000 to pay back the county, and kept him on in his position in the or-
ganization. The first trial jury could not reach a decision in his case, but a
second panel acquitted him. Though he had been forced to resign from his
court clerkship in 1936 by the panicky Democrats, he remained as ward committeeman. His usefulness as a candidate and as PADO director, however,
was greatly curtailed. From then on, the president of PADO, at this time
Judge John Prystalski, and later, in the 1940s, Frank Bobrytzke, began to take
a more active role in leading the organization. The post of managing director
declined in importance.[11]

The Zintak affair marked the beginning of the organization's decline.
The decline hastened in the wake of a disastrous squabble over the reelection
of Judge Jarecki in 1938 (see next chapter). Although, under Frank
Bobrytzke's leadership in the forties, PADO continued to press for more
Polish representation on the Democratic ticket, it graduallly became more
and more of a machine rubber stamp. It exists today in name only.

The Polish-American Democratic Organization was the high point of
political organizing in Polonia's capital, for its efforts represented the highest
unity which Chicago's Polish-Americans ever attained in American politics.
Yet, like the Polonia ideal itself, this political unity was not perfectly realized.
Many Polish-American precinct captains out in the wards barely knew that the
downtown organization existed and continued their own work on a strictly

local basis. More importantly, PADO didn't always work harmoniously with the old-line organizations, especially the Polish National Alliance which still retained much of its Republican or nonpartisan stance and resented the triumph of Resurrectionist political strategy which PADO represented.[12]

Even the impressive unity which PADO did attain in Polonia was not always well directed. Like the other organizations of the recognition drive, it was too concerned with symbolic recognition rather than with political power. Its emphasis on internal solidarity made it useless as a vehicle for forming coalitions with other groups. The unity it gave the Polish voice in Democratic party councils was often more of an advantage to the Kelly-Nash leadership than to Polonia. Had all the political leaders of Polonia sniped away at the machine individually, Kunz-style, they might have achieved more recognition because they would have been a greater nuisance to the party leaders. PADO allowed the bosses to satisfy this one centralized body's minimal demands and then blithely forget the Polish voters and politicians. The reluctance of PADO to rock the party boat facilitated such tactics for Kelly-Nash. A fundamental weakness of the *Dziennik Chicagoski*—PADO strategy was that it contained no threat to the party leaders. Ethnic solidarity within the party, as PADO practiced it, could only be successful if Polish voters were in the majority. This was not the case in Chicago.

Polonia did pick up some significant patronage at both high and low levels during the years when PADO was active. But whether this was due to PADO or would have been attained by individual ward leaders in any case is difficult to determine. That some former Republicans, such as Wencel Hetman, a Deneen man, were converted to the PADO strategy and the Democratic cause is certain; but this might have occurred anyway since the Republicans ceased to present a viable alternative at either the local or the national level in the 1930s.

PADO was most successful in bringing some order to the relief and service activities of the political bosses in the early depression years. In this one instance, the organization clearly saw and met an immediate need in Polonia. But its political strategy merely played into the hands of the party bosses.

17 The Finest Fruit of Recognition: Edmund K. Jarecki

The Polish-Americans from Chicago did not attain top-level elective offices such as mayor, governor, senator, or county board president; but the post of county judge which Edmund K. Jarecki held for thirty-two years, from 1922 to 1954, was a crucial one in the local political system. More important, Jarecki's reputation as a respectable in politics, honest, incorruptible, and independent of the bosses, was a point of pride for Polish-Americans. When the Democratic machine attempted to dump Jarecki midway in his career, the judge marshalled the support of his countrymen and of independent-minded Chicagoans to resist the challenge, enhancing his reputation and his symbolic value for Polonia's capital. Edmund Jarecki, "the Pole who couldn't be dumped," was the finest fruit of the recognition drive, the one Polish-American whom nearly every Chicagoan knew and respected.

Edmund Kasper Jarecki was born in German Poland in 1879 and was brought to Chicago by his parents at the age of five. His father, a skilled butcher, worked at the Chicago stockyards only a few months, then set up in business for himself. The Jarecki family was thus more comfortable than most Polish immigrants. Edmund was first trained as a draftsman and worked at this trade for several years. He later completed the courses at Northwestern University Law School, passed the bar exam in 1908, and set up a law office in Polish Downtown.

Jarecki first entered politics in 1911 at the request of Stanley Kunz and Rev. Francis Gordon, who asked him to run for a one-year vacancy as Sixteenth Ward alderman. Probably without fully realizing it, he was the Sullivan candidate that year against a Polish Harrisonite. Having been elected in a close race with about 52 percent of the Polish vote, he went his own way in the council and was not slated for reelection the following year. But as he himself put it, he "got stubborn and ran independent," losing by only eighty-two votes in a three-way race. The Democratic governor, Edward Dunne, eventually appointed him attorney for the state's pure food commission and then to a vacancy on the municipal court. Jarecki won a full six-year term on that court in the 1914 election but was defeated in the Republican landslide of 1920.[1]

In 1922 Stanley Kunz, as part of an ethnic revolt against Boss Brennan, obtained for Jarecki the Democratic nomination for county judge. The county judgeship was a peculiar hybrid office of considerable importance to the politicians. About half the judge's time was occupied with ordinary judicial duties of the county concerning delinquent tax suits, special assessment judgments, adoptions, insanity hearings, and other legal matters. The other half consisted of supervisory duties over the election machinery.

In the city of Chicago, elections were supervised by a three man Board of Election Commissioners (two from the majority political party, one from the minority party) appointed by the county judge; whereas elections elsewhere in Cook County, outside Chicago, came under the jurisdiction of the county clerk's office. Technically speaking, the city's three election commissioners as well as the thousands of poll judges assigned to the precincts on election days were officers of the county court and subject to the county judge's orders. Any election officer engaged in illegal practices could be summarily held in contempt of the county court. The vast potential power of the county judge over election procedures was what made the office a crucial one for the politicians. Control of the election machinery was estimated to be worth about twenty-five thousand votes to a political party.[2]

The Republicans held this political plum in 1922; but the scandals under Judge Righeimer, a Thompson man, had been so blatant that the Democrats stood a good chance of recapturing it if they put up a man with a good reputation. Jarecki fit the specifications. He had made a good record during his six and a half years on the municipal court, serving most of this time in the newly formed automobile traffic division, where he was known as the terror of speeders. During his campaign against Righeimer, he stressed the urgent need to purify city elections, and he made telling use of the copious evidence of fraud at the election board. Many nonpartisan civic groups endorsed him, as did the Chicago Bar Association and both the major Republican newspapers, the *Tribune* and the *Daily News*.[3]

Thompson threw the whole weight of his machine against Jarecki in a desperate attempt to retain control of the vital election process. Righeimer tried to portray his opponent as a mere puppet of Brennan and Kunz, but he himself was so thoroughly Thompson's puppet that the charge seemed ludicrous. Jarecki and most of the other Democrats on the ticket were winners in a relatively close election. Over 80 percent of the Polish voters supported their countryman.[4]

Judge Jarecki soon proved that he was no political puppet, and both Brennan and Kunz began to think that perhaps they had created a monster. The judge initially cooperated with Brennan by turning over the routine patronage of his office to the Democratic organization, but he broke with Kunz almost immediately. Probably stung by the campaign charges that he was Kunz's creature, he pointedly avoided the congressman and refused to ask for or take any advice from him. Neither of the two Polish appointments which Jarecki reserved for his own authority were Kunz lieutenants. Instead he appointed M. S. Szymczak as his personal secretary and Anthony Czarnecki, a Republican, as the minority member of the election commission. Kunz declared war on Jarecki, and for the next several years the politics of Polonia's capital were wracked by this feud, with Kunz even backing Thompson Republicans on occasion, when it suited his factional purposes.[5]

The county judge's run-in with Boss Brennan came in 1925 over a billion-dollar traction ordinance which the Democrats presented to the voters in a referendum. Widespread bribery and ballot-stuffing occurred on election day, and the county court's hard-hitting investigation indicated that perhaps fifty-thousand votes had been stolen for the ordinance by the Democratic machine. When indictments were brought in against Democratic precinct officials, Brennan looked about for ways of disciplining his honest county judge. The Democratic-controlled county board harassed Jarecki by withholding appropriations for several assistant judges needed to deal with the backlog of cases in his court. Then, early in 1926, it was widely rumored that Jarecki's name would be absent from that year's county ticket.[6]

Boss Brennan had, however, created a monster he couldn't get rid of. Since the 1922 election the Democrats had nearly controlled the county, and their prospects for continued control were excellent. They had stellar vote-getters in the county offices, such as Cermak at the county board, P. J. (Paddy) Carr in the sheriff's office, and Henry Horner as probate judge. Bill Thompson and Republican state's attorney Robert E. Crowe had gone a long way towards destroying the Republican party and pushing honest independents into Brennan's arms. The Boss didn't want to alienate his new-found reform supporters and jeopardize the party's chances for continued success by kicking up a fuss over Jarecki. Furthermore, the Polish voting bloc would be alienated if Jarecki were dumped.

Brennan explored the possibility of slating another Polish-American with respectable qualifications but more regular attitudes for the county judgeship. The post was actually offered to municipal court judge Peter H. Schwaba, who, however, declined to oppose or replace Jarecki. All other efforts to find a willing Polish candidate failed, and Jarecki was therefore renominated. He won easily, the second highest vote-getter on the ticket.

With this reelection triumph, Jarecki established himself as a fixture on the Democratic county slate. In his next two campaigns of 1930 and 1934, he breezed in with easy victories; and in 1934 he actually led the ticket despite continued rumblings from precinct captains and poll judges who resented his watchdog tactics at the ballot box.[7]

Under Jarecki's administration the Board of Election Commissioners gradually became a Polish patronage preserve. The judge appointed a Polish-American, John S. Rusch, as chief clerk of the board. The clerk served as office manager for the clerical staff and was the actual boss in most staff and patronage matters, whereas the judge and the three commissioners dealt mainly with policy decisions and public relations.

After two years of the Jarecki-Rusch regime, twenty Polish-Americans had found work at the election office, forming 17 percent of the 117-man staff. By 1939 Poles had surpassed the Irish as the largest single group of

TABLE 27   NATIONALITY BREAKDOWN OF EMPLOYEES, BOARD OF
             ELECTION COMMISSIONERS

	Total	Polish	Italian	German	Jewish	Irish	Other Slavic	Other*
July 1925	117	20	4	6	5	34	5	39
June 1939	111	36	3	12	6	21	2	31
September 1947	123	49	5	14	4	12	3	32
January 1954	151	54	5	16	5	19	10	46

*Those listed as "Other" have names whose ethnic derivation was not immediately evident upon inspection. Before 1940, most of these would be WASPs or individuals whose names had been changed to sound more "American." After 1940, besides those two categories, it would also include many Negroes.

employees, and in 1947 Polonia's representation reached its high point of almost 40 percent (49 in a 123-man force). At first, Jarecki's influence on the
patronage process was mainly indirect; but after a quarrel with the party
bosses in the late 1930s, the judge handled many appointments personally.
In 1947, when Polish influence was at its height, 34 of the 123 permanent
employees owed their jobs directly to Jarecki's intervention and 22 of these
employees were Polish. Significantly, Stanley Kunz never placed a single employee on the election board; nor did his successor as boss of Polish Downtown, Joseph Rostenkowski, have any more influence on the county judge.
Patronage for this area of the city was handled not by the ward committeeman but by Jarecki himself or by Vincent Zwiefka, an old Kunz adversary
who found a resting place in the election office.[8]

The Polish press exulted over Jarecki's success, his patronage largesse,
and his record of honesty, calling him "The Defender of Honest Elections,"
"The Apostle of True Democracy," "The Model of an American Citizen,"
and "An Honor to the Name of Pole." Polonia's capital had found a "star"
for its recognition drive.[9]

Jarecki irritated party leaders with his independence in both electoral and
patronage matters, yet they tolerated him as a necessary evil during his first
four terms. But in the mid-1930s, as Edward Kelly and Patrick Nash solidified their hold on the Democratic organization, they became increasingly arrogant and intolerant of any opposition within the party. A rift in the organization between Kelly-Nash regulars and more independent-minded
Democrats broke into open conflict which eventually engulfed Jarecki.

The first object of machine wrath was Governor Henry Horner in 1936.
Since his slating for the governorship by Mayor Cermak and his election in
the Democratic landslide of 1932, Horner, a former probate judge, had cooperated with the Chicago machine in most matters but had also shown a
streak of stubbornness and independence. Horner was, in personality and
background, somewhat like Edmund Jarecki. Both were respectable lawyers
and judges of ethnic origin (Horner was a German Jew, Jarecki was from
German Poland). Both had gained advancement through the machine but
were personally honest. Though neither was the crusading type, they stub-
bornly opposed machine fraud when it came to their attention in the course
of administering their offices. Both were "professional honest men," useful
to the machine as window-dressing at the time of their elections but progressively more irritating to the bosses as they served their terms of office.

The break between Horner and Kelly-Nash was precipitated by the governor's veto of a machine-sponsored bill to legalize racetrack bookmaking. Having failed to kick Horner upstairs when the governor refused a judgeship, Kelly-Nash decided to dump him. They thus supported Dr. Herman Bundesen, city health commissioner, for governor in the 1936 spring primaries.

Horner fought vigorously against Bundesen and his sponsors, using state patronage liberally and appealing to downstate resentments against Cook County. He picked up some important allies in the bosses' own bailiwick, most notably State's Attorney Thomas Courtney, who narrowly avoided being dumped in his own right. Chicago's Polish leaders split along the same lines as other Democrats in the city, the good-government, respectable element and the state officeholders backing Horner and the city ward bosses and the Polish-American Democratic Organization staying regular for Bundesen. Judge Jarecki remained neutral, as was his custom in political contests; but his sympathies were known to lie with Horner, for the governor was backing a Jarecki-sponsored bill to institute an innovative permanent registration system against machine opposition.

Horner defeated Bundesen and won renomination on the strength of downstate support; and although he lost the city of Chicago, he made a strong showing there, gaining almost 40 percent of the Democratic vote against the machine's concentrated power. The city's Polish voters, however, were not swayed by the insurgent Horner. He gained only 27 percent of their votes. Though the party closed ranks again for the November elections and Horner was reelected over his Republican opponent, the rift was not really healed between Kelly-Nash and the Horner-Courtney-Jarecki forces.[10]

The party broke wide open again in early 1938 when Kelly-Nash attempted the same treatment on Jarecki that had failed with Governor Horner. The machine bosses finally decided that they could no longer tolerate an independent force in charge of the election machinery. During the 1936 elections, Jarecki's commissioners had summarily dismissed 485 judges and clerks of election, some on suspicion of fraud, others simply because they were careless and incompetent. Also in 1936, after Horner's triumph over Bundesen, the permanent registration law had finally passed. Under competent administration, this new system threatened to cut down sharply on "ghost voting." As the 1938 county slate was being prepared, Jarecki was offered the usual face-saving kick upstairs, a circuit court judgeship. He refused; and then, on February 1, he was dumped from the ticket. Kelly-Nash enlisted Circuit

TABLE 28   ELECTION RETURNS (IN PERCENTAGES):   FIVE INSURGENT CANDIDATES, 1936-1940

Ward	No. of Polish Precincts	1936 Dem. Primary-- Henry Horner, Governor	1938 Dem. Primary-- E.K. Jarecki, County Judge	1938 Dem. Primary-- Scott Lucas, U.S. Senator	1939 Dem. Primary-- T. Courtney, Mayor	1940 Dem. Primary-- B. Adamowski, U.S. Senator
7th Polish vote Ward average	7	32.97 55.75	75.06 64.38	62.44 54.45	48.80 43.18	71.46 46.03
10th Polish vote Ward average	7	32.30 27.16	72.01 56.13	55.70 37.52	51.36 34.79	74.70 47.51
11th Polish vote Ward average	8	27.52 28.62	70.41 47.70	58.18 36.05	40.14 30.71	75.03 47.01
12th Polish vote Ward average	3	33.12 30.10	63.70 63.03	56.61 50.47	34.56 37.32	62.38 53.54
13th Polish vote Ward average	4	19.27 27.65	63.95 48.48	53.48 35.10	42.68 36.26	63.50 43.34
14th Polish vote Ward average	4	29.47 30.41	64.14 45.58	55.21 35.48	39.48 28.23	68.92 36.50
21st Polish vote Ward average	5	19.89 22.72	60.80 47.95	47.93 33.91	31.59 31.59	75.81 62.66
22nd Polish vote Ward average	2	25.50 31.27	56.29 46.23	49.24 35.04	28.37 27.94	59.88 37.30
26th Polish vote Ward average	10	22.76 25.79	59.70 53.76	46.51 41.25	35.79 34.39	72.88 68.86

TABLE 28--Continued

Ward	No. of Polish Precincts	1936 Dem. Primary-- Henry Horner, Governor	1938 Dem. Primary-- E.K. Jarecki, County Judge	1938 Dem. Primary-- Scott Lucas, U.S. Senator	1939 Dem. Primary-- T. Courtney, Mayor	1940 Dem. Primary-- B. Adamowski, U.S. Senator
32nd	14					
Polish vote		23.11	62.13	47.12	32.18	67.17
Ward average		31.59	53.92	43.86	33.04	59.63
33rd	8					
Polish vote		23.36	72.74	60.34	43.03	77.68
Ward average		35.22	65.83	50.92	43.87	65.87
35th	15					
Polish vote		36.02	73.39	56.72	41.17	81.35
Ward average		36.93	66.60	51.02	41.11	72.99
City-wide	87					
Polish vote		27.46	67.50	53.95	39.53	72.89
City average		39.28	50.48	39.01	34.24	39.04

Judge John Prystalski, president of the Polish-American Democratic Organization, to run as the organization candidate for county judge in the April
primaries.[11]

Jarecki had few defenders among the party regulars; only four of the
thirty-one members on the county slate-making committee stood by him. At a
PADO meeting on February 5, just after Jarecki's dumping had been announced, only State Representative Benjamin Adamowski opposed the organization's ratification of the machine decision. Frank Konkowski, boss of
the Twenty-sixth Ward, bitterly summed up the feeling of regular Polish
pols:

Mr. Konkowski said he requested Jarecki for election judges and clerks and
did not get them; that such persons as Mrs. Vittum and Mrs. Graham
[settlement workers at Northwestern University Settlement in Polish
Downtown] have more influence with him; that Jarecki, having received
the support of the Democrats was in some way obligated to them; that he
always thought himself above others, but he is only a judge after all.

The stubborn independence which made Jarecki a leading Polish respectable
seemed like aloofness and ingratitude to the Polish bosses.[12]

But Jarecki quickly picked up allies both inside and outside Polonia.
Governor Horner and State's Attorney Courtney announced their support for
Jarecki within a matter of days, vowing to continue the successful struggle of
two years earlier. Albert J. Horan, bailiff of the municipal court and a Democratic leader in the Polish and Czech area near St. Adalbert's, also announced
his support. Horan demonstrated his commitment by firing John Szumnarski,
the Thirty-fifth Ward committeeman who opposed Jarecki, from his job as
first assistant bailiff. The Chicago Bar Association endorsed Jarecki by more
than a two-to-one margin over Prystalski; and the *Chicago Daily News* editorialized that the Jarecki-Prystalski battle embodied "a clean-cut issue, the
issue of good government versus continued machine rule." Congressman
Scott Lucas from Havana, Illinois, joined Jarecki as an insurgent candidate
for the U.S. senatorial nomination.

Though PADO had deserted Jarecki, the rival Polish Democratic
League of Illinois greeted the embattled judge with a standing ovation when
he spoke at one of their meetings. All three Polish-language dailies in Chicago greeted the news of Jarecki's dumping with violent outrage. On February 1, *Dziennik Zjednoczenia*'s headlines proclaimed, "Polonia Is with
Jarecki 100%"; a *Dziennik Zwiazkowy* article shouted, "We Want Jarecki";
and *Dziennik Chicagoski* echoed, "We Demand Jarecki."[13]

The following day, February 2, there appeared on the front page of

Dziennik Chicagoski a cartoon portraying Judge Jarecki standing on a pedestal while a massed throng, entitled "650,000 Chicago Poles [sic] and the Polish Press," looked on and said, "We're Back of You." Also on that day's front page, the newspaper printed a long editorial, written in English for maximum impact among Polonia's second generation, discussing the challenge to Jarecki:

> We shall be frank—disarmingly frank. The Polish voters are not unaware of the disingenuous pretence of the Democratic bosses.
> For they miss the accents of conviction and high resolve in the selection of one Pole to beat another. Their logic forbids them to appreciate the advantage of driving out Judge Jarecki with Judge Prystalski. . . .
> The Polish voters, therefore, shall reject every suggestion to confuse them among themselves, and shall rally to the support of Judge Jarecki. For they have no intention to allow that profession of honesty in public office and fidelity to duty should be subordinated to party loyalty.

After this initial burst of indignation, however, the editors of the Resurrectionist newspaper, a regular Democratic organ for almost fifty years, obviously had second thoughts. The paper kept an editorial silence about the Jarecki-Prystalski fight for the next two months and accepted numerous paid advertisements from both sides. Then on April 11, the day before the primary, someone in the Jarecki camp cleverly took out a full-page ad in the *Chicagoski,* calling attention to the February 1 headlines supporting Jarecki in all three Polish dailies, including the now silent *Chicagoksi.*[14]

Despite the efforts of the Polish ward bosses, the abandonment of Jarecki by PADO, and the silence of Polonia's leading newspaper, the Polish-American voters stood behind the embattled county judge. In lieu of any more tangible political achievements in Chicago, Jarecki's flinty honesty in a sensitive post was the best Polonia's capital had. Two-thirds of the Polish voters chose to retain Jarecki in the April primary; and in Jarecki's home ward, the thirty-third, the Polish total was almost 73 percent for Jarecki. The Horner-Courtney allies delivered enough other votes in the city and county to renominate Jarecki and deal the Kelly-Nash machine its second straight defeat in a contested primary. Scott Lucas also beat Michael Igoe, the machine choice, for the senatorial nomination. At least some of Jarecki's insurgent strength among Polonia's voters rubbed off on his ally, for Lucas captured 53.95 percent of the Polish vote in the primary. As in 1936, machine and insurgents closed ranks to beat the Republicans in November; and nearly the whole Democratic slate was swept into office with Jarecki far out ahead in total votes.[15]

Jarecki had proven that he could ignore the Democratic bosses with impunity. When he subsequently ran for reelection three more times, the machine left him alone. But ironically, his successful challenge of the machine also exposed the equivocal position of Polonia's organized voice in Chicago politics, the Polish-American Democratic Organization. PADO had at first routinely endorsed Jarecki for renomination in 1938; but when Kelly-Nash dumped him, it meekly and obediently changed its position and backed Prystalski. PADO was caught badly out of step with its constituency, and it appeared as a mere tool of the machine. The Jarecki affair hastened PADO's decline; and thus the highpoint of Polonia's success in Chicago politics, the Jarecki insurgency of 1938, undermined Polonia's organized force for further success and recognition.

The insurgency in the Democratic party did not end with Jarecki. In 1939, State's Attorney Courtney challenged Mayor Kelly himself in the party's mayoral primary. Courtney's campaign, however, never caught fire. Only six of the ward committeemen defected to his side; and although Judge Jarecki publicly campaigned for him, Governor Horner, fatally ill by this time, played no part in the contest and most of his followers stayed with the mayor.[16]

All of the Polish ward committeemen stayed regular in the Courtney-Kelly contest; PADO publicized the great benefits Mayor Kelly had granted Polonia; and all the Polish organizations and Polish newspapers supported the mayor. Courtney had no organized support in Polonia's capital; Jarecki and Adamowski were the only Polish leaders backing him.

PADO had determined before the campaign that a Polish-American must be on the ticket with Mayor Kelly as candidate for either city treasurer or city clerk. A committee drew up a list of possible candidates for both positions, then left the final choice to the mayor. Kelly, eager to placate Polonia after the Jarecki affair, chose Thomas Gordon, Joe Rostenkowski's protégé from Polish Downtown, to make the race for city treasurer. As this was the third time in fifty years that Chicago Democrats had slated a Polish candidate for city treasurer, Polonia had not only a candidate but a symbol of continuity as well. *Dzeinnik Chicagoski's* cartoonist produced a front-page offering entitled "Good Example." In this sketch Thomas Gordon holds up a picture of Peter Kiolbassa, "City Treasurer, 1891, Honest Pete," and Gordon says to Ed Kelly, "I will imitate him, Mr. Mayor." As another bit of symbolic campaigning, Mayor Kelly somehow managed to get the Polish ambassador to the U.S. to award him the Polonia Restituta medal, the Republic of Poland's highest honor. The ever-faithful *Dziennik Chicagoski* again produced the appropriate cartoon, with a Polish-American pointing to Mayor Kelly and his new medal and telling his wife, "Poland has recognized him—he deserves it."[17]

When the votes were counted on primary day, Courtney was buried by an almost two-to-one margin. Polish voters showed that they were not entirely convinced of Mayor Kelly's great service to Poland and Polonia, for almost 40 percent of them voted for Courtney. This was a larger percentage of the Polish vote than Martin Powroznik had gained in the 1935 primary; but it was far less than Judge Jarecki or even Scott Lucas had polled in the most recent challenge to the machine. Courtney did best among Polish voters in South Chicago (wards seven and ten), who, without either a Polish committeeman or alderman, had least reason to be satisfied with Kelly's machine. He also gained a majority in some of the precincts of Clayton Smith's ward (the thirty-third); but in the wards where Committeemen Zintak, Rostenkowski, and J. T. Baran held sway (the twelfth, thirty-second, and twenty-sixth), he lost two to one. This election clearly showed that the antimachine outrage the Polish voters had shown in 1938, though it had not completely subsided, was not readily transferable to another, non-Polish candidate.[18]

The revolt was nearly over. Judge Jarecki did support his friend Adamowski and a few other Democratic insurgents in primary challenges in 1940; but when these fizzled, there was little point left to insurgency. Neither Jarecki nor Adamowski participated in PADO's "Inaugural Special," a three-day holiday and political love-feast in Washington at FDR's third inauguration; but finally, in 1942, both were accepted back into the Polish-American Democratic Organization as full members.[19]

The ultimate failure of the insurgency against Kelly-Nash in no way inhibited Judge Jarecki's personal efforts for honest elections. In 1940, for instance, Jarecki invoked for the first time an obscure passage in the state's election laws giving him the power to take direct charge of the police department on election day. Countermanding the orders of the police commissioner, the judge reassigned five thousand city policemen to guard polling places in neighborhoods far away from their home wards, thus removing them from the watchful gaze of their ward bosses. Jarecki continued the battle for the ballot box until his retirement from office in 1954.[20]

Better known and more respected in non-Polish circles than Kiolbassa, Smulski, or any other Polish respectable, and just as long-lived in political office as Kunz or any ward boss, Judge Edmund K. Jarecki was the finest fruit of the Polish-American recognition drive in Chicago.

18 Limitations of the Recognition Drive

Why has there never been a Polish-American mayor of Chicago? This question is often asked around the city in a tone of reproach to Chicago's largest ethnic group. Anton Cermak, representing a much smaller Czech community, fought his way to City Hall in 1931. Why hasn't Polonia, even in forty years since then, produced a Polish Cermak?

Polish-American politicians have been generally of two types, respectables or bosses. But the history of Chicago politics indicates that the successful mayoral candidate has been a third type, a mixed politician. He has combined the boss's power drive and machine methods with a broker's skill in allying his machine with the respectable elements of the city. Carter Harrison II was a master of this sort of balancing act, combining his river ward allies with reform and independent voters. Though Bill Thompson became almost a caricature of a corrupt boss, in his first race he gained support both from Protestant church leaders and from the lowest underworld elements in the city. And Tony Cermak, Chicago's most successful immigrant politico, also followed this same mixed-politics, broker model.

Cermak's life in Chicago was devoted singlemindedly to the capture of political power, in his own West Side Czech community and later in the city as a whole. Power-seeking was a fundamental trait in his personality, almost a disease inhabiting his body. In fact, this trait may have contributed to his death, for psychosomatic illness weakened his resistance to the assassin's bullet which felled him.[1] But before his tragic end, Cermak's power drive led him to the top in politics.

In seeking power, Cermak used the usual tools of the ward boss, firm ties with his own ethnic power base, control of patronage, and intimate knowledge of the party machinery. But he also developed exquisite skills as a political broker, essential skills in a heterogeneous city like Chicago, where power had to be forged out of many ethnic and economic groups. He first developed the broker's skill as director of the United Societies for Local Self Government, Chicago's leading antiprohibition lobby. In this post he led a coalition of often squabbling and jealous ethnic groups—the Irish, the Germans, and all the new immigrant groups—by focusing their attention on one goal, to keep Chicago wet.

In the 1920s Cermak extended his broker's role and broadened his base by appealing to the conservative establishment and the thrifty middle class with a businesslike image as a master administrator of the county board.

When Boss Brennan died in 1928, Cermak used his skill as a broker to unite all the newer ethnic groups who were dissatisfied with Irish dominance of the Democratic party and thus to capture the Cook County party chairmanship. In the mayoral race in 1931, he successfully united many respectable businessmen and reformers with his ethnic, wet, working-class support by a skillful use of his administrative record and a vigorous campaign against the discredited Thompson administration. Cermak was fortunate in his opposition in 1931, for Big Bill's reputation was so unsavory that the immigrant boss found it relatively easy to look respectable.

Thus the essential elements in Cermak's rise to power were an unquenchable power drive, great skill at the delicate balancing act of broker politics, plus unusually good luck.[2]

An additional, subtle factor may have been involved as well. Cermak's ethnic group, the Czechs, was one of the smaller ones in Chicago. Among the new immigrant nationalities, it ranked roughly in the middle—less numerous than the Poles, Italians, or Jews, but more numerous than the Lithuanians, Greeks, or Yugoslavs.[3] As head of a relatively small ethnic group, he was under no illusions that he could succeed solely as a Czech leader; furthermore, other nationalities, who didn't want to replace Irish and WASP dominance with the tyranny of another large group, did not see the Czechs and their leader as a threat. His leadership of a marginal group assisted his performance as a broker.

Polonia's capital failed to produce a leader who combined a lust for power, skill at political brokering, and good luck, as Cermak did. No Polish-American politician in Chicago successfully played this mixed role, halfway between boss and respectable.

The outstanding leaders of the first generation in Polonia's capital (before World War I) were John Smulski and Stanley Kunz. Kunz, who attained some power and influence as a ward boss, had a distinctly unsavory reputation in the American press and could never have appealed successfully to the community as a whole. Kunz himself must have known this, for never in his long career did he seek an office outside his home district of Polish Downtown. On the other side, Smulski was eminently respectable, a banker, businessman, and attorney; but he was so respectable as to find politics distasteful, and thus he soon abandoned office-seeking. No other Polish leader of the first generation came any closer to combining the necessary ingredients than these two.

The same division between bosses and respectables persisted in the second generation (between the world wars). Polish politicians who became ward committeemen in the late twenties and thirties were generally local figures, powers in their own wards, but either unknown or lowly regarded in the city as a whole. When in 1929, Joe Przybylo, the Thirty-first Ward committeeman, ran for alderman against Frank Konkowski, a future committeeman, the Municipal Voters' League found the former "unfit for council service" and the latter "[despite] natural abilities and educational advantages, disqualified by low standards of public service." The man preferred by the MVL was Stanley Adamkiewicz, "preferred to opponents because of good intentions and willingness to take counsel with better citizens." Obviously none of these ward figures, neither those disapproved nor the one condescendingly tolerated, could have impressed the respectables in a wider contest.[4]

Perhaps the best, and certainly the most influential of the local ward figures, was Joseph Rostenkowski, or "Joe Rosty" as his friends called him. Son of a respected PRCU president and nephew of a former Republican state legislator, Joe Rostenkowski served his political apprenticeship at the precinct level in the Kunz organization while earning a living in insurance and real estate. In 1930 he attained his first elective office, a seat in the state legislature, which he won in a revolt against Kunz's dominance of the district. In 1931 Joe Rosty became alderman of the Thirty-second Ward, the heart of Polish Downtown; and although he did not officially become ward committeeman until the late thirties, he soon established himself as the actual leader of the ward.

When Rostenkowski first ran for the legislature, the *Chicago Daily News* recommended him as a man who "bears a good reputation"; and throughout his career as ward boss, the Polish Downtown ward enjoyed a better press than it had during Kunz's heyday. But, though no major scandals erupted and no charges of corruption were levelled at Rosty, his career was, in most other ways, a classic example of a ward boss. During the hard depression years, Rosty's ward organization kept busy distributing coal and food baskets and helping to pay gas and electric bills for constituents. He was a tireless worker for the Night of Stars gala, a Kelly-Nash fund-raising event held annually at the Chicago Amphitheatre. He attended carefully to the physical appearance of his ward, giving personal attention to garbage pickup and street cleaning, and taking a special interest in the construction of the Milwaukee Avenue subway from his position on the city council transportation committee. And, most important, throughout the thirties and forties, his ward was one of the most productive of Democratic votes in the city.

Apparently the basis of his power at the local level was his personal relationship to his workers and to the voters. All who knew him, ally and political foe alike, emphasized his loyalty to friends and his faithfulness to his word. When the Thirty-second Ward organization brought foreign-born Poles to the federal building for their citizenship tests, it was not uncommon for one of the prospective citizens to answer the question, "Who is the president of the United States?" with the name of Joseph Rostenkowski.[5]

Joe Rostenkowski enjoyed more power and security in his own ward than he did recognition elsewhere in the city. He probably could have been slated for higher office if he had wanted to, for he was personally friendly with Mayor Kelly. He was talked of as a possible successor to Frank Zintak as superior court clerk and also a potential candidate for sheriff. Ed Kelly himself asked Rostenkowski to run for Congress in the early forties, but Rosty refused and put up Thomas Gordon instead. Unlike Anton Cermak or others who transcended a ward-boss background to reach higher office, Rosty was not a power-seeker, except in his own local milieu. Somewhat limited in intelligence and cunning, blunt, straightforward, and emotional, he was as strong as a feudal lord in Polish Downtown but was not the man to appeal to respectable America, any more than the other ward bosses of Polonia's capital were.

In the second generation, the respectables in politics tended to be lawyers and judges. Businessmen like Smulski, Smietanka, or Piotrowski of the first generation rarely went in for officeholding in these later years, since the Democratic machine had begun to centralize the slating process and there was little room for outsiders. Politicians who did not like the nitty-gritty of everyday politics usually played the game for a time in lower offices, but aimed for the relatively nonpolitical spots on the bench as soon as possible.

Thus Walter J. LaBuy, who became the first Polish-American federal judge, had planned for a legal career since high school. After completion of

law school, he served an apprenticeship as assistant city attorney in Carter
Harrison's last administration. He then practiced law privately for fifteen
years, served two terms as a Cook County commissioner at the beginning of
the depression, and finally in 1933 was elected a judge of the circuit court.
Ten years later, the Roosevelt administration, on the advice of Mayor Kelly,
raised LaBuy to the federal bench. When Thaddeus Adesko, a younger lawyer than LaBuy, had his heart set on a judgeship in the 1940s, his ward boss
(an Irishman) arranged the terms with Mayor Kelly—first, two terms for
Adesko in the state senate, then a judgeship. Both Adesko and Kelly kept
their side of the bargain, and Judge Adesko has steadily risen in the ranks of
the judiciary since.[6]

Judge Jarecki was the most noteworthy member of the respectable camp
in the twenties and thirties, and he was occasionally trumpeted by Polonia as
a potential mayoral candidate. Particularly after his successful defiance of the
Kelly-Nash machine in 1938, many thought he should have struck for wider
power in the following year's mayoral race. But such suggestions fundamentally misread both Jarecki and the political situation.

Jarecki's experience had been legal and judicial, not political. He was not
a power-seeker, he had no desire to run for mayor, and he might not have
been an altogether credible candidate if he had. He had thoroughly alienated
the ward bosses of Chicago and would not easily have united the bosses'
muscle with his own respectability. Besides, the Kelly-Nash machine, though
it had made two blunders, was not about to crumble at the attack of respectables alone. Horner in 1936 and Jarecki in 1938 had been able to hold their
offices because they were well-known, respected incumbents dumped gratuit-
ously by an arrogant machine. If Jarecki had challenged Mayor Kelly in 1939,
however, the situation would have been reversed. He would have been trying
to eliminate a popular and successful incumbent and would have been open
to charges of personal arrogance, opportunism, and vindictiveness. Thomas
Courtney's crushing primary defeat by Mayor Kelly in 1939 indicates what
Jarecki's fate would have been had he made the attempt himself.

Judge Jarecki and the other Polish respectables knew enough about
politics to cooperate with the machine and attain the capstone of a legal career,
a seat on the bench. They were respected in both Polish-American and wider
circles as honest, worthy, professional men; but they were not power-seekers.
Edmund Jarecki spoke for all of them in summing up his own career:

It has been my contention that the duties and responsibilities of the
county judgeship are primarily judicial—not political—though they involve

control and supervision of what commonly has been called the "election machinery". . . .

I have never kept silent on the subject of election frauds even when it would have been "good politics" to keep quiet. However, everyone knows by common report that "Jarecki is a bad politician but a lucky fellow."

Such lucky fellows could have prestigious careers, but they could not and did not fight for the mayoralty.[7]

The second generation in Polonia's capital did produce two men, Matt Szymczak and Benjamin Adamowski, who seemed to have the proper combination of political ability and respectable appeal to reach for the mayoral chair; but both, for very different reasons, disqualified themselves along the way.

Matt Szymczak was clearly the leading Polish-American in Chicago politics in the early thirties. He held one of the top positions in Mayor Cermak's inner circle; had Cermak lived to complete one or more successful terms, Szymczak might well have been the heir-apparent. But even after the Czech mayor's death, Szymczak's position remained strong. City controller, ward committeeman on the northwest side, and managing director of PADO, he was the leading voice of the organized Polish-Americans in city politics. Not yet forty years old in 1933, he had time to wait out Mayor Kelly's long tenure in office. As a banker, professor, and businessman, he had the administrative skill and businesslike reputation needed to win the respectable vote. With the actual strength of a ward base and the potential ethnic strength of PADO, he had political muscle as well. As an old precinct captain has phrased it, "Szymczak knew how to speak to bankers in their language and how to speak to the people in the language of the streets."

But his 1933 appointment to the Federal Reserve Board effectively removed him from the political scene. Many in Polonia later viewed this appointment as a shrewd move by the Irish leadership to kick Szymczak upstairs and thus eliminate a serious rival. That this was the actual intention is doubtful. The Irish bosses did not initiate negotiations for this appointment; president-elect Roosevelt himself first made the offer of a position to Szymczak while Mayor Cermak was still alive. Szymczak welcomed the appointment for both personal and professional reasons, happy to remove his family from the burdensome milieu of ward politics and eager to exercise his financial skill at the highest levels. Nevertheless, Szymczak's acceptance removed him from politics as effectively as a kick upstairs. Though possessing far more political potential than John Smulski had, Szymczak, like Smulski, ultimately chose to abandon active politics for more prestigious, respectable activities; and Polonia's capital thus lost an important political opportunity.[8]

Benjamin Adamowski did not abandon politics for a nonpolitical post but rather left the security of the regular party ranks for a career as a political maverick. Considered a "boy wonder" in his early years, Adamowski was admitted to the Illinois bar at the age of twenty-one. With the help of Clayton F. Smith, his ward leader and a second father to him since the death of his own father, alderman Max Adamowski, young Ben went to the state legislature in 1930, still only twenty-three years old. Loyal at first to the Cermak and then the Kelly-Nash leadership, he became majority leader of the legislature in 1935.

Though temperamentally combative and something of a maverick even during these early years in the legislature, he did not oppose the Chicago machine leadership on any issue of importance until 1938, when Judge Jarecki was abandoned by the machine and by the Polish-American Democratic Organization. In that year Adamowski made his first break with the machine. He was one of the few important Polish Democrats to stand by the judge.

At a contentious PADO meeting early in 1938, Adamowski challenged the submissiveness of the organization to machine dictates, bitterly asking, "If the Polish organization refused to give its support to a judge like Jarecki, how can it maintain that it exists only for the good of the Polish people?" Adamowski was later expelled from PADO along with Jarecki; he then began a long career of independence, alternately opposing and making his peace with the Democratic machine, then finally breaking with it altogether and switching parties.

Adamowski retained his seat in the legislature until 1941 on the basis of his own strength in his heavily Polish district; and for a little over a year after 1938, he also served as attorney for the Board of Election Commissioners, a reward from the grateful Judge Jarecki. He unsuccessfully challenged the machine candidate for U.S. Senator in the 1940 Democratic primary, then ran two years later, equally unsuccessfully, for Illinois congressman-at-large with machine backing. After several periods of private law practice and a three-year stint as city corporation counsel under Mayor Martin Kennelly in the late forties, he resumed his maverick role in 1955, futilely challenging Richard J. Daley for the mayoral nomination to succeed Kennelly. Thereafter, he switched parties; as a Republican, he was elected Cook County State's Attorney in 1956, using his full talents as a controversial battler in this crime-fighting office. In 1963, as the Republican candidate for mayor, he held Richard Daley to his smallest margin of victory. As recently as November of 1970, he was still battling the Daley machine, unsuccessfully running on the Republican ticket for county assessor.[9]

From the standpoint of political power in Chicago, Benjamin Adamowski's career was another lost opportunity for Polonia's capital. Even younger than Szymczak, he too had time to wait and work his way up in the organization. He also had political connections—his early rise to House leadership at the age of twenty-eight attests to that—and a reputation as an honest, aggressive lawyer which might have jelled into the proper political combination for a successful mayoral bid. But his frequent bouts of "irregularity" made him anathema to party leaders, killing any chance of a regular party nomination for mayor; and the great strength of the Democratic machine in Chicago since the thirties similarly doomed his independent and Republican bids for the mayoralty.

Democrats in Polonia's capital feel that Adamowski could have been mayor had he not been "impatient." Adamowski's tilting at machine windmills came from both a sensitive conscience and a stubborn personality. He fought the machine both out of principle and because he seems to have enjoyed fighting almost for its own sake. An early experience in the state legislature may have determined much of his later conduct. When he first arrived in Springfield in 1931, Michael Igoe, the Democratic floor leader, told him he was starting off with two strikes against him because his Polish predecessors in the legislature had made a bad record. Adamowski asserts that, then and there, he vowed to prove that a Pole could be honest, capable, and intelligent in public office. This incident seems to have left a permanent chip on his shoulder. He himself has few regrets and has summed up his career thus: "Swimming downstream is easy and pleasant, but it doesn't compare with the exhilaration of swimming upstream and fighting the currents and rapids." Nevertheless, his "impatience" did destroy his early promise as a political "comer"; for Polonia, it meant another lost opportunity.[10]

Such opportunities for Polonia were few. From the second generation, only Szymczak and Adamowski seemed to have the potential for leadership in the city's politics; and the occasions on which they might have made a mayoral bid occurred infrequently. The Irish came to dominate Chicago politics at a rather late date, compared to other Democratic cities; but when they finally solidified their dominance in the early thirties, it remained paramount at a time when Irish leaders of other cities saw power slipping away.

Only two occasions have presented themselves in the last forty years when a non-Irish leader might have made a bid for City Hall: in 1947 when Ed Kelly finally retired amid charges of bossism and rumors of corruption, and in 1955 when the honest successor to Kelly, Martin Kennelly, was eased out of office as a political weakling. At either of these junctures, Szymczak or Adamowski might well have become mayor had they retained an active, regular party presence in Chicago. But since then no opportunities have arisen, for Richard Daley has proven politically invincible for five terms.

Why was Polonia's capital so unsuccessful at producing a leader in the Cermak mold, who could seize political power in the city and give decisive proof that his ethnic group had arrived?

It may have been simply long odds and bad luck. The obstacles against a new immigrant politician rising to power in a large, heterogeneous city should not be down-played. Only the highly unusual situation of Big Bill Thompson's utter degradation allowed Cermak to win in Chicago in 1931. In New York City in 1933, Fiorello LaGuardia achieved a victory similar to Cermak's, using his skills as a broker, his ambition for power, and his passion for reform to become the first Italian-American mayor of that city. But again, only a major scandal and an internal crumbling of the Tammany machine allowed him to win a fusion victory. Victories like LaGuardia's and Cermak's have been rare for new immigrant groups, and the elements of sheer luck and unique personalities cannot be discounted.[11]

Yet there may be deeper reasons for Polonia's failure to elect a mayor than mere chance. Polish-Americans themselves have suggested a number of reasons. Those of a Polish National Alliance persuasion have often berated Polonia for its bloc Democratic voting. The Alliance papers repeatedly implored Chicago's Poles to break their one party allegiance, so that both parties would take them seriously, and to adopt a "swing vote" or "balance of power" strategy, voting for the man or the party which does the most for the group. Such a strategy might have gained Polonia more attention and a bit more patronage, as both parties found they could not take the Polish vote for granted; but it is unlikely that it would have led to more political power or to a Polish mayor. In the 1920s and 30s, when Polonia was first striking for wider recognition, the Republican party in Chicago was a dying institution; and it has been all but dead since then. Neither a total defection of all Polish voters nor an occasional defection of half the Polish voters to the Republicans would have revived their fortunes. And dividing the Polish vote in this way

would have lessened the chances of capturing the Democratic party. Furthermore, if Cermak and LaGuardia are taken as models of successful ethnic
politics, it appears that bloc voting is no disadvantage. LaGuardia used his
life-long Republicanism and Cermak the bloc Democratic vote of the Czechs
as one element in the climb to power. Not a bloc vote, but the failure to move
out from this base seems more pertinent to Polonia's failure.

Polish-Americans, also, have privately blamed their own tendency
towards factionalism for their lack of political success. This trait is supposedly
imbedded deep in the national character and calls up ghosts of the *liberum
veto* in the Polish Diet and the anarchic individualism of Poland's *szlachta*.
Factionalism has certainly been a hindrance in particular local contests, most
notably in the drive to elect Polonia's first congressman. Anarchic individualism and inability to work in harness, another side of the legendary Polish factionalism, also describes Ben Adamowski's maverick career quite well. Perhaps this trait in Polish and Polish-American culture, which militates against
patient, disciplined, broker politics, has been a factor in limiting Polish-
American political success.

But a more fundamental factor, I believe, prevented the recognition
drive from reaching completion in a Polish-American mayor. The whole
thrust of ethnic politics as pursued by the Polish-Americans during the recognition drive and as practiced by other ethnic and racial groups in American
politics was probably misguided. Ethnic politics, when it means closing ranks
in group solidarity and seeking power as a distinct, separate group, has severe
limitations. It only succeeds when the group forms a majority of the voters in
a political division. Even then, success is not often taken seriously by others;
for the group's leaders are then thought of as "big fish in a small pond." Success in larger, more pluralist, sectors of American politics must be coalition,
broker politics.

Polonia's capital suffered from the ironic disadvantage of being the
largest new immigrant group in Chicago yet falling well short of a numerical
majority in the city. Their relatively large numbers were a disadvantage in
two ways: they nurtured the illusion that if Polish voters would only stick together they could gain power and importance in politics by sheer weight of
numbers; second, they made other new groups consider the Polish community
a threat. Had they been more numerous or the city smaller, Polish-Americans
could have eventually dominated politics in Chicago as they did in the small
city of Hamtramck, Michigan.[12] Were they less numerous, they might have
recognized their marginality and played a broker's role as Cermak's Czechs

did. But, as it was, they were a prey to their own illusions and a target of other groups' jealousies.

Dziennik Chicagoski, at the time of Mayor Cermak's death, warned against the illusions inherent in Polonia's large numbers:

A Pole will be mayor of Chicago, only if we continue the politics of the dead mayor Cermak, i.e., if we make alliances with other groups. . . . Unfortunately, the majority among us is now playing at Pan-Slavism and forgetting that mayor Cermak practiced a different kind of politics. In his organization were found next to the Czechs, Jews; next to the Poles, Irish; next to the Germans, Swedes.[13]

However, neither the *Chicagoski* nor the other Polish leaders seem to have taken this advice to heart. Led by PADO, Polish politicians continued to act as if political power would fall to Polonia like a ripe fruit, if only it could perfect its own unity and solidarity.

The political experience of New York's ethnic groups confirms the disadvantage inherent in large numbers which fall short of a majority. Just as Chicago's Poles form the city's largest ethnic group in the twentieth century, yet have never elected a mayor, so too New York's Jews are clearly that city's largest community, but the first Jewish mayor of New York was elected only recently, in 1973. Not a Jew, but LaGuardia, representing the smaller Italian community of New York, was the first to crack the WASP and Irish monopoly in city politics.

For newly emergent groups, solidarity politics is probably a necessary first step; but it reaches a point of diminishing returns. Only through coalition politics, broker politics, the politics of painful compromise and careful bridge-building can a new group be successful at the highest levels in pluralist, polyglot America. Polish-American politicians were dedicated to the Polonia ideal of strength in unity. But in a pluralist society, politics must go beyond the internal unity of one group. The role of politics is to unify all groups in a society, to manage conflicts between groups.

The successful ethnic leader is the one who builds bridges across the hyphen—not a *Polish*-American but a Polish-American.[14] Matt Szymczak probably realized this, and his long service on the Federal Reserve Board, though it removed him from political contention in Chicago, cannot be called a failure. He served his country and his ancestral community well. Had there been more Szymczaks, some would have won prominence in Chicago and others would have gone on to other areas as he did. But too many of his compatriots tried to use the hyphen as a bludgeon rather than a bridge. Polonia's capital remained in the stage of hyphenated politics too long. Why this was so cannot be explained completely without going further into the murky depths of national character. But certainly Polonia's difficult numerical position in Chicago, neither a small, hungry minority nor a clear, dominant majority, has had much to do with its failure to elect a Chicago mayor.

Polonia's capital may not get another opportunity. Among the third generation of Polish-American politicians (men who entered politics after World War II and are active today), only one seems to have the potential combination needed for a mayoral bid after Richard J. Daley retires—Congressman Daniel Rostenkowski. Son of the old ward boss Joe Rosty, Daniel Rostenkowski succeeded his father as Thirty-second Ward committeeman, is widely recognized as Mayor Daley's legislative representative in the U.S. Congress, and is sometimes mentioned as a possible Daley successor. He has both machine connections and a "bright young man" image which could conceivably make him a strong contender for the mayoralty. Yet he has been building up seniority in Congress from a safe seat (a "civil service congressman," as one politician called him); and there is, at present, no indication he would be willing to risk this position in a struggle for city power after Daley leaves the scene.

Ethnic groups move into and out of power in American cities in a fairly regular succession. Old-stock Americans gave way to the Irish, who, in turn, have been challenged by the newer immigrant groups when they became numerous. But as Congressman Rostenkowski himself has said, Poles had better move fast if they wish to take their turn at the helm in Chicago's City Hall; for the "next group up," the blacks, are growing ever more numerous in the city and have begun to elect mayors in other Northern cities. It may well be that, because of the lack of a suitable leader in the second generation, when they were the next group up, Chicago's Polish-Americans never will elect one of their own as mayor.[15]

Participation in American politics was an avenue whereby Polish immigrants and their descendants came inside American life. In the early years of Polonia's capital, Polish-American voting and officeholding gave both individuals and the Polonia community a sense of belonging. Ethnic recognition by Democratic party leaders heightened the Polish-American sense of pride and security. But the recognition drive stalled at lower political levels because of its own inherent limitations. Polish-American political leaders might have achieved more had they moved beyond solidarity to bridge-building, broker politics.

In lieu of the power and prestige of the mayoralty, Polish-Americans in

Chicago have settled for the long career of Judge Jarecki as the symbol of
their attainments in politics. Polonia's capital has made honesty a major
theme of its political history. Honest Pete Kiolbassa, John Smulski, and flinty
old Judge Jarecki, as well as a host of other respectables, are the heroes of this
interpretation. This view, of course, forgets Kunz's reputation as Stanley the
Slugger, omits mention of Frank Zintak's indictment for embezzlement and
Frank Konkowski's conviction for selling city jobs. In fact, Polish politicians
have been neither more nor less honest than others. But when the recognition
drive stalled short of the mayoralty, the honesty theme prevailed among
Polish-Americans. There never was a Polish Cermak, but there was a Jarecki.

Polish-American participation in Chicago politics from 1888 to 1940
was part of a search for bread, a home, security, acceptance, and advancement
in a New World. The success of Jarecki and others like him has assured
Polish-Americans that, despite the limitations of the recognition drive, they
have achieved much of what they sought.

Postscript

I indicated in the preface that Polish-American politics entered a new era after the Second World War which would be best considered as a separate study from the story which appears in these pages. Though I have not pursued this study in any detailed manner beyond 1940, I would like to sketch a few themes I think worth exploring in the recent era and also indicate the problems facing anyone who would undertake such an exploration.

The main problem would be methodological. I have based my estimates of the Polish vote on heavy concentrations of Polish voters in the older neighborhoods of first and second settlement. This necessarily neglects the opinions and voting behavior of Polish-Americans who were scattered in generally non-Polish areas of the city. As long as the number of scattered Polish-Americans is small, as it was before 1940, relatively little distortion results.

But after the Second World War significantly large numbers of Polish-Americans dispersed into middle-class neighborhoods on the fringes of the city and in the suburbs. Though they still clustered together to some extent in these newer areas, they were not sufficiently concentrated to form the majority of voters in any one precinct. Thus the election results from these newer "Polish" areas do not necessarily reflect the voting behavior of the Polish-Americans within them. Heavy concentrations of Polish voters can still be isolated in the older neighborhoods after 1945, but to generalize from the votes of these concentrated neighborhoods to the vote of all Polish-Americans would be seriously misleading.

It seems to me that the political behavior of Polish-Americans after 1945 would have to be examined in two separate ways. The study of Polish voting in more dispersed areas could use contemporary polling techniques to determine the attitudes and votes of a selected sample of still living voters. The vote of those still concentrated in older neighborhoods could be determined by direct inspection of registration lists and election returns, as I have done in this study. Comparison between the votes of these two different groups of Polish-Americans, presumably at different stages of assimilation, would be a major concern of any postwar history of Polish-American politics.

Another major question to explore in the postwar era would be the persistence of Democratic loyalty, both in national and local politics. Nationally, the Republicans attempted in the immediate postwar years to capitalize on Polish-American outrage at the communization of Poland, aiming, in particular, to blame Franklin D. Roosevelt and his advisors at the Yalta Conference for "selling out" Poland to the Russians. There is no question that Yalta became an abrasive issue for Polish-Americans, but a few studies by Samuel Lubell and others have indicated that Polish voters still remained Democratic in the 1948 election. A more detailed study of the impact of Yalta and the early cold war on Polish voting is needed. In the 1950s the great popularity of President Eisenhower may have drawn Polish-Americans from their traditional party allegiance. More recently, white backlash, the law-and-order issue, and the supposed radicalism of the McGovern candidacy in 1972 may also have eroded Democratic loyalty.

Locally, the Republicans also attempted to win Polish-American support. Twice they slated a Polish-American to run for mayor against Richard J. Daley: Benjamin Adamowski in 1963 and John Waner in 1967. Both attempts failed to defeat Daley, and it seems clear that at least in Waner's case Polish-Americans did not give their countryman much support. Waner lost all fifty wards of the city, including his own heavily Polish ward. The staunchly Democratic *Dziennik Chicagoski* endorsed Daley, despite Waner's ancestry. The Adamowski case deserves closer study, however, since Adamowski made a creditable showing against Daley. The Polish Republican aimed his 1963 vote appeal at small homeowners who, he said, paid much of the tax bill for Daley's prestigious downtown projects. Polish-Americans are prominent among city homeowners, and they may well have given significant support to their Republican compatriot in that election.

Overall, I would hazard a hypothesis, which I hope a future researcher will test, that Chicago's Polish-Americans have generally stayed strongly Democratic in local elections since 1945, but that their national voting pattern shows a great deal more variety.

Aside from voting behavior, another significant theme which needs exploration is the changing attitude of Polish-Americans toward politics. After the Second World War, when Polish-Americans entered the middle class in large numbers and left their older, ethnic neighborhoods, they often tried to discard anything which reminded them of their origins. Few continued to read Polish newspapers (*Dziennik Chicagoski,* Chicago's oldest Polish daily, folded in 1971) or to belong to Polonia organizations. It seems to me that ward politics and the appeals of Polish politicians to the old solidarity theme also reminded them painfully of the past.

During the period before 1940, political involvement served an important function as part of Polonia's search for acceptance. Politics was on the leading edge of the Americanization process. But as the limitations of the recognition drive became evident and few Polish politicians were successful in bridging the hyphen, politics became less relevant to upwardly mobile residents of Polonia. More and more "Polish-Americans" were becoming "Americans of Polish descent" through participation in business, labor unions, the professions, and residential dispersal. Polonia's politics, left behind in the hyphenated stage, began to look less like an avenue into America than a barricade keeping American Poles out. The search for acceptance has gone on; but, if my impressions should prove correct, Polonia's politics is no longer a significant part of the search.

A Note on Sources and Method

Manuscript Collections

I discovered only two major manuscript collections dealing with the political activities of Chicago's Polish-Americans. The Edmund K. Jarecki papers at the University of Illinois at Chicago Circle consist primarily of scrapbooks of newspaper clippings. Judge Jarecki seems to have saved every reference to himself which ever appeared in a Chicago paper during his long career. Many of the clippings contain valuable information about other Polish-American politicians as well. Frank Bobrytzke, a former president of the Polish-American Democratic Organization, graciously permitted me to inspect the surviving minutes, financial accounts, and other records of that organization which were in his possession. He has subsequently donated these records to the Chicago Historical Society.

I also consulted the following minor collections on Polish-Americans: The Walter J. LaBuy papers and the Wencel Hetman papers at the University of Illinois at Chicago Circle, scrapbooks in the possession of Martin Powroznik, and a letter file at the Polish Roman Catholic Union Archives and Museum.

Several collections left by non-Polish individuals provided useful information, especially the Carter H. Harrison papers at Newberry Library and the Mary McDowell papers at the Chicago Historical Society, but also the William E. Dever papers at the Chicago Historical Society, the Charles E. Merriam papers at the University of Chicago, and the Graham Taylor papers at Newberry Library.

Election Statistics

The raw materials for determining the "Polish vote" were the official registration lists of voters, preserved in xerox copies at the Board of Election Com-

missioners in Chicago's City Hall, and the official election returns, on microfilm at the Municipal Reference Library in City Hall.

To calculate the Polish vote in any given election, I isolated election
units (precincts) whose voters were indisputably and overwhelmingly Polish
and then used the vote of those units as a sample of the total Polish vote. I
inspected the registration lists in all areas of the city where Poles resided and
counted all the Polish names found on each precinct's list. I then chose as
sample precincts all those in which Polish names comprised at least 60 percent
of the total registration. In most cases, these precincts contained an even
higher percentage (over 80 percent and sometimes as high as 90 or 95 percent) of Polish voters. Whenever there was any doubt as to whether a name
was Polish or not (because of a possible similarity to Czech, Russian, or Jewish names), I adopted a "minimalist" position and omitted it. For this reason and also because some Polish names had probably been Americanized
and thus went undetected, there were undoubtedly more precincts with overwhelming Polish majorities than the ones I selected; but I am reasonably
certain that my minimal sample is composed of indisputably Polish precincts.

Use of voter registration lists to isolate Polish precincts is more accurate
than use of census returns. Census enumeration of persons of Polish origin
includes noncitizens and nonvoters. Thus, a census tract with a majority of
Polish residents would not necessarily include a majority of Polish voters. Inspection of registration lists reveals who was actually a registered voter in each
precinct.

In the earlier part of the study the number of sample precincts with large
Polish majorities is very small; but since the number of Polish voters in the
city is also very small, these few precincts contain a sizable proportion of all
Poles registered. In 1888, for example, my sample consists of only three precincts. These precincts, however, contain about one-third of the two thousand
or so Polish voters in the city. As the study progresses chronologically, the
number of sample precincts increases; but the total number of Polish voters
increases even more. Thus, in the 1930s, the sample consists of over eighty
precincts; but these eighty precincts probably contain a smaller percentage of
the total Polish vote in the city than the three precincts of 1888 did. This
means that, methodologically speaking, the Polish vote figures are less reliable in the latter part of the study than in the earlier part. But, fortunately,
the Polish vote is so monolithically Democratic in the 1930s that it seems unlikely any nuances have been overlooked by this relatively less reliable sample.

Use of the vote in concentrated Polish precincts as a sample of the total

Polish vote can, of course, tell us nothing about how Poles who were scattered in non-Polish areas voted. Theoretically, at least, they may have voted quite differently from Poles who clustered in Polish neighborhoods. But during the time period of this study, most Poles did cluster together.

No attempt was made to apply advanced statistical techniques to the election data. Raw vote totals in each sample precinct were simply converted to percentages, and the mean of all these percentages was determined and used as an approximation of the Polish vote in a given election.

Anyone who wishes to obtain the raw vote totals for Polish precincts in the various elections mentioned in this study can consult Appendix II of my doctoral dissertation, "American Politics in Polonia's Capital" (University of Chicago, Department of History, 1972), to find the ward and precinct numbers of the units I used in my sample. He can then look up the vote totals for those units in the official returns in Chicago's Municipal Reference Library.

Newspapers

Polish-language newspapers published in Chicago provided the most important documentary source for this study. Unfortunately, the files of the *Dziennik Chicagoski* were not available to me due to great confusion at the paper's editorial offices, caused by the paper's move to new quarters and then its subsequent cessation of publication in 1971. I have not been able to determine whether the files have been preserved. However, the editorial morgue of the *Dziennik Zwiazkowy* contained not only a complete file of that paper's back copies but also most issues of the *Dziennik Ludowy* and a partial file of the *Chicagoski* from 1920 on. The Center for Research Libraries of the University of Chicago also contains files of Chicago's Polish papers from 1920 on, including the *Zwiazkowy*, *Chicagoski*, and the South Chicago journal *Polonia*. The Polish Roman Catholic Union Archives possess a file of that organization's weekly journal, *Naród Polski;* and the Polish National Alliance library has a file of the PNA organ, *Zgoda*. A translation of selected articles from Chicago's Polish press, arranged thematically, was made in the 1930s as part of a Federal Writers Project in the Works Progress Administration. It is available on microfilm at the Chicago Public Library under the title *Chicago Foreign Language Press Survey*.

The English-language newspapers of Chicago contained occasional references to Polish-Americans and were valuable for general political information. The *Chicago Tribune* and *Chicago Daily News* were consulted for the entire period of this study; the *Chicago Record-Herald* also proved useful, since it is indexed for the period 1900–1912. Occasional articles in the *Chicago Times, Chicago Journal,* and *Chicago American* also were consulted.

Interviews

I interviewed about twenty-five persons in Chicago's Polish-American community, most of whom were of advanced years and thus had personal recollections of events in this study. These interviews varied widely in usefulness, and most were more important for the attitudes they revealed and the flavor of the past which they evoked than for precise factual information. Five deserve special mention. Benjamin Adamowski spoke long and candidly about his maverick career in politics, and Judge Thaddeus Adesko provided me with a meticulous oral autobiography. Peter Figel, a precinct captain, Frank Zintak, a former ward committeeman, and C. Jack Przybylinski, chief clerk of the election commission, gave me vivid firsthand insights into the day-to-day functioning of a political machine.

Other Sources

The other sources consulted for this study are mentioned and discussed in the footnotes, so a complete listing of them would be repetitious and superfluous. My general indebtedness to writers of American history is, I hope, obvious. A few works which were particularly valuable, however, merit further mention.

The literature on Polish immigrants in America is neither voluminous nor of high quality. No one with an interest in the subject, however, should neglect Emily Greene Balch's pioneering work, *Our Slavic Fellow Citizens* (New York: Charities Publication Committee, 1910); William I. Thomas and Florian Znaniecki's monumental sociological study, *The Polish Peasant in Europe and America* (Chicago: University of Chicago Press, 1919); and Joseph A. Wytrwal's *America's Polish Heritage* (Detroit: Endurance Press, 1961), the closest approach to an adequate general history of Poles in America. Unfortunately, Wytrwal's recent book, *Poles in American History and Tradition* (Detroit: Endurance Press, 1969), is largely a filiopietistic listing of names and milestones. An often neglected source on Polish America is the journal of the Polish American Historical Association, *Polish American*

Studies. The articles are uneven in quality, but they contain much valuable information available nowhere else. Most other historical works published by Polish-American organizations, such as the Annals of the Polish Roman Catholic Union Archives, edited by Miecieslaus Haiman, deal with early Polish-American history before mass immigration and are heavily filiopietist.

Several recent studies have made important contributions to an understanding of ethnic politics in America, particularly John M. Allswang, *A House for All Peoples* (Lexington, Ky.: University Press of Kentucky, 1971); Alex Gottfried, *Boss Cermak of Chicago* (Seattle: University of Washington Press, 1962); Paul Kleppner, *The Cross of Culture* (New York: The Free Press, 1970); Richard Jensen, *The Winning of the Midwest* (Chicago: University of Chicago Press, 1971); Arthur Mann, *LaGuardia Comes to Power* (Philadelphia: J. B. Lippincott, 1965); and Humbert Nelli, *The Italians in Chicago* (New York: Oxford University Press, 1970). Caution should be employed in using the statistics from Allswang's book, since he used census returns as his source for the nationality characteristics of election units. Mann and Nelli used the more satisfactory method of inspecting registration lists.

Notes

Preface

1. The seminal work in developing the "ethnocultural" approach to politics is Lee Benson, *The Concept of Jacksonian Democracy: New York as a Test Case* (Princeton, N. J.: Princeton University Press, 1961). A good review of the recent works using this approach is Robert P. Swierenga, "Ethnocultural Political Analysis: A New Approach to American Ethnic Studies," *Journal of American Studies* (April 1971): 59–79. The works most relevant to my own study are Paul Kleppner, *The Cross of Culture* (New York: The Free Press, 1970); Richard J. Jensen, *The Winning of the Midwest* (Chicago: University of Chicago Press, 1971); and John M. Allswang, *A House for All Peoples* (Lexington, Ky.: University Press of Kentucky, 1971).

1. Polska and Polonia

1. The Congress of Vienna also designated the city of Cracow and its surrounding region a free city, but the three partitioning powers kept a close watch on its theoretical independence. When an abortive revolution broke out in the city in 1846, Austria annexed this last particle of free Poland.

2. Though the broadest outlines of Polish history are familiar to students of Europe, detailed histories of Poland are very scarce in the English language. Much English writing on Poland is by emigrés, who impart a romantic, nineteenth-century spirit of nationalism to it. The best available general history is a translation of a Polish work, Aleksander Gieysztor et al., *History of Poland* (Warsaw: Polish Scientific Publishers, 1968). Two excellent works on the Polish insurrections are R. F. Leslie, *Polish Politics and the Revolution of November 1830* (London: The Athlone Press, 1956), and the same author's *Reform and Insurrection in Russian Poland, 1856–1865* (London: The Athlone Press, 1963). Both these books rely heavily on various works in Polish by Stefan Kieniewicz, Poland's leading authority on nineteenth-century political and social history. Some of my remarks about the history of Poland are drawn from two series of lectures delivered by Kieniewicz at the University of Chicago from January to June, 1968.

3. This discussion of peasant emancipation is based on Gieysztor, *History of Poland*, and, especially, Stefan Kieniewicz, *The Emancipation of the Polish Peasantry* (Chicago: University of Chicago Press, 1969).

4. Gieysztor, pp. 584–86; Kieniewicz, pp. 192, 210–23; Jan Rutkowski, *Historja*

Gospodarcza Polski (Poznan: Księgarnia Akademicka, 1950), 11: 233–40; U.S., Congress, *Reports of the Immigration Commission,* 61st Cong., 2d sess., 1911, Doc. no. 338, vol. 4, "Emigration Conditions in Europe," pp. 338–39, 373–75.

5. William I. Thomas and Florian Znaniecki, *The Polish Peasant in Europe and America* (Chicago: University of Chicago Press, 1918), 5: ix.

6. In this introductory chapter, I am simply trying to give a general idea of the numbers of Polish immigrants. Therefore, the totals given are estimates from Joseph A. Wytrwal, *America's Polish Heritage* (Detroit: Endurance Press, 1961), p. 79. The yearly immigration figures are more precise, taken from Bureau of Immigration reports in *Chicago Daily News Almanac* [hereafter cited as *CDNA*], *1898,* p. 113, and *1915,* p. 463.

7. Thomas and Znaniecki, *Polish Peasant* 5: 113; Wytrwal, *America's Polish Heritage,* p. 212.

8. John Iwicki, *The First Hundred Years, 1866–1966* (Rome: Gregorian University Press, 1966), pp. 10–56.

2. Polonia's Capital

1. See, *Poles in America* (Chicago: Polish Day Assoc., 1937), especially, "A Short History of the Settlement and the Rise of the Poles in the United States," pp. 17–29.

2. "Our Polish Citizens," *Chicago Tribune,* March 14, 1886, p. 3.

3. Thomas and Znaniecki, *Polish Peasant* 5: 63; M. S. Szymczak, "Polish American Statistical Materials," *Polish American Studies* 21 (July-December, 1964): 82–83.

4. Wytrwal, *America's Polish Heritage,* p. 79.

5. Sr. Mary Remigia Napolska, *The Polish Immigrant in Detroit to 1914* (Chicago: Annals of the PRCU Archives, 1946), p. 101; see also, Melvin Holli, *Reform in Detroit* (New York: Oxford University Press, 1969).

6. Iwicki, *First Hundred Years,* pp. 12, 64.

7. Miecieslaus Haiman, "The Poles in Chicago," in *Poles of Chicago, 1837–1937* (Chicago: Polish Pageant, Inc., 1937), p. 1. Bessie L. Pierce, *A History of Chicago,* 1: 183, 2: 22; Anthony G. Tomczak, "The Poles in Chicago," in *Poles in America,* p. 65; "The First Settler of St. Stanislaus," *Dziennik Chicagoski,* April 1, 1942; and numerous references to Anton Smarzewski-Schermann appear in the Polish press and in commemorative books.

8. *St. Stanislaus Kostka Parish Centennial Book, 1967,* pp. 33–34.

9. This and the subsequent listing of Polish parishes can be found in F. Niklewicz, *Historja Polaków w Stanie Illinois* (Green Bay: n.p., 1938), as well as in *Poles of Chicago.* See also the individual parish jubilee books in the PRCU archives.

10. See Table 2. Due to the fact that the U.S. censuses of 1900 and 1910 do not identify Poles, most studies of ethnic groups in America contain no population figures for American Poles in these years. In the table and throughout this chapter, I have relied on my own estimates, based on the Chicago Board of Education school census of May 2, 1910, found in *CDNA, 1912,* pp. 578–86. This school

census listed the number of minors by "mother tongue" in each ward; thus, unlike in the U.S. census, Poles were included. The ratio between all minors in
each ward (from the school census) and the total ward population (from the
U.S. census) provided me with a multiplier to apply to the number of Polish
minors in order to obtain an estimate of each ward's Polish population. This
ratio fluctuated slightly from ward to ward, but it averaged 2.3.

11.   U.S., Bureau of the Census, *Eleventh Census of the U.S.: 1890*, vol. 4, pt. 2, pp.
      170–71; Joseph Parot, "Ethnic versus Black Metropolis: The Origins of Polish-
      Black Housing Tensions in Chicago," *Polish American Studies* 29 (Spring-
      Autumn 1972): 7–14; Edith Abbott, *The Tenements of Chicago, 1908–1935*
      (Chicago: University of Chicago Press, 1936), pp. 176, 187.

12.   *St. Adalbert Parish Diamond Jubilee Book, 1947*, p. 3; "Polish Churches of
      Chicago and Vicinity," in *Poles of Chicago*, pp. 95, 98.

13.   U.S., Bureau of the Census, *Eleventh Census of the U.S.: 1890*, vol. 4, pt. 2, pp.
      164–65; Evelyn M. Kitagawa and Karl E. Taeuber, eds., *Local Community Fact
      Book, 1960* (Chicago: University of Chicago Press, 1963), p. 76. Map 4 in
      Charles J. Bushnell, *The Social Problem at the Chicago Stock Yards* (Chicago:
      University of Chicago Press, 1902).

14.   Paul F. Cressey, "The Succession of Cultural Groups in the City of Chicago"
      (Ph.D. diss., University of Chicago, 1930), p. 79; Louis Wirth, *The Ghetto*
      (Chicago: University of Chicago Press, 1928); Jane Addams, *Twenty Years at
      Hull House* (New York: Macmillan, 1910); *Local Community Fact Book,
      1960*, p. 76.

15.   See Alex Gottfried, *Boss Cermak of Chicago* (Seattle: University of Washing-
      ton Press, 1962), for the story of Cermak's rise to power and his relations with
      the Poles in this area.

16.   *Local Community Fact Book, 1960*, p. 134; *St. Mary of Perpetual Help Parish
      Diamond Jubilee Book, 1961*, and *St. Barbara Parish Silver Jubilee Book, 1935*.

17.   *St. Joseph Parish Golden Jubilee Book, 1937*.

18.   U.S., Bureau of the Census, *Eleventh Census of the U.S.: 1890*, vol. 4, pt. 2, p.
      178; Edith Abbott, *Tenements of Chicago*, pp. 174–75.

19.   Mary E. McDowell, "At the Heart of the Packingtown Strike," *The Commons*
      (September 1904): 398; Edith Abbott, *Tenements of Chicago*, p. 130.

20.   *Reports of the Immigration Commission*, "Immigrants in Industries," pt. 2, pp.
      200–201, 213.

21.   Sophonisba P. Breckenridge and Edith Abbott, "Chicago Housing Conditions V:
      South Chicago at the Gates of the Steel Mills," *American Journal of Sociology*
      17 (September 1911): 145, 173–74.

22.   *Immaculate Conception Parish Golden Jubilee Book, 1932*, and *St. Michael the
      Archangel Parish Golden Jubilee Book, 1942*.

23.   A good contemporary description of the Polish ghettoes in Chicago is in Breck-
      enridge and Abbott, "Chicago Housing Conditions," p. 147. The traditional his-
      torical and sociological view of the ghetto can be found in Louis Wirth, *The
      Ghetto*; Oscar Handlin, *Boston's Immigrants* (Cambridge, Mass.: Harvard Uni-
      versity Press, 1941); and Handlin, *The Uprooted* (New York: Little, Brown and
      Co., 1951). Recent works which question the extent to which ghettoization oc-

curred are Humbert Nelli, *The Italians in Chicago* (New York: Oxford University Press, 1970) and Howard Chudacoff, *Mobile Americans* (New York: Oxford University Press, 1972). The most balanced recent appraisal of the extent of ghettoization is Sam Bass Warner, Jr., and Colin Burke, "Cultural Change and the Ghetto," *Journal of Contemporary History* 5 (October 1969): 173–87.

24. This index has been used most widely to measure Negro segregation, and it has been found that Negro indexes range between 60 and 98 in American cities. Stanley Lieberson, *Ethnic Patterns in American Cities* (New York: The Free Press, 1963) uses it to measure immigrant segregation in ten American cities. He rarely found an index above 60 for an immigrant group. Information on how to compute the index can be found in Charles M. Dollar and Richard J. Jensen, *Historian's Guide to Statistics* (New York: Holt, Rinehart and Winston, 1971), pp. 125–26; and in Karl and Alma Taeuber, *Negroes in Cities* (Chicago: Aldine Publishing Co., 1965), pp. 28–31, 195–245.

25. *Reports of the Immigration Commission,* "Immigrants in Cities," vol. 1, pp. 207, 259–60.

26. See map 3 for an illustration of the concentrated Polish precincts in Polish Downtown. A complete listing of all the precincts with significant Polish majorities, from 1888 to 1940, is found in appendix II of my doctoral dissertation, "American Politics in Polonia's Capital," (University of Chicago, 1972).

27. Cressey, "Succession of Cultural Groups" p. 80; Harold M. Mayer and Richard C. Wade, *Chicago: Growth of a Metropolis* (Chicago: University of Chicago Press, 1969), p. 137; Iwicki, *First Hundred Years* p. 119.

28. *Local Community Fact Book, 1960,* p. 56; *St. Hyacinth Parish Golden Jubilee Book, 1944,* pp. 16–20; Iwicki, p. 100.

29. *Local Community Fact Book, 1960,* p. 56; Mayer and Wade, *Chicago* p. 207; *St. Hyacinth Parish Golden Jubilee Book, 1944,* pp. 28–31.

30. *Local Community Fact Book, 1960,* pp. 130–132; *SS. Peter and Paul Parish Silver Jubilee Book, 1920; Five Holy Martyrs Parish Silver Jubilee Book, 1934.*

31. *Local Community Fact Book, 1960;* "Polish Churches of Chicago and Vicinity," in *Poles of Chicago;* and individual parish jubilee books.

32. Mayer and Wade, *Chicago* pp. 137, 263.

33. *Immaculate Conception Parish Golden Jubilee Book, 1932.* I am not suggesting that Polish neighborhoods were completely closed or self-contained. Stephen Thernstrom and Peter Knights, "Men in Motion," in Tamara K. Hareven (ed.), *Anonymous Americans* (Englewood Cliffs, N.J.: Prentice-Hall, Inc., 1971), pp. 17–47, have suggested that the evidence of population mobility in nineteenth-century cities is so overwhelming that few if any neighborhoods could be closed in a demographic sense. I did not compute the mobility of individual Polish-Americans in and out of Polish neighborhoods; but the rapid expansion of Polonia into new areas indicates that Poles were geographically mobile. Neighborhoods were not completely closed socially either. The economic and social functions of Polish Downtown were city-wide, as indicated earlier. However, impressionistic evidence from the Polish press and from interviews indicates much neighborhood consciousness among Poles as well as a kind of "pecking order" of status among Chicago's Polish neighborhoods, with Polish Downtown at the top and South Chicago at the bottom. The point I wish to emphasize is

that Polish neighborhoods were self-conscious, competitive, and jealous, belying the unity which Polish leaders attempted to foster.

3. Influences and Institutions

1. The Immigration Commission was popularly known as the Dillingham Commission after its chairman, Senator William P. Dillingham of Vermont. It published its findings in forty-two volumes. See chapter five of Oscar Handlin, *Race and Nationality in American Life* (New York: Little, Brown and Co., 1957) for a critical analysis of this report.

2. *Reports of the Immigration Commission*, "Immigrants in Cities," vol. 1, pp. 266, 308, vol. 2, p. 113; "Immigrants in Industries," pt. 2, pp. 209–10.

3. Ibid., "Immigrants and Organized Labor," vol. 1, pp. 417–18; Carroll D. Wright, "Influence of Trade Unions on Immigrants," *Bulletin of the Bureau of Labor*, no. 56 (January 1905), pp. 4–5; Mary McDowell, "A Quarter Century in the Stockyards District," *Transactions of the Illinois State Historical Society* (1920), p. 81. See Victor R. Greene, *The Slavic Community on Strike* (Notre Dame, Ind.: University of Notre Dame Press, 1968), for a discussion of union organizing among Poles in the Pennsylvania coal fields.

4. *Chicago Tribune*, March 14, 1886, p. 3; see the Catholic denunciations of socialism in the columns of the *New World*, Chicago's diocesan newspaper, and the *Dziennik Chicagoski*, in the 1890s. Some of the latter are readily available in English in Chicago Public Library, *Chicago Foreign Language Press Survey* (hereafter cited as *CFLPS*), Polish section, I-E; for circulation figures of *Dziennik Ludowy* and other newspapers, see N. W. Ayer and Sons, *Directory of Newspapers and Periodicals*.

5. *Przewodnik Adresowy Firm Polskich—Polish Business Directory*, (Chicago: W. Smulski Publishing Co., 1905); Sr. Mary Ancilla, "Catholic Polish Book Publishing in U.S., 1871–1900," *Polish American Studies* 16 (June 1954): 3; *CFLPS*, Polish section, II-A.

6. Thaddeus J. Lubera, "Hundred Years of Economic Contributions of the Poles to Chicago's Progress," *Poles of Chicago*, pp. 11–20.

7. Emily Greene Balch, *Our Slavic Fellow Citizens* (New York: Charities Publication Committee, 1910), pp. 307–8; *Reports of the Immigration Commission*, "Immigrants in Cities," vol. 1, p. 308.

8. Thomas and Znaniecki, *Polish Peasant* 4: 103–20.

9. Some American observers understood this phenomenon rather well, The *Chicago Tribune*, in its March 14, 1886, article on the Poles, commented: "The Poles are nearly all devoted Roman Catholics. Their devotion to their pastors sometimes exceeds their devotion to their church. They deem it the highest patriotism to preserve their mother tongue, and as the priest is at the same time the preserver and the teacher all Poles regard him with affection and esteem." The sociologists Thomas and Znaniecki have painted brilliant pictures of the functions of priest and parish in both Poland and America, *Polish Peasant* 4: pp. 103–20; 5: 43, 67–92. As the Poles themselves put it, "Each parish . . . is for us the center of the life and progress, both moral and material. A Polish Catholic not belonging to any parish is homeless; he has no support either religious or national" (*St. Barbara Parish Silver Jubilee Book, 1935*).

10. Wytrwal's, *America's Polish Heritage*, pp. 148–259, contains the best description of both the PRCU and the PNA in English.

11. Edward T. Janas, *Dictionary of American Resurrectionists, 1865–1965* (Rome: Gregorian University Press, 1967), pp. 6–10; Iwicki, *First Hundred Years*, pp. 9–10, 36–38, 61.

12. *St. Stanislaus Kostka Parish Centennial Book, 1967*, pp. 34–36; Iwicki, *First Hundred Years*, p. 64.

13. Iwicki, *First Hundred Years*, p. 62.

14. Ibid., pp. 204–5. Father Gordon, despite his name, was born in Poland, a descendant of Scottish immigrants to Poland.

15. Ibid., p. 13.

16. *Dziennik Chicagoski*, Dec. 15, 1890, p. 2.

17. Iwicki, *First Hundred Years*, pp. 55–56.

18. Ibid., p. 81.

19. "Rzym czy Polska?" A letter from Bishop Francis Hodur to Ignace J. Paderewski, in PRCU archives.

20. Ibid.

4. Politics in Polonia

1. Thomas and Znaniecki, *Polish Peasant*, 5: 127–28.

2. Wytrwal, *America's Polish Heritage*, pp. 212–35.

3. Iwicki, *First Hundred Years*, p. 100.

4. Ibid., p. 71.

5. Ibid., pp. 69–72, 79–89; Niklewicz, *Historja Polaków*, pp. 11–15; *St. Hedwig Parish Golden Jubilee Book, 1938*.

6. Waclaw Kruszka, *Historja Polska w Ameryce* (Milwaukee: Kurjer Publishing Co., 1905), 4: 32.

7. After 1861 Austrian Galicia experienced relatively free political activity. Peasants sat in the provincial diet, and in 1895 an important peasant party was organized. The franchise, however, was not universal, covering only the upper two-thirds of male adult taxpayers. Thus the landless peasants and the poorest third of the landowners, precisely the classes from which most immigrants came, were disfranchised. In Russian Poland a form of communal self-government was granted to peasant villages after the *uwlaszczenie* of 1864; but the communal assemblies had little power and few functions and, again, the landless and small holders were disfranchised. In Prussia, the liberal constitution of 1848 granted universal suffrage in theory; however, a weighted system of voting gave little influence to peasants and artisans. The landless most often did not participate at all. See Kieniewicz, *Emancipation of Polish Peasantry*, pp. 173, 185, 205–6; Felix Gilbert et al., *The Norton History of Modern Europe* (New York: W. W. Norton and Co., 1970), p. 1109.

8. "Another Forgotten Interview," in Carter Harrison papers (hereafter cited as Harrison papers), Newberry Library, Chicago.

5. The Emergence of the Polish-Democratic Bloc

1. *CDNA, 1889,* pp. 157–62; see tables 5 and 6.

2. *Chicago Tribune,* March 24, 1888, p. 6; March 25, 1888, p. 28.

3. Helen Buszyn, "The Political Career of Peter Kiolbassa," and "Peter Kiolbassa— Maker of Polish America," *Polish American Studies* 7 (June 1950): 8–22, and 8 (December 1951): 65–84, respectively.

4. *Zgoda,* March 28, 1888, p. 4.

5. *Chicago Tribune,* April 4, 1888, p. 2; see table 6.

6. *Zgoda,* April 11, 1888, p. 4.

7. See table 7 and, for national elections, table 17.

8. Claudius O. Johnson, *Carter Henry Harrison I: Political Leader* (Chicago: University of Chicago Press, 1928); "The Carter Harrison Dynasty in Chicago," *Review of Reviews* 28 (September 1903): 342–343.

9. *Chicago Daily News,* March 30, 1889, p. 1; *CDNA, 1895,* pp. 183–84. Paul Kleppner, *The Cross of Culture,* and Richard J. Jensen, *The Winning of the Midwest,* argue that throughout the Midwest at this time Catholic groups identified strongly with the Democratic party on religious and cultural grounds.

10. *Dziennik Chicagoski,* November 3, 1894, in *CFLPS,* Polish section, I-F.

11. The political affiliation of ethnic newspapers listed in N. W. Ayer's directories can be misleading. Both *Zgoda* and *Dziennik Zwiazkowy* listed themselves as independent, but a reading of these papers reveals Republican leanings.

12. *Chicago Tribune,* March 29, 1889, p. 3, and March 27, 1891, p. 1; *Dziennik Chicagoski,* December 15, 1890, p. 1.

13. Act of May 24, 1889, *Illinois Laws, 1889,* pp. 237–38; Bessie Pierce, *History of Chicago* 3: 367–68; John Patrick Walsh, "The Catholic Church in Chicago and Problems of an Urban Society, 1893–1915" (Ph.D. diss., University of Chicago, 1948); *Prominent Democrats of Illinois* (Chicago: Democrat Publishing Co., 1899), pp. 85–86; Ray Ginger, *Altgeld's America* (Chicago: Quadrangle Books, 1965), pp. 73–75, 143–67; see Kleppner, *Cross of Culture,* p. 161, and Jensen, *Winning of Midwest,* pp. 122–53, for a similar school controversy in Wisconsin.

14. *Illinois Staats-Zeitung,* November 5, 1892, in *CFLPS,* Polish section, I-F.

15. *Dziennik Chicagoski,* April 3, 1896, in *CFLPS,* Polish section, I-F.

16. Bessie Pierce, *History of Chicago* 3: 369–70.

17. *Chicago Times,* March 27, 1891, p. 1; *Chicago Tribune,* March 27, 1891, p. 1.

18. Buszyn, "Political Career of Peter Kiolbassa," p. 11; *Chicago Tribune,* April 10, 1891, p. 4; see table 8.

19. *Chicago City Council Proceedings, 1890,* p. 1754, and *1891,* pp. 20–22.

20. Ibid., *1892,* p. 144; V. O. Key, "Techniques of Graft: Memorandum on Interest on Public Funds," manuscript in Charles E. Merriam papers, University of Chicago.

21. *Chicago City Council Proceedings, 1901,* p. 89, *1902,* pp. 1594–95, *1905,* p. 891.

6. The Banker and the Boss

1. Pierce, *History of Chicago,* 3: p. 378; Joseph Bush Kingsbury, "Municipal Personnel Policy in Chicago, 1895–1915" (Ph.D. diss., University of Chicago, 1925), pp. 4–7.

2. William T. Stead, *If Christ Came to Chicago* (Chicago: Laird and Lee, 1894); Lloyd Wendt and Herman Kogan, *Lords of the Levee* (Garden City, N.Y.: Garden City Publishing Co., 1944), pp. 91–96; Charles N. Glaab and A. Theodore Brown, *A History of Urban America* (New York: The Macmillan Co., 1967), pp. 212, 218–19.

3. *Chicago City Council Proceedings, 1894,* pp. 2666–70, and *1895,* pp. 38–42; Wendt and Kogan, *Lords of the Levee,* pp. 117–20; Joel A. Tarr, "The Urban Politician as Entrepreneur," *Mid-America* 49 (January 1967): 63.

4. Lincoln Steffens, *The Shame of the Cities* (New York: Hill and Wang, 1965), pp. 162–73; Wendt and Kogan, pp. 119–20, 144–50.

5. Steffens, *Shame of the Cities,* pp. 175–77; Harold L. Ickes, *The Autobiography of a Curmudgeon* (Chicago: Quadrangle Books, 1969), pp. 82–88; John A. Fairlie, "The Street Railway Question in Chicago," *The Quarterly Journal of Economics* 21 (May 1907): 378–80.

6. Steffens, *Shame of the Cities,* p. 177; Fairlie, "The Street Railway," pp. 400–402.

7. Ralph Russell Tingley, "From Carter Harrison to Fred Busse" (Ph.D. diss., University of Chicago, 1950), pp. 4–9.

8. Ickes, *Autobiography,* p. 34; Charles E. Merriam, *Chicago: A More Intimate View of Urban Politics* (New York: The Macmillan Co., 1929), pp. 21–22; Carter Harrison, II, *Stormy Years* (Indianapolis: The Bobbs-Merrill Co., 1935), p. 191. The *Chicago Tribune* played a major role in defeating Lorimer, through a series of exposés starting on April 30, 1910, and continuing until Lorimer's expulsion from the Senate on July 14, 1912. Throughout this period the *Tribune* and the *Record-Herald* (more accessible because it is indexed) provide valuable political background.

9. Basic biographical material on Smulski can be found in most of the commemorative books on Polonia in Chicago. See, for instance, chap. 3 in *Poles in Chicago;* the chapters on Poles in Chicago and Poles in politics in *Poles in America;* and biographical sketches in Karol Wachtel, *Polonja w Ameryce* (Philadelphia: Polish Star Publishing Co., 1944); *St. Stanislaus Kostka Parish Golden Jubilee Book, 1917;* and Francis Bolek, ed., *Who's Who in Polish America* (New York: Harbinger House, 1943). Fuller information can only be gleaned from newspaper articles which appeared at various stages in his career.

10. *Chicago Tribune,* April 4, 1896, p. 9, and April 4, 1898, p. 7.

11. *The Commons* (April 1901): 15; idem (May 1901): 15; "Chicago Commons: A Social Center for Civic Cooperation," (1904), p. 42, and "Chicago Commons," (1899), pp. 32–33, pamphlets in the Graham Taylor papers (hereafter cited as Taylor papers), Newberry Library, Chicago.

12. *Chicago City Council Proceedings, 1898,* p. 1198, *1900,* pp. 650–52, 998–99, *1902,* p. 1127; *The Neighbor* (Northwestern University Settlement House Bulletin), February 1903.

13. See table 9.

14. *Chicago Tribune,* March 21, 1903, p. 6; Ickes, *Autobiography,* pp. 94–100.

15. See table 9.

16. *Chicago Record-Herald,* March 12, 1906, pp. 1–2, October 4, 1906, p. 1, and October 5, 1906, p. 8.

17. *Chicago Record-Herald,* April 6, 1905, p. 2.

18. *Chicago Journal,* February 6, 1904, p. 4; *Chicago Record-Herald,* October 5, 1906, p. 4; Illinois, *Journal of the Senate,* 1907, pp. 1361, 1457, 1564.

19. Smulski died in 1928. He committed suicide after a series of painful intestinal operations had driven him to the verge of insanity. See *Chicago Tribune,* March 19, 1928, p. 1, and March 20, 1928, p. 16; *Chicago Daily News,* March 19, 1928, p. 1, and March 20, 1928, pp. 4, 10; *Chicago Herald and Examiner,* March 19, 1928, p. 1.

20. Biographical information on Kunz is as scarce as it is for Smulski. Again, see the above-mentioned commemorative books on Poles in Chicago. The newspapers provide the most interesting details. See *Chicago Record-Herald,* June 11, 1906, p. 2, and *Chicago Tribune,* July 28, 1929, for information on Kunz as a horse fancier.

21. *Chicago Record-Herald,* January 19, 1906, p. 2, April 5, 1906, p. 8, and April 1, 1907, p. 2; *Chicago Journal,* March 9, 1904, p. 2, and March 16, 1904, p. 1; *Chicago Tribune,* February 2, 1911, p. 2.

22. Jane Addams, "Why the Ward Boss Rules," *The Outlook* 58 (April 2, 1898): 879; Robert A. Woods, in *The Commons* (May 1902): 21; Merriam, *Chicago,* pp. 101, 137.

23. *Dziennik Zwiazkowy,* October 30, 1920, p. 9.

24. *St. Stanislaus Kostka Parish Centennial Book, 1967,* p. 37.

25. *Chicago Tribune,* March 17, 1903, p. 2, and April 8, 1903, p. 3; *Chicago Record-Herald,* April 4, 1903, p. 9.

26. *Chicago Tribune,* April 7, 1903, p. 2, and April 8, 1903, p. 3; *The Commons* (May 1903): 2.

27. *Chicago Record-Herald,* March 31, 1904, p. 8; April 4, 1905, p. 3; April 5, 1905, p. 1; *Chicago Tribune,* April 3, 1905, p. 3.

28. *Chicago City Council Proceedings, 1905,* p. 2249.

29. Ibid., pp. 2580–81, 2688–89, 2790.

30. Ibid., pp. 2250–52; Tingley, "From Harrison to Busse," pp. 194–96; *Chicago Record-Herald,* January 19, 1906, p. 2.

31. *Chicago Record-Herald,* April 5, 1906, p. 8.

32. *Chicago Record-Herald,* November 7, 1906, p. 3, and November 20, 1906, p. 5; *Chicago Herald and Examiner,* February 9, 1932. Kunz continued running unsuccessfully for his old offices of congressman and ward committeeman throughout the 1930s. He died in 1946 at the age of eighty-two. See obituaries in *Chicago Tribune* and *Chicago Daily News* on April 24, 1946, and in the *New York Times,* April 25, 1946.

33. Program, the Aldermanic Club, Third Monthly Dinner, February 14, 1900, in Harrison papers.

7. The WASP as Ethnic Leader

1. Ickes, *Autobiography*, p. 128.
2. Harrison, *Stormy Years*, pp. 25–26, 31, 75.
3. Ibid., p. 106.
4. Ibid., p. 118; *Chicago Tribune*, March 16, 1897, p. 7; Merriam, *Chicago*, pp. 21–22, 191–92.
5. "Speeches for and about Poles," in Harrison papers.
6. "Another Forgotten Interview," in Harrison papers.
7. *Dziennik Chicagoski*, April 1, 1911, p. 4.
8. See table 11.
9. "Chicago's Campaign for Municipal Ownership," *The Commons* (March 1905): 137–43; Fairlie, "The Street Railway," pp. 390–91; *Chicago Tribune*, April 5, 1905, p. 8.
10. Fairlie, "The Street Railway," pp. 392–402; *Chicago Tribune*, March 27, 1907, p. 3; Kingsbury, "Municipal Personnel," pp. 70–78.
11. Ickes, *Autobiography*, pp. 117–20.
12. *Chicago Tribune*, January 5, 1911, p. 1.
13. *Chicago Tribune*, January 16, 1911, pp. 1–2, and April 3, 1911, p. 8.
14. The Republican totals in the primary were: Merriam—53,089; Thompson—26,406; Smulski—23,138; Murray—2,799; Scully—1052; party vote—110,721 (*CDNA, 1912*, p. 462).
15. The Democratic totals were: Harrison—55,116; Dunne—53,696; Graham—38,758; party vote—149,219 (*CDNA, 1912*, p. 461). See also table 12 and map 4.
16. *Chicago Tribune*, January 29, 1911, p. 2; "The Platform of Carter H. Harrison, 1911," in Harrison papers.
17. *Chicago Tribune*, April 1, 1911, p. 2, March 13, 1911, p. 1, and March 26, 1911, p. 4.
18. The complete returns were: Merriam (R)—160,672; Harrison (D)—177,997; Brubaker (Pro.)—2,239; Rodriguez (Soc.)—24,825; Prince (Soc. Lab.)—1058 (*CDNA, 1912*, p. 460).
19. *Chicago Tribune*, April 5, 1911, pp. 1–2.
20. Harrison, *Stormy Years*, p. 294; Merriam, *Chicago*, p. 284; *Chicago Tribune*, April 5, 1911, p. 2; *Chicago Journal*, April 5, 1911, p. 2. See table 13.
21. Information on these various officeholders has been gathered from three sources: a series of articles on "Our Progress in Politics," in *Dziennik Chicagoski*, running from January 19 to March 1, 1935; the civil lists published yearly in the *CDNA*; and the *Pay Rolls of the City of Chicago*, a complete and official civil list published by the city up to 1915, inclusive. Information on Board of Education members is from a list of appointees to the board found in the Harrison papers.

22. *Chicago Tribune,* March 26, 1911, p. 4.

23. Kingsbury, "Municipal Personnel," p. 81; Wendt and Kogan, *Lords of the Levee,* pp. 294–300; "Carter Harrison and the Gray Wolves," in Harrison papers; Carter Harrison to Graham Taylor, January 7, 1936, in Taylor papers; Graham Taylor, *Pioneering on Social Frontiers* (Chicago: University of Chicago Press, 1930), pp. 93–94.

24. *Dziennik Zwiazkowy,* February 17, 1915, p. 5, and February 19, 1915, p. 8.

25. Carter Harrison to Graham Taylor, January 7, 1936, in Taylor papers.

26. See table 14.

27. *Dziennik Zwiazkowy,* February 27, 1915, p. 8; Program of the Testimonial Dinner given to Honorable Carter H. Harrison, May 4, 1915, in Harrison papers.

8. Polonia and Progressivism

1. *Dziennik Zwiazkowy,* February 28, 1911, p. 1.

2. Ibid., February 24, 1911, p. 1.

3. Ibid., December 8, 1911, and April 7, 1910, in *CFLPS,* Polish section, I-F and I-E, respectively.

4. *Dziennik Chicagoski,* April 1, 1895, in *CFLPS,* Polish section, I-F.

5. See table 15.

6. See table 16.

7. See, especially, the discussions of this topic in Richard Hofstadter, *The Age of Reform* (New York: Vintage Books, 1955), pp. 181–85; Oscar Handlin, *The Uprooted* (New York: Little, Brown and Co., 1951), chap. 8; and Edward Banfield and James Q. Wilson, *City Politics* (New York: Vintage Books, 1963), pp. 38–43.

8. *Dziennik Zwiazkowy,* February 27, 1911, p. 8.

9. *Dziennik Ludowy,* October 25, 1912, p. 4, and November 2, 1918, p. 1.

10. The first Irish mayor of an important city was elected in Scranton, Pennsylvania, in 1878. The Irish then elected one of their own in New York in 1880 and Boston in 1884. Chicago's first Irish mayor was elected in 1893. In interviewing Polish politicians and journalists, I was struck by the grudging respect which most of them paid to the political skill of the Irish. Many expressed the opinion that the Irish have a "natural talent" for politics.

9. "Roofs of Silver, Fences of Polish Sausage"

1. This percentage varies, depending on which presidential election is compared with which mayoral election. In order to obtain a rough average, I compared each presidential election from 1888 to 1912 with the mayoral election closest to it in point of time (using only those Polish precincts whose boundaries did not change between the two elections). In all cases except one (comparison of the 1912 presidential election with the 1911 mayoral election), the turnout was clearly higher for the presidential race. The mean of all these ratios was 30%.

2. See table 17 for this and subsequent figures on presidential elections; *Zgoda,* July 4, 1888, p. 5, and October 3, 1888, p. 1.

3. *Chicago Tribune,* October 27, 1896, p. 1.

4. *Chicago Tribune,* October 28, 1896, p. 2, and October 30, 1896, p. 4.

5. Any of the standard accounts of the 1896 campaign, for instance, Matthew Josephson, *The Politicos* (New York: Harcourt, Brace, and World, 1938), pp. 702–8, or Herbert Croly, *Marcus Alonzo Hanna* (New York: The Macmillan Co., 1912), pp. 209–27, detail the threats of Hanna against the workers. See also Paul Glad, *McKinley, Bryan, and the People* (Philadelphia: J. B. Lippincott, 1964). *Chicago Tribune,* November 3, 1896, p. 6, and November 4, 1896, p. 1.

6. *Chicago Tribune,* July 6, 1900, p. 12, and November 2, 1900, p. 1.

7. *Naród Polski,* October 24, 1900, p. 1.

8. George Mowry's two books on Roosevelt, *The Era of Theodore Roosevelt* (New York: Harper and Row, 1958), and *Theodore Roosevelt and the Progressive Movement* (Madison, Wis.: University of Wisconsin Press, 1946), as well as John M. Blum, *The Republican Roosevelt* (Cambridge, Mass.: Harvard University Press, 1954), describe in detail the image which T. R. presented to the electorate in 1904.

9. J. Rogers Hollingsworth, *The Whirligig of Politics* (Chicago: University of Chicago Press, 1963) contains the best account of the Democratic "reorganization."

10. *Chicago Tribune,* November 9, 1904, p. 5, and November 10, 1904, pp. 1–2.

11. Ibid., November 10, 1904, p. 2; *Chicago Record-Herald,* November 10, 1904, p. 3.

12. *Chicago Record-Herald,* November 10, 1904, p. 3.

13. Roosevelt to Lyman Abbott, May 24, 1908, in Elting E. Morrison et al., eds., *The Letters of Theodore Roosevelt* (Cambridge, Mass.: Harvard University Press, 1952), 6: 1041–43; Roosevelt to Charles Evans Hughes, October 4, 1906, ibid., 5: 442–43; *Dziennik Chicagoski,* May 9, 1908, in *CFLPS,* Polish section, I-F.

14. Woodrow Wilson, *A History of the American People* (New York: Wm. H. Wise and Co., 1931; first published in 1901 by Harper and Brothers), 5: 212–13.

15. *Dziennik Zwiazkowy,* July 5, 1912, p. 4.

16. *Chicago Record-Herald,* September 28, 1912, p. 4; *Dziennik Zwiazkowy,* September 29, 1912, p. 8, and October 16, 1912, p. 7.

17. *Dziennik Zwiazkowy,* April 3, 1912, p. 8.

18. *Chicago Journal,* October 31, 1912, p. 6, and September 5, 1912, p. 3; *Dziennik Zwiazkowy,* October 31, 1912, p. 4.

19. *Immaculate Conception Parish Golden Jubilee Book, 1932; Dziennik Zwiazkowy,* April 8, 1912, p. 5; Personal interview, C. Jack Przybylinski.

20. *Chicago Record-Herald,* October 27, 1912, p. 4, and October 28, 1912, p. 2; *Chicago Journal,* October 26, 1912, p. 2.

21. *Dziennik Ludowy,* October 25, 1912, pp. 1, 3.

22. See table 18.

23.	The Polish turnout in 1912 was lighter than in the 1911 mayoral election or in the 1908 presidential election. Jensen, in *The Making of the Midwest,* p. 10, indicates that in the late nineteenth century, when committed party voters were displeased with their party's candidate, they stayed away from the polls rather than switch parties. The Polish voters in 1912 seem to have done some of each; many switched parties, others stayed away from the polls.

10. The Politics of Wartime

1.	John F. Smulski, "Poland's Role During the World War," *Poland* (April, 1927): 211.

2.	H. H. Fisher, *America and the New Poland* (New York: The Macmillan Co., 1928), pp. 62–64; Louis L. Gerson, *Woodrow Wilson and the Rebirth of Poland, 1914–1920* (New Haven, Conn.: Yale University Press, 1953), pp. 10–15.

3.	Thomas and Znaniecki, *Polish Peasant,* 5: 131–33.

4.	Ibid., pp. 132–36; "The Central Relief Committee," *Free Poland* 1 (February 20, 1915): 8; Gerson, *Woodrow Wilson,* pp. 48–52.

5.	"The Central Relief Committee," *Free Poland* 1: 8–9; *Dziennik Zwiazkowy,* December 29, 1914, and January 12, 1915, in *CFLPS,* Polish section, II-D.

6.	The immense influence of Paderewski on Poland's cause in America is explored in Fisher *America and the New Poland,* and Gerson, *Woodrow Wilson,* see also, Louis L. Gerson, "The Poles," in Joseph L. O'Grady, ed., *The Immigrants' Influence on Wilson's Peace Policies* (Lexington, Ky.: University Press of Kentucky, 1967).

7.	Fisher, *America and the New Poland,* p. 104; John F. Smulski, "Poland, The Land of Promise," an address to the Chicago Association of Commerce, July 7, 1920, in PRCU archives; Graham Taylor, *Chicago Commons Through Forty Years,* p. 108.

8.	Arthur S. Link, *Wilson: Campaigns for Progressivism and Peace, 1916–1917* (Princeton, N.J.: Princeton University Press, 1965), pp. 135–40.

9.	*Dziennik Zwiazkowy,* October 25, 1916, p. 4, and October 26, 1916, p. 4.

10.	Ibid., June 9, 1916, p. 8, June 12, 1916, p. 8, and October 26, 1916, p. 4.

11.	Link, *Campaigns,* pp. 327–28; O'Grady, *Immigrants' Influence,* p. 277; *Dziennik Zwiazkowy,* November 4, 1916, p. 10; "Text of Wilson's Letter to the Allied Powers," *Free Poland* 3 (October 26, 1916): 3.

12.	O'Grady, *Immigrants' Influence,* p. 278; *Dziennik Zwiazkowy,* October 20, 1916, p. 8.

13.	*Naród Polski,* October 25, 1916, p. 6.

14.	See table 19.

15.	Louis L. Gerson, *The Hyphenate in Recent American Politics and Diplomacy* (Lawrence, Kansas: University of Kansas Press, 1964), p. 69.

16.	See point thirteen in the Fourteen Points address, reprinted in many places, e.g., Daniel Boorstin, ed., *An American Primer* (New York: New American Library, 1968), p. 803.

17. *Dziennik Zwiazkowy,* February 25, 1919, p. 1, and February 29, 1919, p. 4;
     Dziennik Chicagoski, June 2, 1920, p. 4.

18. *Dziennik Chicagoski,* October 23, 1920, p. 5, and October 30, 1920, p. 4;
     Polonia, October 21, 1920, p. 5, and October 28, 1921, p. 1; *Dziennik Zwiaz
     kowy,* October 29, 1920, p. 4.

19. Stephen Horak, *Poland and Her National Minorities, 1919–1939* (New York:
     Vantage Press, 1961), pp. 111–26; Fisher, *America and the New Poland,* pp.
     147, 155–59; W. F. Reddaway et al., eds., *The Cambridge History of Poland*
     (Cambridge: At the University Press, 1951), pp. 505–10; *Dziennik Zwiazkowy,*
     October 14, 1920, p. 4; October 30, 1920, p. 1, and October 28, 1920, p. 8.

20. Moses Rischin, *The Promised City* (New York: Harper and Row, 1970), pp.
     20–31.

21. Inspection of polling lists in heavily Polish areas shows that in many precincts
     the population was nearly 100 percent Polish except in the precincts near busi-
     ness streets such as Milwaukee Avenue, where the names of many Jews, who un-
     doubtedly lived above or behind stores, appear on the lists. *Dziennik Chicagoski,*
     December 17, 1895, in *CFLPS,* Polish section, II-A; Frederic Thrasher, *The
     Gang* (Chicago: University of Chicago Press, 1927), pp. 132–36; personal in-
     terview, Judge Thaddeus Adesko.

22. *Naród Polski,* April 28, 1920, and August 17, 1921; *Dziennik Zwiazkowy,*
     February 15, 1919, all in *CFLPS,* Polish section, I-E.

23. See table 20.

24. *Dziennik Chicagoski,* November 4, 1920, p. 4; *Polonia,* November 4, 1920, p. 1.

11. Ethnic and Economic Heroes

1. *Zgoda,* October 3, 1888, p. 1, and June 28, 1900, p. 401.

2. *Dziennik Zwiazkowy,* October 19, 1920, p. 5, and October 25, 1920, p. 1.

3. *Dziennik Chicagoski,* October 25, 1924, p. 4. See table 21 for all election re-
    sults in this chapter. Among the many general studies of American politics and
    society in the interwar period, William E. Leuchtenberg, *The Perils of Prosperity*
    (Chicago: University of Chicago Press, 1958), and *Franklin D. Roosevelt and
    the New Deal* (New York: Harper and Row, 1963) are standards. A recent
    synthesis by George Mowry, *The Urban Nation* (New York: Hill and Wang,
    1965), deals with the period 1920 to 1961, but is especially perceptive in the
    first three chapters, on the 1920s. Walter Johnson, *1600 Pennsylvania Avenue*
    (Boston: Little, Brown, and Co., 1960) is a lively account of presidential politics
    from 1929 on. J. Joseph Huthmacher, *Massachusetts People and Politics* (New
    York: Atheneum, 1959) deals with many of the same issues of ethnic politics as
    the present study and has far wider usefulness and relevance than its title might
    imply.

4. *Dziennik Zwiazkowy,* October 25, 1924, p. 4; *Dziennik Chicagoski,* October 21,
    1924, p. 4; *Polonia,* October 2, 1924, p. 2.

5. *Dziennik Ludowy,* October 25, 1924, p. 7. Third-party percentages of Chicago's
    Polish vote: Roosevelt Progressive, 1912—20.09%; La Follette Progressive,

1924—14.41%; Debs Socialist, 1912—12.53%; Debs Socialist, 1904—10.88%; all other third-party efforts from 1888 to 1936 fell below 5%.

6. *Dziennik Zwiazkowy,* June 6, 1924, p. 4, June 14, 1924, p. 4; November 6, 1924, p. 4. John M. Allswang, in *A House for all Peoples,* pp. 44, 76–79, somewhat over-estimates the Polish swing toward the Republicans in the early twenties. Though Polish allegiance to the Democrats weakened during the candidacies of Cox and Davis, there was no decisive switch to a Republican allegiance. The highwater marks for Republican presidential candidates in Chicago's Polonia were: Roosevelt, 1904—46.15%; Harding, 1920—44.22%; Taft, 1908—37.44%; Coolidge, 1924—37.43%; Taft, 1912—33.13%; all other Republicans from 1888 to 1936 fell below 30%.

7. *Dziennik Chicagoski,* October 17, 1924, p. 1, and October 18, 1924, p. 1; *Polonia,* October 2, 1924, p. 2; *Dziennik Zwiazkowy,* October 25, 1924, p. 4.

8. *Dziennik Zwiazkowy,* October 20, 1924, p. 4.

9. *Dziennik Ludowy,* October 25, 1924, pp. 2, 7.

10. *Dziennik Chicagoski,* November 7, 1924, p. 4.

11. *Dziennik Zwiazkowy,* June 16, 1928, p. 4; June 18, 1928, p. 4; November 1, 1928, p. 4.

12. Fisher, *America and the New Poland,* pp. 121–23, 162, 174–75, 194.

13. *Dziennik Zwiazkowy,* June 9, 1920, p. 4; June 18, 1928, p. 4; June 28, 1928, p. 4; October 17, 1928, p. 5; October 22, 1928, p. 1; N. L. Piotrowski to E. Kolakowski, October 10, 1928, PRCU Archives.

14. *Dziennik Chicagoski,* November 2, 1928, p. 4; *Polonia,* October 11, 1928, p. 2, and November 1, 1928, p. 6; *Dziennik Zwiazkowy,* November 2, 1928, p. 14.

15. *Dziennik Zwiazkowy,* July 2, 1928, p. 4; November 2, 1928, p. 14; *Polonia,* July 5, 1928, p. 2, and September 27, 1928, p. 2.

16. V. O. Key, Jr., and other political scientists have described the 1928 election as a "critical election," in which, for the first time in the twentieth century, the Democrats won a majority of the big-city vote and united most of the European ethnic groups into a party coalition. The Democratic breakthrough in this critical election is viewed as the basis of the later New Deal coalition. In Samuel Lubell's phrase, "before the Roosevelt revolution, there was an Al Smith revolution." See V. O. Key, Jr., "A Theory of Critical Elections," *Journal of Politics* 17 (February 1955): 3–18; Samuel J. Eldersveld, "The Influence of Metropolitan Party Pluralities in Presidential Elections Since 1920," *American Political Science Review* 43 (December 1949): 1189–1205; Samuel Lubell, *The Future of American Politics* (New York: Doubleday Anchor, 1955), pp. 29–43.

Allswang, *House for all Peoples,* pp. 56, 59, 61, 207–8, has revised this theory for Chicago election data, arguing that the entire decade of the 1920s was a "critical period" for the formation of the Democratic urban-ethnic coalition.

Both these viewpoints, however valid they may be in general, have little relevance to the Polish vote. Polish voting had been normally Democratic for decades. Although Polish-Democratic strength did drop off in the early 1920s, there was no decisive shift to the Republicans. Smith's percentage of the Polish vote in 1928 was not a critical Democratic breakthrough for Polonia but a return to older, more normal, patterns. See my article, "The Emergence of the Polish-

Democratic Vote in Chicago," *Polish American Studies* 29 (Spring-Autumn 1972): 67–80.

17. Arthur M. Schlesinger, Jr., *The Crisis of the Old Order* (Boston: Houghton Mifflin Co., 1957), pp. 155–269, effectively describes the effects of depression on all classes of Americans. For the situation in Chicago and other major cities, see Johnson, *1600 Pennsylvania Avenue*, pp. 12–24; also for Chicago, Gottfried, *Boss Cermak*, p. 241.

18. *Dziennik Zwiazkowy*, June 9, 1932, p. 4, and June 18, 1932, p. 4; *Dziennik Chicagoski*, June 30, 1932, p. 4; *Polonia*, June 23, 1932, p. 1. *Dziennik Chicagoski*, on June 27, 1932, printed a front-page cartoon showing a map of the U.S. covered with eyes and ears. The caption read: "All Eyes and Ears on Chicago."

19. *Polonia*, June 23, 1932, p. 1; *Dziennik Zwiazkowy*, June 28, 1932, p. 4.

20. *Dziennik Zwiazkowy*, June 27, 1932, p. 4; *Dziennik Chicagoski*, June 30, 1932, p. 4.

21. *Dziennik Chicagoski*, July 5, 1932, p. 4; *Polonia*, October 28, 1932, p. 1.

22. Letter in the Polish-American Democratic Organization Papers (hereafter cited as PADO papers), Chicago Historical Society; *Dziennik Zwiazkowy*, June 11, 1936, p. 4, and October 23, 1936, p. 4.

23. *Dziennik Chicagoski*, October 15, 1936, p. 1; *Dziennik Zwiazkowy*, June 27, 1936, p. 4; October 22, 1936, p. 4; October 29, 1936, p. 4, November 4, 1936, p. 4.

12. Big Bill the Boisterous

1. *Chicago Tribune*, February 21, 1915, sec. 2, p. 4; February 25, 1915, p. 6; and April 2, 1915, p. 9.

2. William L. Cheney, "The Fall of a Mayor," *New Republic* 2 (May 13, 1916): 36; "Members of the Chicago Board of Education Appointed by Carter H. Harrison, 1897–1905, 1911–1915," in Harrison papers.

3. *Chicago Tribune*, March 23, 1919, p. 10; "The Chicago Election," *The Outlook* 109 (April 21, 1915): 901; Lloyd Wendt and Herman Kogan, *Big Bill of Chicago* (New York: Bobbs-Merrill Co., 1953), p. 108.

4. *Dziennik Chicagoski*, March 30, 1895; *Dziennik Zwiazkowy*, March 28, 1918, April 25, 1917, and January 17, 1918, all in *CFLPS*, Polish section, I-F and I-A, respectively.

5. *Dziennik Zwiazkowy*, February 15, 1915, p. 7, and April 5, 1915, p. 8.

6. Wendt and Kogan, *Big Bill*, pp. 81–86.

7. *Chicago Tribune*, February 21, 1915, sec. 2, p. 4; "The Chicago Election," *The Outlook* 109: 902; Wendt and Kogan, *Big Bill*, pp. 15–56.

8. Wendt and Kogan, *Big Bill*, p. 42; Harold Gosnell, *Negro Politicians* (Chicago: University of Chicago Press, 1935), pp. 37–62.

9. Cheney, "The Fall of a Mayor," pp. 36–37.

10. *Chicago Tribune*, April 5, 1915, p. 1, and sec. 2, p. 4; April 6, 1915, p. 6.

11. See table 22.

12. Wendt and Kogan, *Big Bill*, pp. 120–23, 143–47, 163; Cheney, "The Fall of

a Mayor," p. 37; Leonard D. White, "Conditions of Municipal Employment in Chicago," Report to Chicago City Council, June 10, 1925, pp. 20–21.

13. Wendt and Kogan, *Big Bill,* pp. 150–70.

14. *Chicago Tribune,* February 23, 1919, pp. 1, 8; February 26, 1919, pp. 1, 6; February 28, 1919, p. 5.

15. *Chicago Tribune,* March 24, 1919, p. 8; Eugene Perlstein, "The Progressive Movement in Chicago, 1919–1924" (M.A. thesis, University of Chicago, 1948), pp. 5–6.

16. *Chicago Tribune,* March 19, 1919, p. 11; March 23, 1919, pp. 1, 10; *Dziennik Zwiazkowy,* April 8, 1915, p. 1; *Polonia,* March 13, 1919, p. 1; *Dziennik Ludowy,* March 29, 1919, p. 2.

17. See table 23.

18. Wendt and Kogan, *Big Bill,* pp. 172, 206, 213–14; *Chicago Tribune,* February 28, 1923, p. 3, and February 24, 1923, p. 6.

19. *Chicago Tribune,* February 28, 1923, p. 3; March 16, 1923, p. 5; March 21, 1923, p. 5; March 22, 1923, p. 5; March 29, 1923, p. 6; April 1, 1923, p. 8; and April 4, 1923, p. 3.

20. *Dziennik Chicagoski,* February 27, 1923, p. 4; March 20, 1923, p. 4; March 30, 1923, p. 4; *Polonia,* March 22, 1923, p. 1; *Dziennik Zwiazkowy,* March 31, 1923, p. 4; April 5, 1923, p. 4. See table 24.

21. Wendt and Kogan, *Big Bill,* pp. 234–39; *Chicago Tribune,* October 21, 1923, p. 6; *The American Issue,* October 13, 1923, p. 2, in the William E. Dever papers (hereafter cited as Dever papers), Chicago Historical Society.

22. Board of Election Commissioners figures show over 80 percent of Polish voters voted No on the referendum. See Allswang, *House for All Peoples,* pp. 118–29, for a detailed treatment of the prohibition issue among nine ethnic groups.

23. *Chicago Tribune,* February 8, 1926, p. 6, and April 9, 1926, p. 3; Carroll Hill Wooddy, *The Chicago Primary of 1926* (Chicago: University of Chicago Press, 1926), pp. 258–59.

24. The Carter Harrisons, father and son, always spoke of the right of "personal liberty"; the leading wet pressure group in Chicago, headed by Anton Cermak, was called the United Societies for Local Self Government. *Dziennik Zwiazkowy,* March 16, 1923, p. 4, and March 20, 1923, p. 4.

25. Wendt and Kogan, *Big Bill,* p. 248; *Chicago Tribune,* March 28, 1927, p. 4, and April 3, 1927, p. 1; *Dziennik Zwiazkowy,* March 18, 1927, p. 18.

26. *Dziennik Zwiazkowy,* February 23, 1927, p. 8; March 18, 1927, p. 18; March 23, 1927, p. 8; *Polonia,* April 19, 1923, p. 1.

27. Mayor Dever's speech in the Dever papers; *Chicago Tribune,* February 23, 1927, p. 2, and March 16, 1927, p. 4.

28. Final election returns for mayor: Dever (D)—432,678; Thompson (R)—515,716; Robertson (Ind. R.)—51,347. Returns for city treasurer: Szymczak (D)—435,055; Peterson (R)—480,815; Wolff (Soc.)—40,359. See table 24 for comparison of the Polish vote with the vote in other mayoral elections. *Chicago Tribune,* April 6, 1927, p. 1, and *Dziennik Chicagoski,* April 6, 1927, p. 7, give nearly identical analyses of the election. Allswang, *House for All Peo-*

ples, pp. 43–46, 125–26, agrees with this analysis in general while differing in some details. Humbert Nelli, in *The Italians in Chicago,* p. 231, presents statistics which indicate that the falling off in Democratic strength among Italians was even more marked than among Poles.

29. *Chicago Tribune,* March 12, 1927, p. 1, and March 28, 1927, p. 4; *Polonia,* March 31, 1927, p. 4; Wendt and Kogan, *Big Bill,* p. 256; *Dziennik Chicagoski,* March 19, 1927, p. 1; April 1, 1927, p. 4; March 11, 1927, p. 1; March 15, 1927, p. 1; March 16, 1927, p. 6; March 25, 1927, p. 12.

30. A crude sociological survey of Poles in Buffalo, by Niles Carpenter and Daniel Katz, reported as "The Cultural Adjustment of the Polish Group in the City of Buffalo," *Social Forces* 6 (September 1927): 76–85, and "A Study of Acculturation in the Polish Group in Buffalo," *The University of Buffalo Studies* 7 (June 1929): 103–33, though based on a small sample and thus not very reliable, agrees with the contention that anti-Negro bias is a sign of Americanization; for racial prejudice seemed to increase with the length of residence in America. Smulski said: "Carter Harrison says he [Merriam] has been here only seven years. Bathhouse admits he was here eleven years. Well, I hope the colored voters get to hear about that connection, seven and eleven, sounds pretty good to them" ("Transcripts of a speech by J. F. Smulski at Merriam mass meeting, April 1, 1911," in Merriam papers). See also *Polonia,* June 17, 1920, p. 2.

31. See Allan Spear, *Black Chicago* (Chicago: University of Chicago Press, 1967), pp. 11–27; and Chicago Commission on Race Relations, *The Negro in Chicago: A Study of Race Relations and a Race Riot* (Chicago: University of Chicago Press, 1922). The maps on pp. 116 and 120 of the latter study illustrate the expansion of the Black Belt, and the map on p. 8 pinpoints the location of each incident in the 1919 riot. In the 1927 mayoral election, the average vote from Polish precincts in the Eleventh Ward (Bridgeport) was 51.26 percent Republican; in the Twelfth Ward (Brighton Park and beyond), 41.21 percent; Thirteenth Ward (Back of the Yards), 45.38 percent; whereas in Polonia as a whole, the voters gave the Republican Thompson 42.20 percent of their votes.

13. The End of the Republican Alternative

1. *Dziennik Zwiazkowy,* February 16, 1931, p. 4; personal interview, Marion Kudlick, Sr., attorney.

2. The rise of the Democratic party during the latter years of the Thompson era is generally well known in its broad outlines, though no definitive work has yet appeared. Harold Gosnell, *Machine Politics: Chicago Model* (Chicago: University of Chicago Press, 1937), examines the origins and structure of the machine; Gottfried, *Boss Cermak,* is the standard biography of Anton Cermak; John M. Allswang, *A House for all Peoples,* and Arthur Thurner, "The Impact of Ethnic Groups on the Democratic Party" (Ph.D. diss., University of Chicago, 1966), treat the role of the ethnic vote in the Democrats' rise.

3. Wendt and Kogan, *Big Bill,* pp. 329–33; Gottfried, *Boss Cermak,* pp. 205–6; *Chicago Tribune,* March 29, 1931, p. 7.

4. *Polonia,* April 16, 1931, p. 2; *Dziennik Chicagoski,* April 11, 1931, p. 4; *Dziennik Zwiazkowy,* April 4, 1931, p. 4; March 24, 1931, p. 4; April 3, 1931, p. 4.

5. *Chicago Tribune,* April 9, 1931, p. 14.

6. Gottfried speaks of a "heyday of Czech and generally of all Slavic participation in city offices" during Cermak's administration. This ignores, however, the importance of Carter Harrison's last term in giving the Slavs an entree into city government. Allswang's discussion of Cermak's importance in "the cementing of the ethnic vote into the Democracy" (pp. 152–62), is probably correct; but it should not be applied too literally to the Polish voters, who were among the most consistently Democratic of groups. See tables 11 and 24 for comparative percentages of the Polish vote.

7. *Dziennik Zwiazkowy,* February 18, 1933, p. 4. The rumor was that Cermak sought a post on either the Federal Reserve Board or the Federal Civil Service Commission for Szymczak, and a federal judgeship for Jarecki. After Cermak's death Szymczak was appointed to the Board of Governors of the Federal Reserve, but Jarecki did not receive a promotion.

8. *Chicago Tribune,* March 13, 1933, p. 3; March 22, 1933, p. 11; March 25, 1933, p. 12; March 31, 1933, p. 1; April 14, 1933, p. 1; April 15, 1933, p. 12; *Dziennik Chicagoski,* March 13, 1933, p. 1; March 28, 1933, p. 1; April 14, 1933, p. 1; April 15, 1933, p. 4.

9. *Chicago Tribune,* March 31, 1935, p. 14.

10. *Chicago Tribune,* February 24, 1935, p. 1; February 27, 1935, p. 1.

11. Personal interview, Martin Powroznik; articles in *Real Estate News,* March 1926, and *Chicago Tribune,* February, 1935, in scrapbook in the possession of Martin Powroznik.

12. *Polonia,* October 18, 1928, p. 1; *Chicago American,* January 2, 1932, and April 20, 1932, clippings found in Edmund K. Jarecki papers (hereafter cited as Jarecki papers), University of Illinois at Chicago Circle.

13. *Chicago American,* December 6, 1933, p. 18; April 23, 1934; April 24, 1934; *Public Service Leader,* April 5, 1934, all found in Jarecki papers.

14. *Chicago American,* December 8, 1933, p. 18; *Dziennik Zwiazkowy,* March 29, 1935, p. 5; personal interview, Stanley J. Piotrowicz, real estate agent. See table 25 for detailed returns from the 1935 primary.

15. The phenomenon of neighborhood taxpayers' associations is a subject which needs further study by social historians. I am indebted for some of my ideas on the subject to a study of ratepayers' associations in York Township, outside Toronto, by one of my students at Carleton University, Ottawa, Ontario—J. Steven Mould.

16. *Chicago Tribune,* March 14, 1886, p. 3; Julius John Ozog, "A Study of Polish Home Ownership in Chicago" (Ph.D. diss., University of Chicago, 1942); Thaddeus J. Lubera, "Hundred Years of Economic Contributions of the Poles to Chicago's Progress," in *Poles of Chicago,* p. 15. Stephan Thernstrom has suggested in *Poverty and Progress* (New York: Atheneum Press, 1970), pp. 201, 274, that the homeowning drive was strongest in Catholic immigrant groups whereas Protestant immigrants tended to put a higher priority on occupational mobility.

17. As an indication that defense of personal liberty was more than a code word for booze, even in the Thompson era, consider one of the minor issues of the 1927 campaign: water meters. The federal government instructed Mayor Dever that

the city would be allowed to continue pumping its water supply from Lake Michigan only if a system of universal water metering were introduced. When Dever attempted to comply, many suspicious Poles and other immigrants viewed this as another invasion of the home and another attack on personal liberty. Thompson tried to play on this feeling by promising to "strip the meters from the homes." *Chicago Tribune,* March 28, 1927, p. 4; "Campaign speech of Mayor Dever, March 18, 1927," in Dever papers.

14. A Changing Polonia

1. *CDNA, 1923,* p. 798; U.S., Bureau of the Census, *Fourteenth Census of the United States: 1920. Population,* 2: 730–33.

2. Ernest W. Burgess and Charles Newcomb, eds., *Census Data of the City of Chicago, 1930* (Chicago: University of Chicago Press, 1933), pp. 626–34; *CDNA, 1924,* p. 724.

3. Lubera, in *Poles of Chicago,* p. 15.

4. *Dziennik Zwiazkowy,* March 24, 1919, p. 4.

5. Wytrwal, *America's Polish Heritage,* pp. 236–37; "History of New City," in McDowell papers.

6. John F. Smulski, "O Stanowisku Wychodstwa Polskiego w Stanach Zjednoczonych Ameryki Pólnocnej," unpublished address delivered to the Polish Emigration Congress, Detroit, April 21, 1925, in PRCU archives.

7. Carpenter and Katz, "Cultural Adjustment," p. 80; and "Study of Acculturation," pp. 119–20.

8. *Dziennik Zwiazkowy,* October 25, 1920, p. 4; Wytrwal, *America's Polish Heritage,* pp. 196, 250–52.

9. Wytrwal, *America's Polish Heritage,* p. 253; *N.W. Ayer and Sons Newspaper Annual and Directory* for 1928 lists the total circulation for Chicago's three Polish dailies at about 92,000, roughly equivalent to the circulation of the four dailies which existed in 1920; Bolek, *Who's Who,* pp. 11, 78–82; Iwicki, *First Hundred Years,* p. 178.

10. "Polish Days and Other Demonstrations of Civic and National Character," and "Polish Organizations of Chicago," in *Poles of Chicago,* pp. 137–44, 148–82; Wytrwal, *America's Polish Heritage,* pp. 236–59; personal interview, Jane Palczynski, former president of Polish Teachers' Club; list of Polish-American organizations in PADO papers.

11. *Polish-American,* February 20, 1971; personal interview with Marion Kudlick, Sr., former president of Chicago Society; constitution of the Chicago Society, in the possession of Marion Kudlick.

15. The Drive for Recognition

1. *Dziennik Zwiazkowy,* November 2, 1928, p. 4.

2. See, for example, *Polonia,* March 2, 1922, p. 2; April 6, 1922, p. 2; December 7, 1922, p. 1; October 23, 1930, p. 2; *Dziennik Chicagoski,* January 19, 1935, p. 4.

3. Rev. M. J. Madaj, "The Polish Immigrant, the American Catholic Hierarchy, and

Father Wenceslaus Kruszka," *Polish American Studies* 26 (January 1969): 16–29; Polish Clergy Association to George Cardinal Mundelein, July 9, 1917, in PRCU archives.

4. *Dziennik Zwiazkowy,* October 23, 1920, p. 8, and October 29, 1920, p. 10.

5. *Chicago Record-Herald,* May 4, 1904, p. 3; *Chicago Journal,* June 6, 1904, p. 2; October 17, 1904, p. 2; November 8, 1904, p. 3. The district totals were: Charles McGavin (R)—20,107; Preston Harrison (D)—13,025; others—5,761. The Polish vote in the Sixteenth Ward was 51.23 percent for McGavin and 38.73 percent for Harrison.

6. *Chicago Record-Herald,* November 7, 1906, p. 3, and November 20, 1906, p. 5. The district totals were: McGavin (R)—11,421; Kunz (D)—11,336; others —5,792. Polish votes in the Sixteenth Ward were distributed 74.16 percent for Kunz and 21.37 percent for McGavin.

7. *Dziennik Zwiazkowy,* October 28, 1908, p. 8; October 29, 1908, p. 2; November 4, 1908, p. 8. The district totals were: Ksycki (R)—14,660; Gallagher (D) —15,963; others—1,820. Polish votes in the Sixteenth Ward were distributed 54.92 percent for Ksycki, and 43.25 percent for Gallagher.

8. The totals in the 1914 primary were: Kunz—2,125; Czekala—2,860; Gallagher —4,494; in the 1916 primary: Gallagher—3,772; Kadów—965; Piotrowski— 2,968; others—2,810.

9. *Dziennik Zwiazkowy,* November 8, 1916, p. 1.

10. The Polish bloc-voting was well known to contemporaries and often lamented by the Polish National Alliance, which was alternately Republican or nonpartisan. The tendency toward factionalism was also noted by contemporaries, e.g., "Stupid Politics in the 27th Ward," *Dziennik Zwiazkowy,* February 25, 1915, p. 8; and it was also emphasized in personal interviews with Polish-American leaders today, such as Rev. Marion Kaleth, pastor of St. Stanislaus Kostka, and Congressman Daniel Rostenkowski (D.—Ill.).

11. *Chicago Daily News,* January 4, 1922, p. 7; January 13, 1922, p. 3; January 30, 1922, p. 3; February 1, 1922, p. 3; February 3, 1922, p. 7; and two columns by Arthur Evans in the *Chicago Tribune,* July 12, 1929, and July 28, 1929, found in Jarecki papers.

12. *Dziennik Chicagoski,* April 14, 1927, p. 4, and April 16, 1927, p. 10; lists of Polish-Americans holding city offices in the 1930s and 40s, as well as partial lists of those they employed in their bureaus, were found in PADO papers.

13. Leonard D. White, "Conditions of Municipal Employment."

14. This information for 1915 was gleaned from the official city payroll lists for that year. Librarians at the Municipal Reference Library in Chicago City Hall informed me that these payrolls were no longer published after 1915 because Mayor Thompson had no desire to make his personnel policies public. Such suppression of civil lists was not unusual. New York's Boss Tweed did it as one of his first actions upon taking power. See Alexander B. Callow, *The Tweed Ring* (New York: Oxford University Press, 1965), p. 173.

15. See a series of articles in *Dziennik Chicagoski,* from January 19 to March 17, 1935, entitled "Our Progress in Politics"; *Poles in America,* p. 223.

16. See patronage lists in PADO papers.

17. The records of the Chicago Civil Service Commission are quite complete, but they are not arranged in a way that is very useful for researchers trying to determine the ethnic makeup of the service at any particular point in time. All workers who were ever employed under civil service from 1895 to the present, literally hundreds of thousands, are listed alphabetically, with the job and year of appointment noted after each name. To get a rough indication of Polonia's progress, I tabulated all Polish names starting with several letters of the alphabet (for example, names starting with C and K, where Polish names are particularly numerous) and calculated how many were hired in each decade.

18. White, "Conditions of Municipal Employment," pp. 13–19.

19. *Chicago City Council Proceedings, 1923,* p. 1029; *1926,* pp. 762, 782, 1630; *1928,* pp. 2459–60; *1936,* p. 1628; *Dziennik Zwiazkowy,* April 5, 1935, p. 1; and clippings from the Polish-American file in the editorial morgue of the *Chicago American* (later called *Chicago Today*).

20. *Chicago Tribune,* October 1, 1933; *Chicago City Council Proceedings, 1933,* pp. 945, 1207, 1272.

21. "Peter Crawford," and "Where Do You Stand?" pro-Pulaski pamphlets in the PRCU archives.

22. Pamphlet, Gads Hill Settlement House, at the Chicago Historical Society.

23. The data for this section were obtained from the lists of aldermen in the *Chicago City Council Proceedings* and the lists of ward committeemen in the *CDNA.*

16. Organizing the Recognition Drive

1. *Dziennik Chicagoski,* November 18, 1893, in *CFLPS,* Polish section, I-F; *Dziennik Chicagoski,* December 1, 1952, p. 5.

2. "Polish Organizations of Chicago," in *Poles of Chicago,* pp. 166–68; "Work Done by the Polish American Democratic Organization at its Headquarters," manuscript in PADO papers.

3. PADO minutes, October 7, 1932, and December 27, 1932, in PADO papers.

4. Szymczak to Louis Howe, October 20, 1932; Szymczak to James Farley, November 7, 1932; Max Drezmal to Franklin Roosevelt, October 10, 1932; "Message from Governor Roosevelt," all in PADO papers.

5. The various estimates wired into PADO headquarters indicated a 90 to 93 percent Democratic vote. This was probably a little high. In Chicago, Polish-Americans voted 83.29 percent for FDR.

6. Szymczak to James Farley, November 7, 1932; Szymczak to Anton Cermak, November 7, 1932, in PADO papers.

7. PADO minutes, September 24, 1936; October 8, 1936; May 1, 1939.

8. *Poles of Chicago,* p. 167; PADO minutes, April 24, 1937.

9. Job-seeker dossiers, personal letters, and a manuscript of "Work Done by PADO at its Headquarters," all in PADO papers.

10. Thomas Pawloski to Szymczak, January 18, 1933; *Wiadomosci Codzienne* (Cleveland), December 13, 1932; *The North Side News,* June 15, 1933; *Dziennik Zwiazkowy,* December 14, 1932; June 12, 1933; *Dziennik Chicago-*

ski, December 15, 1932; June 17, 1933; June 19, 1933; all found in PADO papers.

11. *Dziennik Chicagoski,* October 3, 1936, p. 12; September 28, 1936, p. 1; *Chicago Tribune,* September 17, 1936, p. 11; September 18, 1936, p. 1; September 21, 1936, p. 7; September 25, 1936, p. 4; October 2, 1936, p. 3; November 26, 1936, p. 6; December 2, 1936, p. 1; December 11, 1936, p. 17; February 4, 1937, p. 1.

12. Personal interviews, Frank Bobrytzke, Matthew Bieszczat, former presidents of PADO; and Peter Figel, precinct captain in Polish Downtown; PADO minutes, May 1, 1939.

17. The Finest Fruit of Recognition: Edmund K. Jarecki

1. Stanley Pieza, "Edmund K. Jarecki: Portrait of an Honest Politician," manuscript biography in Jarecki papers; *Dziennik Chicagoski,* December 1, 1952 (special issue commemorating Jarecki's thirtieth anniversary as county judge); *Chicago Daily News,* October 27, 1926, p. 4.

2. Edward M. Martin, *The Role of the Bar in Electing the Bench in Chicago* (Chicago: University of Chicago Press, 1936), pp. 263–65; *Chicago Daily News,* October 28, 1926, p. 4; Wooddy, *The Chicago Primary of 1926,* p. 93.

3. *Chicago Daily News,* November 1, 1922, p. 8; November 4, 1922, pp. 3–4; November 6, 1922, p. 8; *Chicago Tribune,* November 2, 1922, p. 4; November 5, 1922, p. 8; Martin, *The Role of the Bar,* p. 177.

4. *Chicago Daily News,* November 4, 1922, p. 1; *Chicago Tribune,* November 1, 1922, p. 6. The election results for county judge were: Righeimer (R)— 355,554; Jarecki (D)—388,176; the Polish vote for Jarecki was 81.50 percent.

5. Two unidentified clippings, 1922 and 1926, and *Chicago American,* January 2, 1923, in Jarecki papers.

6. *Chicago American,* September 12, 1925; *Chicago Journal,* January 13, 1926, and unidentified clipping, February, 1925, in Jarecki papers.

7. *Chicago American,* January 6, 1926, and *Chicago Journal,* January 13, 1926, in Jarecki papers; also, *Chicago Daily News,* January 15, 1926, p. 5; January 27, 1926, p. 8; February 8, 1926, p. 6; November 1, 1926, p. 3; *Chicago Tribune,* November 1, 1926, p. 3; November 3, 1926, p. 2; Wooddy, *The Chicago Primary of 1926,* p. 96.

8. See table 27 for a nationality breakdown of election employees. It was possible to determine the various influences on patronage because the employee lists in the Jarecki papers note the political "sponsor" of each individual employee. The election board has remained heavily Polish. When Jarecki retired in 1954, Judge Otto Kerner, a Czech and a son-in-law of Anton Cermak, succeeded him as county judge. Kerner, in turn, was succeeded by a Polish judge, Thaddeus Adesko, who sat until the county judgeship disappeared in a court reorganization. Throughout the 1960s, a South Chicago Polish-American, C. Jack Przybylinski, served as chief clerk of the board; and in 1970, Stanley Kusper, Jr., another Polish-American, became chairman of the three-man Board of Commissioners.

9. *Dziennik Zjednoczenia,* October 27, 1926; *Dziennik Zwiazkowy,* October 29, 1926; *Dziennik Chicagoski,* November 1, 1926, clippings in Jarecki papers.

10. Thomas B. Littlewood, *Horner of Illinois* (Evanston, Ill.: Northwestern University Press, 1969); Gosnell, *Machine Politics,* pp. 21–24; *Dziennik Chicagoski,* April 11, 1936, p. 3; April 17, 1936, p. 4.

11. *Chicago Examiner,* August 5, 1936, p. 1; *Chicago Daily News,* August 7, 1936, February 1, 1938, March 3, 1962; *Chicago's American,* March 31, 1963, clippings in Jarecki papers.

12. *Chicago Daily News,* February 1, 1938, p. 1; PADO minutes, February 5, 1938.

13. *Chicago Daily News,* February 4, 1938, p. 1; April 4, 1938; *Chicago American,* March 17, 1938; March 18, 1938; April 9, 1938; *Chicago Herald and Examiner,* April 2, 1938; *Dziennik Zjednoczenia, Zwiazkowy,* and *Chicagoski,* February 1, 1938; all clippings in Jarecki papers.

14. *Dziennik Chicagoski,* February 1, 1938, p. 1; April 11, 1938, in Jarecki papers.

15. Jarecki polled an average of 67.50 percent of the Polish vote; see table 28. *Chicago Daily News,* November 9, 1938, in Jarecki papers.

16. *Chicago Tribune,* January 26, 1939; February 23, 1939; *Chicago American,* February 7, 1939, in Jarecki papers.

17. *Chicago Daily News,* January 18, 1939; *Chicago Herald and Examiner,* February 8, 1939; *Chicago Tribune,* February 19, 1939—all in Jarecki papers; PADO minutes, November 28, 1938; January 9, 1939; January 16, 1939; February 6, 1939; February 14, 1939; March 20, 1939; March 27, 1939; *Dziennik Chicagoski,* January 9, 1939, p. 1; January 12, 1939, p. 1; January 19, 1939, p. 1; February 18, 1939, p. 1; February 27, 1939, p. 4.

18. See table 28.

19. PADO minutes, March 27, 1942; "Inaugural Special Program," in PADO papers.

20. *Chicago Tribune,* November 2, 1940, p. 1; November 3, 1940, p. 3; November 5, 1940, p. 1; November 6, 1940, p. 8; *Chicago Daily News,* November 1, 1940, p. 4.

18. Limitations of the Recognition Drive

1. Gottfried, Cermak's biographer, discusses in an appendix entitled "Leadership and Psychosomatic Analysis," pp. 365–78, Cermak's power drive and its role in his chronic suffering from colitis. He concludes that Cermak did not literally die of his gunshot wound but from complications brought on by colitis.

2. Gottfried, *Boss Cermak,* p. 351.

3. In 1930 the population figures for the new immigrant groups in Chicago (with percentage of total city population) were: Poles—401,316 (12%); Italians—181,861 (5%); Russians (Jews)—169,736 (5%); Czechs—122,089 (4%); Lithuanians—63,918 (2%); Yugoslavs—32,291 (1%); Greeks—26,384 (1%). Burgess and Newcomb, *Census Data of the City of Chicago, 1930,* p. xv.

4. *Chicago Tribune,* February 19, 1929, p. 4.

5. *Dziennik Zjednoczenia,* February 12, 1929, in *CFLPS,* Polish section, II-B-3;

Chicago Daily News, November 1, 1930, p. 7; personal interviews, Charles Roz-marek, former PNA president; Stanley Piotrowicz, realtor; Congressman Daniel Rostenkowski; Peter Figel, precinct captain; Walter Nega, personal secretary to Congressman Rostenkowski.

6.   "Report to the Chicago Bar Association," May 15, 1939, and assorted newspaper clippings, in Walter J. LaBuy papers, University of Illinois at Chicago Circle; personal interview, Judge Thaddeus Adesko.

7.   *Chicago Daily News,* October 20, 1936, p. 4.

8.   Personal interviews, Aloysius Mazewski, PNA president; Charles Piatkiewicz, former editor of *Dziennik Zwiazkowy;* Frank Bobrytzke, former PADO presi-dent; Peter Figel, precinct captain; Walter Nega, secretary to Congressman Rostenkowski; Matthew Bieszczat, county commissioner and former PADO president. All of these individuals stressed that Szymczak was the man most likely to be Chicago's first Polish mayor; many of them blamed the Irish for "kicking him upstairs." Personal interview with M. S. Szymczak. Szymczak denies that he was kicked upstairs, and the sequence of events supports this.

9.   PADO minutes, February 5, 1938; biography of Adamowski, *Chicago Daily News,* February 7, 1955, in PADO papers; Mike Royko, *Boss: Richard J. Daley of Chicago* (New York: E. P. Dutton and Co., 1971), pp. 85, 98, 119.

10. Personal interviews, Thaddeus Adesko, Matthew Bieszczat, Daniel Rostenkowski, Benjamin Adamowski.

11. See Arthur Mann, *LaGuardia Comes to Power* (Philadelphia: J. B. Lippincott Co., 1965), for the story of LaGuardia's election in 1933.

12. Arthur Evans Wood, *Hamtramck* (New Haven, Conn.: College and University Press, 1955), pp. 46–114, discusses the factionalism of Polish-American poli-tics in Hamtramck and the city's low reputation in the greater Detroit area.

13. *Dziennik Chicagoski,* March 14, 1933, p. 4.

14. I am greatly indebted, in my discussion of hyphenization and broker politics, to Arthur Mann's analysis of LaGuardia as a "marginal man," a political hybrid, and a "balanced ticket all by himself" in *LaGuardia Comes to Power,* pp. 24–27.

15. See Robert A. Dahl, *Who Governs?* (New Haven, Conn.: Yale University Press, 1961), and Donald S. Bradley and Mayer N. Zald, "From Commercial Elite to Political Administrator," *American Journal of Sociology* 70 (September 1965): 153–67, for typologies of the succession of various kinds of mayors. Bradley and Zald, dealing specifically with Chicago, divide the mayors into the following chronological and typological categories: commercial elite (1837–68); transi-tion mayors (1868–75); personalized politics vs. party machine (1876–1930); political administrators (1931–   ). Though the authors do not emphasize the ethnic origins of the mayors, it is clear that both the commercial elite and the transition mayors were WASPs; the battle between personalized politics and party machine was a battle between individual WASPs (the two Harrisons and Thompson) and an Irish clique; and the political administrators, with the ex-ception of the first, Cermak, were all Irish. It is during this last period that the new immigrants were the next group up. To succeed in this type of politics, a mayor would have to practice broker politics among many differing groups.

Index

Paderewski, Ignace J., 64, 74, 111–12,
  127
Panna Maria (Texas), 12
Pańszczyzna, 5–6, 41
Parker, Alton B., 102–3, 107, 122
Patronage. *See* Recognition
"Personal liberty": in Al Smith's campaign, 126–28; issue used by the Harrisons, 49–50, 73, 79, 83; in Mayor
  Dever's administration, 145–50
Pilsudski, Joseph, 38, 110, 127
Piotrowski, N. L., 63, 84, 105–6, 127,
  178, 211
Poland: attitudes of American Poles
  toward, 10, 33, 35, 36, 39, 122, 125,
  127–28, 129, 131, 168–69; emigration from, 7–8; insurrections in, 3–5,
  6, 31, 33; liberation of, 38–39, 110–
  12, 115, 127; partitioned, 3; re-
  emigration to, 168–69; social structure, 5–7, 30
Poles in America. *See* Polonia; Politics
  and Chicago Poles
Polish-American Central Committee, 189
Polish-American Democratic Organization (PADO): history, 174, 189–95;
  political endorsements by, 201, 204–
  6; mentioned, 213, 214, 218
Polish Catholic parishes: founding dates
  and locations, 15–26, 165–68. *See also*
  individual parishes
Polish Central Relief Committee, 64, 111
Polish Clergy Association, 174
Polish Constitution Day, 182–83, 188
Polish Democratic League, 189, 204
Polish Downtown: described, 15–19, 23;
  expansion from, 25–26, 165–68;
  mentioned, 149
Polish gentry. *See Szlachta*
Polish language, 30–31, 33, 38, 52
Polish National Alliance (PNA): attitudes toward Germans, 113, 136;
  attitudes toward Jews, 117–19; attitudes toward Wilson, 105, 115;
  founded, 10, 13; political endorsements by, 46, 121, 127–28, 131, 177;
  political strategy, 51–52, 93–95, 173,
  216; purposes of, 33, 35–37, 39, 40,
  168–69; Taft visits college of, 106–7;
  mentioned, 170, 171–72, 190, 195.
  See also *Dziennik Związkowy; Zgoda*
Polish National Catholic Church, 34–35
Polish National Department, 64, 111,
  117

*The Polish Peasant in Europe and
  America* (Thomas and Znaniecki), 8
Polish Publishing Company, 32
Polish Roman Catholic Union (PRCU):
  founded, 10, 13, 32; political activities,
  46, 111, 117, 124–25, 190, 195;
  political strategy, 93–95; purposes of,
  31, 40; mentioned, 55, 105, 112, 170.
  See also *Naród Polski*
Polish Socialist Alliance. *See* Alliance of
  Polish Socialists
Polish Socialist Party (PPS), 38, 110–11
Politics and Chicago Poles: career of
  Carter Harrison II, 72–85; career of
  Edmund Jarecki, 197–200, 201–6;
  careers of Smulski and Kunz compared, 60–71; early political successes,
  45–47, 53–55; failure to elect a
  Polish mayor, 208–19; functions of
  politics, 40–42; Horner-Bundesen
  primary fight, 200–201; issues in the
  1920s, 121–22; Polish attitudes
  toward Progressivism, 87–92; Polish
  drive for recognition, 173–88, 189–
  95; political allegiances, 47–48, 48–
  52, 60; post-World War II politics,
  221–23. *See also* Election campaigns
Polonia: defined, 8–9; changing self-
  image, 168–70; as fourth province of
  Poland, 8, 10, 36, 168; growth of, 9–
  10, 38, 39–40, 165–68, 170–72; as
  ideal of strength in unity, 10–11, 26–
  27, 171–72; as new society, 8–9; political strategies, 93–95
Polonia (newspaper), 27, 124
Polonia's capital. *See* Polonia; Chicago,
  city of
Polonja Amerykańska. See Polonia
Polska: defined, 8
Pomerania, 3, 15
Powers, Johnny, 57
Powroznik, Martin, 155–61, 171, 207
Poznań (city), 60
Poznań (grand duchy), 3
Progressivism: issues in Chicago politics,
  57–60; and Polish voters, 60, 71, 87–
  93; in mayoral elections, 77–83, 144–
  45; in presidential elections, 104,
  122–26
Prohibition. *See* "Personal liberty"
Prystalski, John, 194, 204–5
Przybylo, Joseph, 210
Pulaski, Casimir, 73, 100, 182
Pulaski Road, 183–85, 188